Exhibiting

Māori

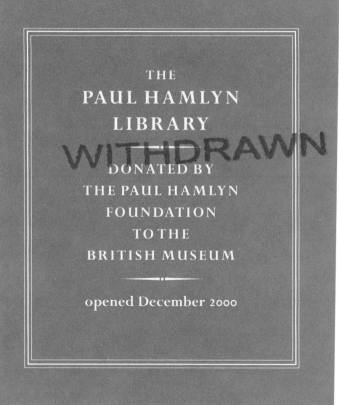

Augustus Hamilton, Dominion Museum bookplate, c.1908 (Museum of New Zealand Te Papa Tongarewa B.010327).

Exhibiting Māori

A History of Colonial Cultures of Display

Conal McCarthy

BERG

Oxford • New York

English edition
First published in 2007 by
Berg
Editorial offices:
First Floor, Angel Court, 81 St Clements Street, Oxford OX4 1AW, UK
175 Fifth Avenue, New York, NY 10010, USA

Berg is the imprint of Oxford International Publishers Ltd.

Library of Congress Cataloging-in-Publication Data

McCarthy, Conal, 1961-
    Exhibiting Maori : a history of colonial cultures of display / Conal
McCarthy. — English ed.
        p. cm.
    Includes bibliographical references and index.
    ISBN-13: 978-1-84520-474-7 (cloth)
    ISBN-10: 1-84520-474-3 (cloth)
    ISBN-13: 978-1-84520-475-4 (pbk.)
    ISBN-10: 1-84520-475-1 (pbk.)
    1. Maori (New Zealand people)—Exhibitions—History. 2. New Zealand—
Exhibitions—History. I. Title.

    DU423.A1M44 2007
    305.89'9442--dc22

                                                                        2006100889

British Library Cataloguing-in-Publication Data

A catalogue record for this book is available from the British Library.

ISBN   978 1 84520 474 7 (Cloth)
         978 1 84520 475 4 (Paper)

Typeset by JS Typesetting Ltd, Porthcawl, Mid Glamorgan
Printed in the United Kingdom by Biddles Ltd, King's Lynn.

www.bergpublishers.com

CONTENTS

ILLUSTRATIONS

ACKNOWLEDGEMENTS

E ngā reo
E ngā waka
E ngā taonga whakahirahira
Tēnā koutou katoa!

Kei te mihi atu au ki ngā mea katoa e tautoko rā i te kaupapa. Ahakoa he pukapuka tēnei e whakapā atu ki ngā taonga Māori, ko te mea nui e kōrerotia nei ko ngā mahi whakawhiti whakaaro kei waenganui i ngā Māori me ngā Pākehā i Aotearoa nei. He koha tēnei ki a koutou e titiro whakamua rā i te hitoria o ngā whakaaturanga Māori o ngā whare taonga o Aotearoa.

(Customary greeting and acknowledgement)

There are many people I have to thank for their help with the task of completing this book, which is drawn from my PhD thesis: my supportive and encouraging supervisors at Victoria University of Wellington, Dr Michael Volkerling and Associate Professor Jenny Harper, my expert advisors Pou Temara and Dr Wendy Cowling at the University of Waikato, where I was Research Associate in the Anthropology Department from 2001 to 2003; my examiners Dr Peter Brunt, Professor Roger Neich and Professor Barbara Kirshenblatt-Gimblett who all provided engaged and perceptive comments that helped immeasurably in the revision of the manuscript; and Sally Reweti-Gould and Dr Lee Davidson in the Museum and Heritage Studies programme for collegial assistance of many forms. I received research grants for this book from the Faculty of Humanities and Social Sciences at Victoria University. The original research was funded by The Allan Laidler Scholarship from the Sports Fitness and Recreation Industry Training Organization. Thanks to Pat Sargison for compiling the index. I am immensely grateful to Ross O'Rourke, Jim Te Puni, Arapata Hakiwai, Awhina Tamarapa, Te Ikanui Kapa, Eamonn Bolger, Jennifer Twist, Kate Button, Jo Moore, Sean Mallon and all the current and former staff at Te Papa who helped with interviews, research and other essential forms of support and encouragement.

I owe a huge debt of gratitude to the staff of the institutions where I carried out my research and who gave permission to reproduce material from their collections: Te Papa Archives, Archives New Zealand, the Alexander Turnbull Library, the Auckland Museum, the New Zealand Film Archive and the Hocken Collections, University of Otago. I am most obliged to the *iwi* and *whānau* who allowed me to use images of their *taonga:* including Te Iwi Moriori, Tainui, Tūwharetoa, Ngāti Pōneke, Ngā Puhi, Kai Tahu, Ngāti Pikiao, Te

Aupōuri, Ngāti Hinewaka; as well as to the artists and their *whānau* who allowed me to reproduce images of their work: Hec Busby, Ralph Hōtere, Selwyn Muru, Lisa Reihana, Carol Nin, the Brian Brake estate, Ans Westra, and Cliff Whiting.

Most of all, heartfelt thanks to my family and to Bronwyn Labrum, my partner in scholarship and in life.

A NOTE ON THE MĀORI LANGUAGE

Many Māori words are in commmon usage in New Zealand English. Where they are not translated in the text, the reader is referred to the glossary. Translations are my own, except where otherwise stated. Māori texts have been edited to conform to modern conventions, including the addition of macrons. In English texts Māori words have been left in the original form in which they appear.

He whare maihi tū ki roto ki te pā tūwatawata, he tohu nō te rangatira; he whare maihi tū ki te wā kei te paenga, he kai nā te ahi.

A carved house standing inside a palisaded *pā* is the mark of a chief; one standing in the open is food for a fire.

ABBREVIATIONS

AFA	– New Zealand Academy of Fine Arts
AGMANZ	– Art Gallery and Museums Association of New Zealand
AJHR	– *Appendices to the Journals of the House of Representatives*
AM	– Auckland Museum
ANZ	– Archives New Zealand
AR	– Annual Report
ATL	– Alexander Turnbull Library
Dom	– *The Dominion*
EP	– *The Evening Post*
Herald	– *New Zealand Herald*
JPS	– *Journal of the Polynesian Society*
MP	– Member of Parliament
NZFA	– New Zealand Film Archive
NZPD	– *New Zealand Parliamentary Debates*
OED	– *Oxford English Dictionary*
TNZI	– *Transactions and Proceedings of the New Zealand Institute*
TP	– Te Papa
TPA	– Te Papa Archives

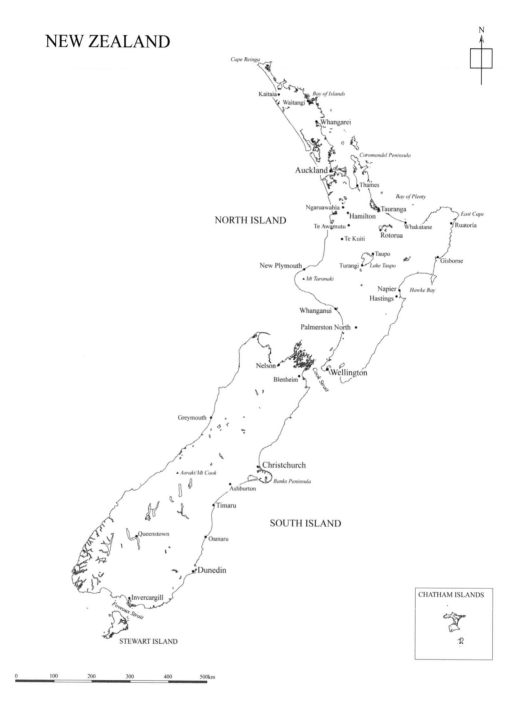

NEW ZEALAND
AOTEAROA

Simplified iwi (tribal) map
Source: Roger Neich and Te Warena Taua
(Starzecka 1996: 159-160)

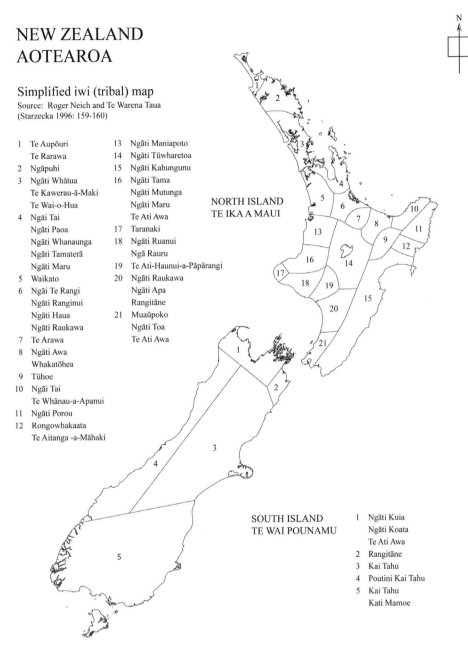

1	Te Aupōuri	13	Ngāti Maniapoto
	Te Rarawa	14	Ngāti Tūwharetoa
2	Ngāpuhi	15	Ngāti Kahungunu
3	Ngāti Whātua	16	Ngāti Tama
	Te Kawerau-ā-Maki		Ngāti Mutunga
	Te Wai-o-Hua		Ngāti Maru
4	Ngāi Tai		Te Ati Awa
	Ngāti Paoa	17	Taranaki
	Ngāti Whanaunga	18	Ngāti Ruanui
	Ngāti Tamaterā		Ngā Rauru
	Ngāti Maru	19	Te Ati-Haunui-a-Pāpārangi
5	Waikato	20	Ngāti Raukawa
6	Ngāi Te Rangi		Ngāti Apa
	Ngāti Ranginui		Rangitāne
	Ngāti Haua	21	Muaūpoko
	Ngāti Raukawa		Ngāti Toa
7	Te Arawa		Te Ati Awa
8	Ngāti Awa		
	Whakatōhea		
9	Tūhoe		
10	Ngāi Tai		
	Te Whānau-a-Apanui		
11	Ngāti Porou		
12	Rongowhakaata		
	Te Aitanga -a-Māhaki		

NORTH ISLAND
TE IKA A MAUI

SOUTH ISLAND
TE WAI POUNAMU

1	Ngāti Kuia
	Ngāti Koata
	Te Ati Awa
2	Rangitāne
3	Kai Tahu
4	Poutini Kai Tahu
5	Kai Tahu
	Kati Mamoe

0   100   200   300   400   500km

INTRODUCTION: THE CULTURES OF DISPLAY

The very nature of exhibiting, then, makes it a contested terrain.

(Karp and Lavine 1991)

The colonial encounter on the cover of this book took place in the Town Hall of New Zealand's capital city, Wellington, in 1923. To our eyes, the East and West Missionary Society Exhibition belongs to an earlier age. The scene of Europeans and Polynesians meeting on the shores of a new-found land was staged as a tableau of civilized progress. Exhibitions today seem natural to us only because they are dressed in a familiar style. Historical exhibitions, on the other hand, expose the continuing artifice of display. They are instructive because they show us how differently our ancestors saw the world and how contested the process of exhibiting was.

Exhibiting Māori traces such changes in exhibition display from the mid-nineteenth century to the end of the twentieth century. It shows how the meaning of Māori things in New Zealand museums has been transformed at different times, shifting from curio, to specimen, to artefact, to various forms of art, to *taonga*. Consider the transformation of a *waharoa* or gateway, for example. This postcard (Figure I.1) shows a six-metre high structure carved out of wood. It formed the entrance to the Māori *pā*, a model village built for the 1906–7 New Zealand International Exhibition in the city of Christchurch in the South Island. The gateway was made for the exhibition and not a Māori community – it looks old but is new, an antiquarian idea of Māori life. Journalist James Cowan wrote that the exhibition illustrated the 'material progress of New Zealand since it was first redeemed from barbarism by the white man'. The ethnological section provided not only 'novel entertainment' for the visitors but also a 'scientific' record of the 'linguistics, primitive customs and folklore' of the Māori people (Cowan 1910: 308). Presented for the curiosity of visitors, the *waharoa* operated as a foil for the progress of the settler colony, remnant of a dying culture that, like the long extinct native bird the *moa*, survived only in museums.

The next photograph (Figure I.2) shows the same object displayed in 1998 at the Museum of New Zealand Te Papa Tongarewa (Te Papa) in Wellington. Positioned prominently near the entrance of the new national museum, it was the symbolic realization of Te Papa's '*waharoa*' policy – the museum's 'gateway' to New Zealand's cultural and natural heritage. Whereas previously this object was seen through the disciplinary framework of ethnology, it was now viewed in aesthetic terms. Dramatically lit and isolated against the wall behind, the installation focused attention on its singular, sculptural qualities as a work of art. In

N.Z. International Exhibition, 1906-7.   No. 5—The Gateway, Maori Pah.

Figure 1.1   A postcard showing the *waharoa* (gateway) of the Māori
pā at the New Zealand International Exhibition Christchurch, 1906–7
(Alexander Turnbull Library Eph-POSTCARDS-Ellis-04).

addition, its Māori status as a *taonga* (treasure) was acknowledged by Māori staff: the bilingual label uses the word *'waharoa'* and identifies the carvers and their tribal affiliation. The carving was interpreted in mythological terms as a representation of ancestor figures who are shown challenging visitors in the stance of the *haka* (*Te Papa Our Place* 1998: 41).

In the ninety years that separates these displays, the exhibition of Māori things has been reworked. The *waharoa* was once a specimen and now it was art. Most surprising of all, the gateway has become a *taonga*, a treasure. The position of Māori people has shifted, from exhibits to exhibitors, from spectacle to audience. The social context of the display is also very different. At the turn of the twentieth century, indigenous people, plants and animals were part of 'Maoriland', an exotic image of New Zealand that furnished a local identity for Pakeha (European New Zealanders) and a distinctive spectacle for tourism. At the end of the twentieth century the museum was seen as a showcase for biculturalism, a state ideology of Crown-Māori partnership founded on the Treaty of Waitangi, New Zealand's founding document signed in 1840.

Many see the shift from curio to *taonga* as a sign of progress, and point to the famous 'Te Maori' exhibition as the turning point. This exhibition, which toured the US and New Zealand from 1984 to 1987, gave people a new appreciation of 'the beauty of Maori

Figure I.2 *Waharoa* on display, level 2, Te Papa, Wellington, 1998
(Museum of New Zealand Te Papa Tongarewa CT.9997/01).

artistry and the spiritual qualities associated with the taonga' (Simpson 1996: 253). Before this, it is claimed, Māori had little to do with museums and Pakeha did not value Māori collections lying neglected in their basements (Mead 1997b; Hakiwai 2005). But, as Barbara Kirshenblatt-Gimblett (1995: 148) warns, when artefacts are suddenly enshrined as art, then we know that 'the revolution was not in the objects but in our categories'. Current understandings of display are uniformly presentist, taking little account of the historical trajectories of objects (Tapsell 2000; 2006). In this book, I examine material things as part of a culture of display, showing how New Zealanders exhibited themselves. The history of Māori exhibitions tells us as much about those who exhibit as it does about those who are exhibited.

It is the same *waharoa* in all these images but the object eludes any fixed meaning because of the different ways in which it is displayed at various times, and the manner in which it is seen by different viewers. If, for example, we look again at the *waharoa* as it was being made in 1906 (Figure I.3), a quite different reading is possible. Commissioned to replicate an

Figure I.3   *Waharoa* with Neke Kapua and his sons, International Exhibition, Christchurch, 1906 (Museum of New Zealand Te Papa Tongarewa Hamilton C.1659).

'authentic' pre-European relic, Neke Kapua and his sons from the Ngāti Tarāwhai tribe have dared to improvise, making a hybrid work that was also a product of their own imagination. From the Māori point of view carving was a living cultural practice that conveyed ideas of identity and *mana* (power, prestige). In a speech on the *marae* during the exhibition, Kapua declared that 'Our works of ancient times have been brought here, so that the peoples of the earth may know that the Maori is still living' (Hamilton in *Dominion Museum Bulletin* 1911: 13). This message of survival provides abundant evidence of Māori agency long before the events of the 1980s and casts exhibition history in a new light.

In the 1930s, we can see the *waharoa* in yet another context at the new Dominion Museum in Wellington (Figure I.4), a forerunner of the Museum of New Zealand. This time it was seen as an artefact, a frozen fragment of the Māori 'as he was' set within a timeless ethnographic past. The Māori hall was positioned in the centre of the museum, representing an ancient past as a prelude to the settler society's present. 'The white man, in designing his national treasure house', declared a journalist who visited the space, 'has certainly given pride of place to the storied history of a proud race' (*The Dominion*, 1 August 1936). Though the photograph may suggest these hallowed halls were an exclusively Pakeha temple of culture, how do we know that there were no Māori visitors, or indeed Māori staff?

Figure I.4 Māori Hall, Dominion Museum, Wellington, 1936
(Alexander Turnbull Library PAColl-3033-1-13).

For these Māori people, did the museum celebrate the glories of their past, or did it signal their absorption into modernity and the nation state?

This ambiguity was captured in a contemporary photograph of a Māori visitor (Figure I.5). The caption described the well-groomed young man as a 'modern Maori', looking 'back into the past' at 'the Masterpieces of his Ancestors' (Cowan 1939). Kingi Tahiwi, shown here admiring the carvings in the museum, was in fact a state welfare officer, broadcaster and member of the Ngāti Pōneke culture group, who was at the forefront of the urban migration when many Māori people left their rural homelands for a new life in the cities. It is too easy to 'read' this image as a Pakeha recipe for Māori assimilation, a reading that overlooks what part Māori played in museum display, let alone what future aspirations they had within the New Zealand of their day. Did not Māori also regard their old carvings as 'masterpieces'? Their response to exhibiting, which like all heritage products marked off the past from the present, expressed a desire to take part in contemporary society through a *Māori* modernity.

Figure I.5   Kingi Tahiwi in the Māori Hall, Dominion Museum, Wellington, 1937 (Alexander Turnbull Library BK-690-7).

How and why has the display of Māori culture changed? How can we explain these extraordinary transformations – from curio to taonga – in the ways that Māori things have been exhibited? James Clifford reminds us that these taxonomic shifts require 'critical historical investigation, not celebration' (Clifford 1985: 169). By adopting a critical rather than celebratory approach, *Exhibiting Māori* examines exhibits within a culture of display which is shaped by the complex relations of colonization, modernity and nationhood. In the process, this book uncovers a history of active Māori engagement with Western culture, which complicates current orthodoxies about cultural politics and indigeneity.

THE CULTURES OF DISPLAY

Museum display has an important but little-known history. Exhibitions as we know them today are not only relatively recent but 'distinctively modern' in their form (Vergo 1989: 47). The exhibition has been described as 'the characteristic construction of the modern age, like the printed book, the framed picture . . .' (Pearce 1992: 139). Despite this acknowledgement, much was said about exhibition content but very little about its form (Ward 1996: 451). In most books about exhibition design, display is treated as a self-evident category (Newhouse 2005). Exhibition catalogues and illustrated histories of museums have long focused on objects and collections, overlooking the displays which are their public face, and the people who look at and interact with them (Rogoff and Sherman 1994; Wollen in Wollen and Cooke 1995). The exhibition was often regarded as a 'natural form' and the actual work exhibitions do 'on and through audiences' was largely neglected (Ferguson in Greenberg, Ferguson and Nairne 1996: 178, 175). Recently, scholars have paid more attention to the history of exhibiting through specific studies that attend more to the exhibition itself as a form of display than merely what is exhibited (Karp and Lavine 1991; Greenberg et al 1996; MacLeod 2005). It follows that after the 'pictorial turn', a picture is analysed not as a self-evident category but as a 'complex interplay between visuality, apparatus, institutions, bodies and figurality' (Mitchell 1994: 16). The same can be said of exhibitions. In this book, therefore, display is understood within the broad range of visual culture (Foster 1988; Crary 1990; Evans and Hall 1999).

The critical study of exhibitions proceeds from the idea that vision is something historical and social. 'The eye', wrote Michael Foucault, 'was not always intended for contemplation' (cited in Rabinow 1984: 83). Foucault has been described as a 'visual historian' who examined the way that objects and subjects were 'shown' (Lidchi in Hall 1997: 195). His books trace 'a history not simply of what was seen,' said critic John Rajchman, 'but of what could be seen, of what was seeable or visible' (Rajchman 1988: 91). Just as hospitals, poorhouses and asylums in Foucault's historical work are 'spaces of constructed visibility,' museum display can be seen as something that produces the 'categories through which art was given to be seen' (Rajchman 1988: 103).

Looking at things on display is a cultural practice that is imbedded in a field of social production. 'The eye is a product of history reproduced by education', declared Pierre

Bourdieu (1984: 3). By treating 'historical schemes of perception and appreciation' as the 'product' of social divisions, Bourdieu's work provides tools for an historical analysis of social institutions and visitor reception (1984: 468). One of the most fruitful applications of this theory has occurred in studies of the historical formation of cultural institutions and their relations with social groups (Bennett 1995: 99–102). Nick Prior has investigated the history of museums as realms of 'distinction' (2002: 5) and Gordon Fyfe has examined art galleries as 'accumulations of cultural capital' (2000: 4). The sociology of cultural reception has begun to be integrated into theoretical and historical studies of exhibitions (Taylor 1999; McClellan 2003; Hill 2005).

Exhibiting is socially and historically determined. The 'visualizing technologies' peculiar to modernity have not only displayed the world but have constructed the modern way of comprehending it as if it were an exhibit (Macdonald in Macdonald and Fyfe 1996: 7). Sharon Macdonald complains that exhibitions are often presented as 'unequivocal state-ments rather than as the outcome of particular processes' and calls for an analytical approach which takes their social context into account. 'The task', she wrote, 'is also to explore the consequences of particular forms of representation in terms of the distribution of power: who is empowered or disempowered by certain modes of display?' (Macdonald 1998: 4). Mary Anne Staniszewski's history of exhibitions at the Museum of Modern Art in New York is an example of this approach. By treating installation design as 'an aesthetic medium and historical category', her work questions how historical shifts in display at certain periods transformed the meaning of things:

> What aesthetic, cultural, and political discourses intersected with these exhibits? What sorts of viewers, or 'subjects,' do different types of installation designs create? What kinds of museums are constituted by particular installation practices? (Staniszewski 1998: xxiii)

The history of how things have come to be displayed as they are teaches us about the 'madeness of all categories' (Kirshenblatt-Gimblett 1998: 264). But display is more than a trace of the past, it is an active agent in the encounter of people with things. 'Display not only shows and speaks', writes Kirshenblatt-Gimblett, 'it also *does*' (1998: 128). She draws our attention to the agency of display and the reflexive quality of exhibited objects, how indigenous styles of presentation operate in festivals and performances in contrast to ethnographic exhibitions which are implicated in the 'disappearance of what they show' (1998: 162). Like these histories of exhibitions, this book attempts to go beyond condemnations of primitivism to look for evidence of the ways in which colonized peoples mediated representations of their culture (Jonaitis 1981; Clifford 1988; Stainforth 1990; Mitchell 1991; Jackson Rushing 1992).

Questions about the agency of display, and how it enacts social relations with viewers and objects, are central to this study. Consideration of these questions led me to formulate a model for cultural reception drawn from Emma Barker's (1999: 13–15) idea of a 'culture of display'. Her work demonstrates the *productive* capacity of display, and treats exhibitions as things that actively produce meaning, which are 'a form of representation as well as mode of presentation' (Barker 1999: 13). Things are constructed through words: the discourses which make them available to be seen and interpreted. Although these objects certainly exist outside us, they are only meaningful for us in terms of some concept or discursive framework through which they make sense. The culture of display makes things visible to viewers, by putting objects into a context in which they are interpreted by the people who look at them.

The nexus of the culture of display is the subject–object interface: the encounter of visitors (subject) with artefacts on display (object).[1] Foucault states that discourse constitutes objects (1972: 47–9). For Kirshenblatt Gimblett (1998: 128), in addition, display constitutes subjects. In the space of the museum, display comprises the subject who sees, and the object which is seen, as mutually constitutive entities. Exhibitions include what is looked at as well as viewers who look – they are contested sites where visitors, exhibited objects, cultural practices and discourses come together.[2] Visitors are at once subject to the power of display, shaped by what they see, and active agents who construct the meanings of objects. But the object is no less a social agent: it mediates social relations just as people do (Gell 1998: 17–19).

In this model, ideology, social structure and individual agency are integrated into a single theoretical framework. The analysis of representations in an institutional setting, together with sociological data on the reactions of individuals, reveals how audiences actually

The culture of display:

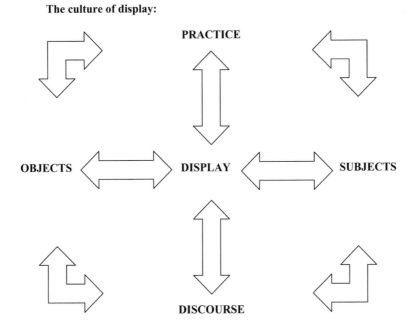

responded to exhibits, which in turn were shaped by their social context. It can be applied to many examples of what we might call the 'exhibitionary apparatus' including museums, worlds fairs, exhibitions and performances, tourism and popular culture (McCarthy 2006). Using this understanding of display as a culture, I examine the relationship of objects to subjects, how things on show shape, and are shaped by, the people who showed them.

In this book, I apply this model to a specific historical case study of an ethnic group in a colonial context. I trace the many different ways in which Māori culture has been represented in association with New Zealand's national museum over 150 years. Audience responses to exhibitions illuminate the ways in which categories of visual display – from curio to *taonga* – were constituted through visitors who accepted, mediated, or contested them. In the process I uncover a new and more nuanced history of exhibitions, and the objects (and subjects) they created.

There are a number of factors that make this book's methodology distinctive. First, each chapter includes a wide and deep range of sources – newly discovered images, primary documentary material from archives, a broad range of secondary historical sources, and specially conducted oral histories – that enables me to present detailed reconstructions of exhibitions within their social context. Interviews with museum staff, for example, provide a very important insider's view of the process of exhibition development. Second, archival sources, audience surveys and social theory are used to explore the historical and contemporary reception of exhibitions by Māori audiences. Visitor research has provided a wealth of information on current responses to current Māori exhibitions. Third, I have consulted Māori language sources, such as the rich archive of newspapers now available, in order to assess Māori responses. Finally, a key element in this research is my professional involvement from the point of view of a participant as well as an external observer. During the 1980s and 1990s I experienced first hand most of the exhibitions discussed in the book and worked at the national museum either back of house developing exhibitions or front of house interacting with visitors in the exhibitions. Far from compromising my account, this adds significant depth to this study, because I am able to set the theory, the archival evidence and the survey data against my own experiences of the museum, the objects, the exhibitions and the staff.

MUSEUMS, GENEALOGY AND MODERNITY

This book is not a conventional history of museums or exhibitions but an 'effective' history, a Foucauldian genealogy of discontinuities and breaks rather than chronological progress. Foucault's theory of genealogy (1984) is the process of understanding how taken-for-granted ideas have a history that is not preoccupied with origins but with contingencies (Racevskis 1989: 230; Smart 2002: 56). Genealogical critique is a powerful tool for tracking the workings of power and knowledge in museum history (Jordanova in Vergo 1989; Hooper-Greenhill 1992; Crimp and Lawler 1993; Coombes 1994; Bennett 1995). However, as Andrea Witcomb notes, Foucauldian critiques sometimes overlook evidence of other histories such as resistance, pleasure and consumption (Witcomb 2003: 15–17). The view of museums as instruments of colonial power can obscure the ways in which minority groups such as Māori engage in international networks and the exchange of ideas (Henare 2005: 210). Writers now stress the adaptive, hybrid and contested nature of objects in colonial encounters (Thomas 1991, 1994; Sissons 1998). New work in museum studies overcomes these problems by combining theoretical and empirical interpretations of museums, examining social relations within a historically grounded analysis (Macdonald and Fyfe 1996; Whitehead 2005). Scholars balance discursive and materialist approaches without losing sight of either words or things (Prior 2002: 11; Hill 2005: 3).

While the constructionist position has successfully countered transcendent theories of art and culture, critics have warned against underestimating objects and the power they exercise over people (Mitchell 1996; Gell 1998; Latour 2004). There is a growing interest in material culture – what Appadurai (1986) has called 'the social life of things'. Exploring the material evidence provided by physical objects, scholars show how they acquire new meanings in different situations (Fisher 1991: 3–6; 1996: 16; Hooper-Greenhill 1992: 194–5). For example, Amiria Henare (2005: 3) has recently described *taonga* as a special category of objects that instantiate social relationships through time, while Gell (1998: 253) has suggested how Māori *whare* embody agency in ways that are collective, ancestral and political.

Although the idea of controlling and regulating visitors, including indigenous ones, is certainly part of the critical analysis of museum history (Duncan 1995; Bennett 1995; 2001), there is a risk of overdetermining the colonial encounter and denying Māori agency and the potential for indigenous action and response. Many Māori writers are hyper-critical of colonial culture (Graham 1995; Allen 1998; Tuhiwai Smith 1999). However, a number of scholars now present more complex views of colonial encounters in the Pacific (Salmond 1991; Thomas 1991; Erikson, Neumann and Thomas 1999; O'Regan 1999; Sissons 2005; Thomas and Losche 1999; Teaiwa 2005). James Belich, whose work is part of a re-evaluation of imperial history, points out that simplistic views of New Zealand's past often overlook the dynamic Māori adaptation to European settlement (Belich 1996, 2001). Far from being passive victims of European power, the Māori reaction may be seen as an 'eager, adaptive and innovative engagement with the things and thoughts of Europe' (Belich 1996: 271). The following chapters follow historical developments in New Zealand society using the periodization introduced by Belich: from colonization in the 1860s to what Belich calls 'recolonization' in the 1880s, and from recolonization to decolonization in the 1960s and 1970s, a process that continues up to the present.

A growing body of literature describes the contemporary relationship between museums and Māori but lacks a historical and theoretical analysis (Brown 1995; Corbey 1995; Bishop 1998; Hakiwai 1999; Kernot 1999). For example, Paul Tapsell has recounted the journey of a famous Ngāti Whakaue gateway *Pukaki* from Ohinemutu *pā* on the shores of Lake Rotorua to Auckland Museum and its eventual return home, describing the 'life, times and transformations' from 'mortal human to carved ancestor, museum curiosity to national icon' (Tapsell 2000: 16). *Exhibiting Māori* also pursues the journey of individual objects through time but goes further in accounting for the social formation of each of these stages of display. There is an a-historical assumption underlying museum practice today that *taonga* remained unchanged through all their 'mis-representations' until recently, when they resumed their true status, implying that the rightful acknowledgement of *taonga* as *taonga* is the end of history, and their repatriation the end of museums (Tapsell 2006). A more critical analysis is demonstrated in Jeffrey Sissons's work on the 'traditionalization' of the Māori meeting house, using the Māori concept of *whakapapa* and the theory of genealogy:

> The carved meeting house is, then, a traditionalized object with a genealogy in both Foucauldian and Māori senses. Foucauldian, because its genealogy traces links between new forms of power/knowledge associated with cultural commodification and colonial state formation; Māori, because, in symbolizing ancestral connections, it embodies a history of kin-based engagement with these new forms of power. (Sissons 1998: 46)

In this book I argue that changes in the Māori culture of display in the late twentieth century should be seen, not as 'inauthentic' but as a creative recoupling, or rearticulation, of constituent elements in response to social and political forces in settler colonies (Clifford 2001; Slack 1996; Grossberg 1986). The startling history of Māori exhibitions puts forward an indigenous critique of Western perspectives on culture, social change and modernity. Museums and 'heritage' create modern culture by providing a space where the present can mark off the past as 'a foreign country' (Lumley 2005; Prior 2002: 9–10; Kirshenblatt-Gimblett 1998: 149–50). Whereas ethnographic exhibitions portrayed indigenous peoples as distant in time and place, as 'over there' and 'back then' (Dias 1994: 166; Thomas 1999: 259–60), Māori represented themselves in the here and now. For Māori, the past was recycled as a claim on the present, and whether in myth or in museum display, they always 'found themselves in history' (Johansen in Sahlins 1995: 250). Marshall Sahlins (1993: 21) has called this the 'indigenization of modernity'. The following story of Māori resistance to, involvement in, and eventual capture of, the culture of display represents the 'indigenization of the museum'.

NOTES

1. This model is based on three sources: Hall's 'circuit of culture' (1997: 1); Harker's model of cultural reproduction based on Bourdieu (Harker in Harker, Mahar and Wilkes 1990: 101); and Clifford's art-culture system (Clifford 1988: 224–6).
2. My thinking here is indebted to Nicholas Thomas's 'ethnography of colonial projects', which combines Foucault's discourse, describing how large social structures operate in society, with the work of Bourdieu, detailing how people actually reproduce, practice or adapt these structures on a day to day level (Thomas 1994: 58–64).

1 'COLONIALISM'S CULTURE', 1865–1913

Obviously enough, there could be no Orientalism without, on the one hand, the
Orientalists, and on the other, the Orientals.

(Said 2001)

Figure 1.1 shows a display at the Colonial and Vienna Exhibition of 1872–3 in Christchurch.
On the end wall of the hall, two large *poupou* frame an assemblage made up of carving
and weaving surrounded by flax and other native foliage. A shorter *pou* in the centre has
kākahu and *korowai* draped around it, and wooden clubs are laid across these at an angle.
This *pou* is topped by a *tauihu* facing out into the hall and is crowned by a fan of weapons:
taiaha, *tewhatewha* and *hoe*. These Māori objects are treated as interesting shapes, which
are combined into an artful composition to delight the curiosity of the spectator. In front
a group of Canterbury worthies are lined up in their formal clothes, members of the social
elite and landed gentry. Dr James Hector, director of the Colonial Museum in Wellington
and the man who organized the exhibition, stands in the centre shuffling his speech notes.

This style of display, called a 'trophy,' was a common sight in colonial exhibitions and,
as the name suggests, owes its origins to the fanlike arrangements of game and war booty
that adorned the grand houses of soldiers and collectors (*Catalogue of the Colonial and
Vienna Exhibition* 1873: 22). Exhibiting Māori implied the possession of the people and
their land who, like the native flora and fauna, were apparently doomed to extinction. This
image is not merely a record of an historical occasion but makes visible connections between
material culture and imperial power, between objects and subjects. What the exhibition
puts on display is the colonizing culture of Pakeha settlers.

Carvings were variously described by Europeans at this time as specimens, curios and
even art. Their display expressed European understandings of Māori culture but did not
give any sense of the original functions or settings that Māori people would be familiar
with. But exhibits like this did not always go unchallenged, nor were European categories
of display the only ones at work here. To its carver Raharuhi Rukupō, the meeting house
from which the carving came was a 'great *taonga*' or treasured possession. Rukupō, chief of
the Rongowhakaata people, protested vigorously in a petition when this house *Te Hau ki
Tūranga* was 'carried off without pretext' by the government (*Appendices to the Journals of the
House of Representatives* 1867 G:12).

No responses have been recorded from Māori visitors to this exhibition, but other sources
suggest Māori responses to the public display of their culture were not always negative.

Figure 1.1   Trophy display, Colonial and Vienna Exhibition, Christchurch, 1872 (Alexander Turnbull Library Barker PA1-q-166-052).

When carver Hone Tāhu was present in Christchurch the following year to complete the house *Hau-te-ana-nui-a-Tangaroa* set up within the Canterbury Museum, his work was praised by a prominent Māori leader, who wrote that the *whare* would show 'the learned works of the ancestors of this land' (Wahawaha in *Te Waka Maori,* 11 August 1874). The Reverend James Stack commented on the curious designs and fanciful resemblance of the house to the human form, in Māori terms literally the body of an ancestor with the rafters representing his ribs (Stack 1875). Though Stack called it art, to Māori eyes they were 'carved histories' (Neich 2001), what Mead (1986b:12) calls '*te toi whakairo*' or genealogical knowledge (1986b: 12).

My reading of the exhibition shows that different discourses produce different objects, at times overlapping and at times in conflict (Hooper-Greenhill 1998: 130). In this chapter

I examine the colonial culture of display from the mid-nineteenth to the early twentieth century, explaining how and why the presentation of Māori objects changed. I follow the ebb and flow of colonization throughout the century and trace the tidemark left on the collections and displays of museums in New Zealand. The chapter begins by situating display in the context of New Zealand's 'progressive colonization' from the 1860s to the 1880s. The first half examines the Māori exhibits at the Colonial Museum in Wellington and then at international exhibitions in Britain, America and Australia. In the second half I consider the discourse of 'recolonization' from the 1880s to 1913 and how it affected cultures of display, examining ethnographic exhibitions, as well as Māori 'art' and antiquities, at the Colonial and later Dominion Museum. I incorporate the Māori perspective on these changes in display and argue that around 1900 Māori ideas converged with Pakeha campaigns for the preservation of cultural heritage.

COLONIZATION AND DISPLAY, 1860s TO 1880s

In 1840, with the signing of the Treaty of Waitangi, New Zealand became a British colony. At first European interest was focused on extraction through a series of rushes to exploit natural resources: whales, seals, timber, flax, gold and coal. Great tracts of land were acquired after the New Zealand wars, a period of armed conflict between government and Māori tribes from the 1840s to the 1860s. Planned European settlement and mass migration were encouraged and extensive public works were embarked on with unbounded confidence, financed by foreign banks caught up in the progress industry. The very idea of progress drove the headlong development of the settler colony, until the depression of the 1880s punctured the illusion of prosperity. 'Progressive colonization', an astonishingly rapid process of cultural reproduction, created a 'greater Britain' which Pakeha people felt would surpass the old country (Belich 1996: 358–60). But this 'neo-Britain' was formed at the cost of the indigenous people. From 1840 to 1890, the European population exploded from 2,000 to 500,000, while the Māori population declined from perhaps 100,000 to less than 50,000 (Belich 1996: 250, 374). Despite the Treaty's promise to recognize Māori sovereignty, they became marginalized in their own country and by the end of the century had lost most of their land and political independence.

The New Zealand Exhibition of 1865 in the southernmost city of Dunedin provides a graphic example of progressive colonization and its attendant culture of display. In a city not yet twenty years old, but eager to show off the new wealth created by the Otago gold rush, the city fathers organized a large-scale exposition that attracted thousands of people to a grandiose Italianate building. A scaled-down version of the Great Exhibition of 1851 in London, it expressed the vaunted aspirations of a young colony that believed it would one day be bigger and better than 'Home'. Medals were given not for services to science and industry but for services to the exhibition. This symbolized, Belich argues, the power of progressive colonization 'to make futures by celebrating them' (1996: 448). The exhibition brought New Zealand into existence by putting the settler colony on display.

The exhibition included a section containing 'Maori and other Aboriginal manufactures and implements' (*New Zealand Exhibition* 1866: 321–32). These were donated by private collectors such as Sir George Grey, the Premier who had recently overseen the invasion of the Waikato in the North Island and the confiscation of land for settlers. It is difficult not to see such exhibitions as a triumphal display in which the dispossession of indigenous people is carried out through the possession of their culture (Healy 1997). But closer inspection reveals that Māori people were *exhibitors* as well as being *exhibited* (Eccles 1925: 5). Several prominent chiefs lent weapons, weaving and carving, passing on the names and histories that were associated with them (*New Zealand Exhibition* 1866: 321–32). Amidst a Pakeha celebration of conquest that assumed indigenous absence, these voices and things declared a Māori presence.

As the Great Exhibition of 1851 begat the Victoria and Albert Museum, the New Zealand Exhibition of 1865 gave birth to the Colonial Museum in Wellington, the nation's new capital. One of the key exhibition commissioners was Dr James Hector, a Scot originally appointed as a geologist by the Otago provincial government, and he became the museum's first director later that year. Hector was the most prominent scientist in the government service, who stamped his influence on a range of fields through the functions of the Colonial Museum: the Geological Survey, the Colonial Laboratory, as well as botanic gardens, meteorology and other activities (Dell 1972: 887–901; Dell 1990). In addition to Hector's material from Dunedin, this museum brought together several collections from former short-lived bodies, such as the Wellington Philosophical Institute and the New Zealand Society, which already had links with contemporary developments in British natural history (Henare 2005: 146–7, 149). The Colonial Museum's activities were implicated in the colonial project of exploring, describing and classifying the country. To Hector, it would be like a library of natural specimens that classified the natural resources of the colony in order to advance colonization:

> My desire is not to make an extensive and showy collection but to organise for the Colony a complete typical museum of reference that will illustrate all the branches of its natural history and mineral resources. (Dell 1965a: 8)

In the British Empire, the cultural models of the Imperial metropolis were faithfully reproduced on a smaller scale in colonial outposts. The design of the Colonial Museum, both inside and out, reflected the current models of Victorian architecture. Early sketches and plans show a squat building with round arches, quoins and a grand colonnaded entrance, which conveys the utilitarian character of the geological museums that were probably its model (Richardson 1997). Photographs of the completed museum depict a rather more elegant Italianate design, most likely by Colonial Architect William Clayton (Figure 1.2). Despite its modest size, the Classical elements were in keeping with provincial museum buildings in Britain. These recalled the British Museum's façade with its temple-front portico, an architectural style associated with learning and tradition. For European

Figure 1.2   Colonial Museum and Dr Hector's house, Museum Street, Wellington, 1874 (Museum of New Zealand Te Papa Tongarewa Salmond 1937 B.5880).

settlers in far flung colonies, visual echoes of the Old World in stark new townscapes were reassuring reminders of the roots of their civilization (McCarthy 2002).

The Colonial Museum's interior (Figure 1.3) consisted of a central hall rising through two floors surrounded by a gallery on three sides and lit by a skylight. The ground floor area contained table cases and mounted skeletons. Standing cases were placed against the outside walls. Smaller items were arranged in permanent wall cabinets in the gallery, while pictures and specimens were hung or suspended from the railing and the roof. This layout, common in Australasian museums of the period, was again based on British models (Rasmussen 2001; Hill 2005).[1] The design of department stores, arcades, exhibition buildings and museums was part of an 'exhibitionary complex' that had developed out of the arcades and galleries of Paxton's Crystal Palace building. It reflected the 'disciplinary' society and was responsible for 'ordering objects for inspection and ordering the public that inspected' (Bennett 1995: 61). Society was configured as a spectacle in ways that reinforced the power of dominant social groups (Marsh 1999; Black 2000). British museums from the mid-nineteenth century

Figure 1.3   Interior of Colonial Museum, c.1870 (Alexander Turnbull Library Sebley PA4-1063).

offered free access for the general public in contrast to their private antecedents. Museum buildings were designed with large internal spaces allowing visitors to walk past objects arranged in series inside rows of glass cases. They were part of the practice of 'showing and telling' that made visible, through the layout of objects in space, discourses associated with the notion of progress (Bennett 1995: 6).

As with the architecture, the design of the exhibits at the Colonial Museum can be traced back to Britain. Nineteenth-century museum interiors did not have 'exhibitions' as we know them today and are notable for what the modern viewer often interprets as cluttered disorder. Like the abundance of material possessions seen in photographs of domestic spaces, this clutter is partly an expression of bougeois acquisitiveness and wealth (Conn 1998: 13) but also reflects a different culture of display at work. In the Colonial Museum objects were crowded on walls, into cases and onto shelves, much as they were 'back of house' in the store rooms. At this time the collection *was* the exhibition: the museum always had the collection on permanent display 'front of house'. Museum staff did not make a distinction between storage and display, and regarded the museum halls as semi-permanent reference collections like books in a library, designed to keep the public occupied while they carried out their more important scientific duties behind the scenes (Bouquet 2000: 179).

International exhibitions, or world's fairs as they are often called, formed an integral part of the culture of display in the nineteenth century. The word 'exhibition', a public display of objects, was first applied specifically in the late-eighteenth century to pictures hung at the Royal Academy. After the Great Exhibition of 1851, however, it was widely used to describe general exhibitions on a large scale. The term 'exhibit,' referring to objects sent to or making up an exhibition, only came in to use late in the nineteenth century (*Oxford English Dictionary* 1989, vol. 15: 536–7). International exhibitions were immensely popular in the Victorian era and New Zealand participated in many overseas, as well as hosting a number at home (Johnston 1999: 323–5). Much of the Colonial Museum's time and resources were spent in organizing or contributing to these exhibitions. They received more government support than museums in New Zealand because they were intimately associated with trade, tourism and the prestige of the colony. As a result the displays sent abroad were more comprehensive, dynamic and open to new influences than the static installations at home, although this experimentation often shaped the form that local museums subsequently took. There is a very close historical interrelationship between museums and the exhibitionary apparatus of the world's fairs, with colonial institutions employing display practices that were initially used with better funded exhibitions abroad. One example mentioned later in this chapter is the emergence of separate ethnological displays as a result of their popularity at world's fairs.

FROM CURIO TO SPECIMEN AT THE COLONIAL MUSEUM

When visitors saw Māori objects on display in museums and exhibitions, how did they interpret them? The terms most often used by Pakeha viewers to describe and name Māori objects were 'curio' and 'specimen'. The process of exhibiting Māori took place within a history of European spectatorship. Curio is a word that carries traces of shifts in meaning over the last few centuries (Impey & MacGregor 1985; Hudson 1987; Pomian 1990; Findlen 1994). The curiosity cabinet, the Renaissance proto-museum, was not, as the current meaning of the word suggests – a heterogeneous jumble of oddities – but places where learned naturalists were encouraged to give free reign to their 'curiosity', their openness to discover new things, a valid premise for inquiry in the early modern culture of science (Findlen 1994: 94; Hudson 1987: 21). The word 'curiosity', encompassing the commonplace and the unusual, suggested both the inherent qualities of a material object and the response of viewers to it (Greenblatt 1991: 22). There was little connection between objects in combined collections until the Enlightenment when they began to be reordered within the systematic disciplines of history and biology (Foucault 1970: 128; Hides 1997: 18–28). By this time, a gap had opened up between legitimate scientific inquiry and the mere curiosity of amateurs (Findlen 1994: 398–9).

From the Renaissance period Europeans understood the material culture of non-European peoples through their curiosity or strangeness (Hides 1997: 18). When Europe came into contact with the 'Other' something merely interesting or cleverly made came to be seen as marvellous or strange. The term 'curio,' not necessarily used perjoratively, was duly applied to objects from the Far East and the Americas that found their way back to

European collections (Greenblatt 1991; Shelton 1994). By the eighteenth century the idea of 'artificial curiosities' recognized a distinction between natural and human categories but much of the man-made exotica was not valued highly (Kaeppler 1978: 43), although the British Museum grouped together Pacific objects under the title 'miscellanea' in a South Seas Room (Chapman 1985: 23), while at the Leverian Museum they were sometimes admired for their 'artistic' qualities (Smith 1989: 127). Among European explorers in the Pacific, the word 'curious' was used as an adverb to express interest in things without passing aesthetic judgement (Smith 1989: 123–5). By the mid-nineteenth century, curio was a noun, with connotations of the odd, bizarre, and exotic. In 1851 Henry Melville wrote of 'balmed New Zealand heads' as 'great curios' (*OED* 1989, vol. 4: 143).

In Victorian New Zealand, the term 'curio' was freely used to describe Māori objects but in museums this was less common because professionals sought to illustrate the principles of natural history rather than evince fascination with cannibal trophies or evoke wonder at God's creation. Museum staff rarely used the word, generally adopting the more scientific term 'specimen' to describe the contents of museum display cabinets, or new additions to the collection. Hector distinguished between 'popular' and 'scientific' museums, which were prevented from lapsing into 'unmeaning collections of curiosities' by the means of 'accurate information instructively arranged' (*AJHR* 1866 D-9). Throughout the nineteenth century, the term 'curio' was more likely to be found in the commercial sphere of collectors and 'curio dealers' than in the scientific realm of the museum, and even there it was more common in personal correspondence than in official records.

As a visual category of display, 'specimen' was constructed within the scientific disciplines of natural history that paralleled the colonization of the physical world by Europe. The term implied that, as an illustration of a species, the object stood for all the other objects of that type (Dias 1994: 166). Although for much of the nineteenth century British museums continued to display disparate plants and animals together, gradually they adopted Darwin's controversial new ideas about how life forms changed and separated out different species in exhibition halls designed for the general public rather than the specialist (Hudson 1987). The labelled specimens laid out in seried ranks of glass cases were intended to illustrate evolutionary development to visitors through an 'object-based epistemology' (Conn 1998: 3). This new category of display was accompanied by new technologies of vision and techniques of observation. The antiquarian slowly gave way to the scientist; tables and catalogues replaced wonder cabinets, and classified collections superseded their miscellaneous forebears (Foucault 1970: 129; Dias 1994: 167–8). These practices were familiar to Hector and his contemporaries in New Zealand, through personal contact with Darwin, Owen and other progressive figures in British science.

If specimens illustrated the laws of the natural world, by extension this applied to human society because primitive peoples were considered 'children of nature'. Human history, as Stephen Bann has observed, also came to be seen as a specimen (1984). The particular disciplines through which 'man' was invented were the new 'human sciences' of ethnology and ethnography (Foucault 1970: 313).[2] At the Bethnall Green Museum in the 1870s and then at Oxford University in the 1880s, A.H.L.F. Pitt Rivers' display of types, influenced by Charles Darwin's theories, illustrated the evolution of culture. Social Darwinists looked at ethnographic specimens for proof that 'savages' occupied a lower rung of the evolutionary ladder, thus justifying their colonization by a superior European race (Hudson 1987: 65–75). Tony Bennett has traced in detail the deployment of the 'archaeological gaze' in 'evolutionary' museums in Britain, the US and Australia (Bennett 2004). These ideas saturated Pakeha perceptions of Māori people in colonial New Zealand. When the New Zealand Institute was founded at the Colonial Museum in 1868, Governor George Bowen made a point of referring to the need to throw light on 'that very complicated and difficult, but highly interesting subject – the past and future of the Maori race' (*The Wellington Independent,* 6 August 1868). Yet despite circumstantial evidence of this type, historians warn against the assumption that all Pakeha believed Māori were inevitably doomed to evolutionary oblivion (Stenhouse 1996).

How did these categories of display operate in practice at the Colonial Museum? In its early days the Museum met with general approval from staff, colleagues in other museums and visitors. 'The museum looks pretty' declared James Hector proudly in 1868 (Letter 17 May 1868 ATL Ms 0305). A visitor who was shown over the museum in the same year was impressed by the exhibits, reporting that the director and his museum were 'immensely popular.' He described a large moa display, an unusual stuffed *kurī* (Polynesian dog), photographs and paintings on the walls and vases with native shrubs, trees and plants. The only Māori material mentioned was 'a large quantity of native weapons', which he thought 'handsomely arranged' (Holmes in Von Haast 1948: 567–8).

A floorplan shows the main hall with table cases in orderly ranks, and standing cases around the walls, with the feature display the feathered model of a *moa* on a stand at the south end (*Catalogue* 1870, n.p.). Models and skeletons of the extinct native *moa*, the flightless giant birds, were the star attractions of early museums in New Zealand and were eagerly sought by foreign collectors (Figure 1.3). Hector's colleague Walter Mantell sent *moa* bones to Richard Owen and returned to England in 1856 to work with him on constructing a skeleton at the British Museum (Sorrenson 1990). Around the *moa* there were glass cases crammed with rocks and fossils; above them a walrus sat on top of the railing and a skeleton of a dolphin hung from the ceiling. Despite the fact that Hector was busy identifying and classifying these new species in his scientific articles, the ramshackle nature of the public displays retained a sense of awe at the strange beasts discovered in a new found land. They help us to understand 'why wonders and curiosities never ceased', despite the best efforts of scientists to do away with them (Glenn Penny 2002: 7).

There are few Māori objects in these images. They were of secondary importance in what was essentially a natural history museum, and were classified as natural rather than cultural entities. Early exhibits grouped Māori objects with geology, flora and fauna in a

'New Zealand collection,' which was generally displayed in the main hall. In the floorplan, 'Maori implements' were placed in a table case with 'moa bones,' and 'Maori mats' placed on a wall with birds, fossils, wood, wool and other 'anatomical preparations'. Annual Reports referred to them as part of the 'natural history' collections in the 1860s, and only used the term 'ethnology' consistently from the late 1870s, without making any distinction between foreign and Māori acquisitions ('Memorandum', *AJHR* 1866 D-9). It is likely that W.B.D. Mantell took more interest in Māori collections than Hector in the early years of the Museum. Mantell was a Māori-speaking collector and gentleman scientist who was Minister of Native Affairs in several governments. He was involved in efforts to establish the Museum, helped to set up the first displays, and was honorary curator during Hector's frequent absences on geological surveys (Simpson 1964: 27; Dell 1965a: 4).

The Colonial Museum building reached its final form after extensions in 1875–6. The gallery now ran around three sides of the main hall and the railing was still being used to hang framed paintings, photographs and mounted heads. The main hall was devoted to 'general, typical and foreign' collections, the north wing given over to natural history, and the south wing to geology (Annual Report 1876). A photograph from just after this period shows rows of cases on the ground floor, which was also dotted with feature objects such as busts, animal skulls and decorative art (TP B.004141). Images of museums in the British Empire at this time show a mix of things that, though bewildering to modern eyes, reflect shifting values about visual culture that had not yet hardened into the modern dichotomy of art and craft. To the Victorians, 'art' was a word more loosely applied than today. There was debate over a diverse range of industrial and domestic 'arts', over original sculptures and plaster casts, and the relative artistic merits of womens' work and the products of non-European peoples (Taylor 1999; Hill 2005; Whitehead 2005). Care should be taken with the use of the term 'art' before 1900, which reflected the liberal impulse of the Arts and Crafts movement rather than the formalist aesthetics of the twentieth century.

Te Hau ki Tūranga, or the 'Maori house', as it was called, was the most important Māori object in the collection. Reconstructing the context surrounding its display shows the fluidity of visual categories in the colonial cultures of display, in which Māori objects occupied multiple and seemingly contradictory positions within several discursive formations. Built in the 1840s with steel tools by leading Rongowhakaata chief and master carver Raharuhi Rukupō, the meeting house was a strikingly innovative combination of indigenous tradition and imported technology. The *whare whakairo* developed in the early nineteenth century as symbol of social unity, representing an ancestor's body in which descendants gathered together to express an emerging sense of tribal identity (Walker 2001: 43). The immediate background to *Te Hau ki Tūranga's* acquisition was the military conflict on the East Coast between 'rebel' Māori and government forces backed by loyalist Māori. Circumstances suggest that it was displayed in the capital during the New Zealand or 'land wars' as a trophy of colonial conquest. Nevertheless the *whare* is a classic example of what Thomas has called an 'entangled object' (Thomas 1991) and its complex story involves a large cast of characters involved in an episode that is almost impossible to unravel (Barrow 1976; O'Rourke 1994; Binney 1995: 29).

After it arrived in Wellington in 1867, Hector decided not to reconstruct it because a costly and 'unsightly' detached building would not allow the carvings to be seen clearly nor allow space for 'other exhibits'. Instead he lobbied the Colonial Secretary's Office to get the Museum's north wing built as originally planned, in order to 'incorporate' the carvings within the building and so 'exhibit them to most advantage as specimens of native carving' (Hector 6 June 1867 ANZ IA 1, 1868/450). A groundplan shows the resulting enclosed annex attached to the new north wing, with the surviving carvings raised up off the floor and enclosed within an exterior skin of wood and iron by a carpenter, who placed 'reeding' between the *poupou* and *heke* as a substitute for *kākaho* reeds and the missing *tukutuku* panels (*Catalogue of the Colonial Museum* 1870). A photograph apparently taken at the time of construction shows a *poupou* from the house, described as a 'fine specimen' of Māori carving, mounted on a base and fixed between the fluted wood work that passed for *tukutuku* (Figure 1.4).

In July 1868, a visitor described the recently completed exhibit in glowing terms, noting that it was 'worth coming a long way to see' (Holmes in Von Haast 1948: 569). Hector seemed pleased with this solution, and wrote that the 'interior presents as much as possible the original character which its designers intended' (AR 1868: 4). But his response to *Te Hau ki Tūranga* itself remained ambiguous. He found its carvings 'grotesque' yet he referred to the *whare* as a 'wonderful specimen of Native Art' (AR 1868: 4). Although the director intended to use the interior as a setting for the display of Māori objects, little evidence has survived of the form that this took. A card with 'Tareha's account' (see below) of the house was placed inside 'for the information of visitors' (Hector 15 January 1869 TPA MU 147, 2/62). There is also evidence that the space contained table cases (Gordon 20 January 1899 TPA MU 94, 8/47), and that Māori flags were draped along the ceiling (Hamilton 11 November 1909 TPA MU 152, 3/5). Later photographs (Figure 1.5) show objects such as *rākau whakapapa*, *taiaha* and even large carvings placed casually against the *poupou*. The interior of the Māori house at the Canterbury Museum in Christchurch was a similar space with clothing and weapons casually hung on the walls between the *poupou*, and table cases with smaller objects (Walker 1991: fig 1). Certainly the general public seemed to regard it as a curiosity, which is understandable given the patterns of European colonization in the South Island where Pakeha swamped the small Kai Tahu population. 'To a Southern Colonist a Maori is quite a novelty', declared a newspaper report, 'and such a thing as a "rununga-house" is almost unknown' (*Illustrated New Zealand Herald*, 6 November 1875). Despite this reaction from European visitors, the *whare* received the praise of Ngāti Porou leader Ropata Wahawaha who saw it being carved (*Te Waka Maori* 10.16, 11 August 1874).

Nearly all early museums in New Zealand were supported by learned societies rather than public rates as in Britain's municipal museums (Hill 2005). The Colonial Museum

Figure 1.4 *Poupou* from *Te Hau ki Tūranga*, Colonial Museum, c.1868
(Alexander Turnbull Library Mundy PA1-f-039-32).

Figure 1.5   Interior of *Te Hau ki Tūranga*, Colonial
Museum, c.1901–2 (Alexander Turnbull Library Cowan
PAColl-3033-1-14).

was linked to the New Zealand Institute, with James Hector also acting as manager and
the editor of its journal (Dell 1965a: 4–5). In August 1868, the Colonial Museum was the
venue for the inaugural meeting of the New Zealand Institute, a *conversazione* attended by
the Governor and 'all the fashion and elite of the city' (*The Evening Post* 5 August 1868). In
Victorian England, soirees and like events were related to the formation of new urban elites
who marked off the museum as a socially exclusive space (Hill 2005: 135). In colonial New
Zealand society, the Institute was similarly 'class based and class-defining' (Reid 2005). After
the formal speeches, the company proceeded to 'promenade the Museum' and the recently

installed meeting house was one of the 'objects of interest' (*Transactions and Proceedings of the New Zealand Institute* 1868 1: 3). At a later meeting, in addition to the papers presented by learned gentlemen, two Māori speakers described the house for their Pakeha audience. Tāreha Te Moananui said it was a 'sign of chieftainship' and a man identified only as Kiekie said that it was one of the 'distinguishing marks of a New Zealand chief'. The other aspect stressed by Tāreha was that each *pou* represented 'certain individuals, ancestors of mine.' Tāreha, chief of Ngāti Kahungunu and MP for Eastern Māori, was closely involved in the purchase of *Te Hau ki Tūranga* and his speech implies that this 'important and valuable property among the Maori' had come into Pakeha hands because of the misdeeds of the rebel natives (*TNZI* 1868 1: 445–6). In contrast to its Pakeha status as a spectacle, Māori emphasized its importance in terms of political and genealogical efficacy.

Despite the circumstances of its sale and the varying views of Māori, Pakeha visitors and museum staff about its worth, *Te Hau ki Tūranga* remained popular with New Zealand commercial photographers for the rest of the century. Individual *poupou* from the house were photographed out of doors with other objects for several *cartes de visite* or Victorian postcards, which often depicted exotic subject matter for sale to visiting tourists. An early example of these images featuring another *poupou* from the house was probably taken at the time of the Colonial and Vienna exhibition in Christchurch in 1872–3 (Figure 1.6). The ancestor figure is 'clothed' in a *kaitaka* cloak with its decorated *tāniko* border, creating an effect like drapery on a classical statue. A greenstone *mere*, *pūtorino*, fish hook and lure are laid against the figure. Though there are many such examples of decontextualized Māori objects depicted as curiosities, this was not always the case. In the late nineteenth century, the same objects received a more positive response from Pakeha viewers as the image of the noble savage displaced the ignoble one in the colonial culture of display.

TAONGA, TRADE AND EXCHANGE: MĀORI RESPONSES TO DISPLAY

Just as Māori successfully resisted and adapted to Pakeha control in war and politics, the visual categories within which Māori objects were constituted in museums were equally open to contestation and change. Exhibiting was central to the construction of colonial discourse but it was by no means immune from Māori involvement. There are many examples of Māori contact with museums and exhibitions in the period from the 1860s to the 1880s. Māori responses to museum display reveal much about their own categories of visual culture, and how these too changed in response to new social forces.

Although it is difficult to obtain a clear picture of Māori practices of display in the nineteeth century, the evidence suggests that they were closely related to *mana*, that most central of Māori values, which can be understood as power, prestige, authority, influence, and control (Williams 1971: 172; Barlow 1991: 60–2; Mead 2003: 29–30). In the following proverb, the heavens bedecked with clouds are compared to the bird that is 'adorned' with feathers, namely the chief whose mana is enhanced when he stands to speak in his feather cloak: '*He ao te rangi ka uhia, he huruhuru te manu ka tau*' (Mead and Grove 2001: 65).

Figure 1.6   *Poupou* from *Te Hau ki Tūranga*, c.1872–3
(Alexander Turnbull Library Preston PA1-0-423-05-1).

In the Māori language the verbs *whakakite* ('reveal', 'display') *whakaatu* ('show,' 'call attention to') *whakatakoto* ('lay down,' 'place') were used to denote displays, exhibits or exhibitions (Williams 1971: 120, 20, 374). For Māori exhibiting was about power – display demonstrated *mana*. This can be seen in images of *kai* piled high on huge platforms for visitors; of *tūpāpaku* covered in cloaks and *pounamu* during *tangihanga*; and of groups of people standing in front of *whare* presenting their weapons and finery (Figure 1.7). In fact *Hinemihi* was known as the house with the 'golden eyes' because the *pāua*-shell eyes of the carved figures were replaced with coins by the local people made wealthy from the tourist trade, an example of Māori 'conspicuous consumption' (Neich 2001: 194). Another example

Figure 1.7   The meeting house *Hinemihi* at Te Wairoa, near Rotorua,
1880–1 (Alexander Turnbull Library PA7-19-19).

was the display of cloaks, flags and other prized possessions at the *tangi* of a Whanganui
chief, with a local man performing the traditional *pūkana* as if to show off in front of the
impressive spectacle (Figure 1.8). Carved and woven heirlooms such as *waka taua, pātaka*
and later *whare whakairo* were the pre-eminent means of exhibiting the *mana* of a *rangatira*,
but it is telling that these images of public wealth often included such objects right alongside
European trinkets or commercial produce (ATL 3042 (½-008439G)). Numerous portraits
commissioned by Māori patrons make it clear that Pakeha clothes and jewellery, and indeed
oil painting and photography itself, were also popular ways of exhibiting status and prestige
(Bell 1992).[3]

   Despite its historical breadth of usage, current interpretations of the word '*taonga*' define
it as the 'treasures' of Māori cultural and natural heritage, albeit encompassing things as
diverse as the natural environment, people, objects, and non-material entities (Hedley
2004). Anne Salmond calls *taonga* a 'fixed point in the tribal network of names, histories,
and relationships'. They connected the living to the living, and the living to the dead, in the
shape of *waiata*, proverbs, heirlooms, or garments that bring down the past into the present
(Salmond in Mead 1984a: 118). *Taonga* are said not only to collapse spatial and temporal

Figure 1.8 Cloaks and flags at Porokoru Patapu's *tangi* at Pūtiki *pā*, Whanganui, 1917 (Alexander Turnbull Library Tesla Studios PAColl-3046 (1/1-016457-G)).

boundaries but to blur the Western separation of the material and immaterial world. Māori people respond to *taonga* as living rather than inanimate things – carvings do not just represent ancestors, they *are* those ancestors (Mead 1997a). It is helpful to understand this complex and ambiguous concept through the work of Alfred Gell. Following Gell's (1998: 25) analysis of the 'network of social relationships' that occurs in the vicinity of art objects, I explore how the agency of display is articulated through the response of Māori to exhibiting Māori.

The indigenous category of '*taonga*' operated outside museums in Māori contexts throughout the period under discussion. As with other aspects of Māori culture, the concept of *taonga* was nevertheless profoundly affected by the experience of colonization, and documents show a subtle shift in meaning away from the economic towards the cultural field. The current legalistic definition of *taonga* (Tapsell 1997, 2000) has led to claims for repatriation based on notions of stolen patrimony but there is abundant evidence that things were freely exchanged in networks of trade and commerce from the first contact between Māori and Europeans (Henare 2005: 47–8, 33–6). Anthropologist Annette Weiner has analysed *taonga* in the context of broader Polynesian practices, suggesting it was more fluid and contingent than current orthodoxies indicate (Weiner 1992: 48).[4] Early English dictionaries and other texts stress the sense of 'property' or 'anything highly prized' (Kendall and Lee 1820: 207; Williams 1971: 381; Orange 1987: 257–8, 264).[5] In articles, letters and advertisements in Māori newspapers from the 1860s to the 1900s, it is most commonly used to describe 'goods' (Simpson 1994; Orbell 2002). An 1885 government notice soliciting contributions for an industrial exhibition used the word *taonga* for agricultural produce as well as handmade crafts (Pānui 30 April 1885 ATL Williams 709a). Dictionaries and glossaries in the late nineteenth century and early twentieth century indicate a drift from 'property' to 'treasure' (Williams 1871: 152; Tregear 1891: 468; Hamilton 1901a: 413). By the early twentieth century, Māori texts refer to *taonga* specifically as selected items of cultural heritage.

For Europeans, the meaning of Māori objects in museum display moved gradually from curio to specimen in the nineteenth century but there is evidence that for Māori their commercial display as curios outside museums was closer to Māori concepts of material culture. Māori who made or dealt in *taonga Māori* moved in the business world rather than museums. The Kai Tahu people offered curios for sale at Joubert and Twopenny's commercially-oriented New Zealand International Exhibition in Christchurch in 1882. Ngamotu Wiremu, who could only be described as a Māori curio dealer, offered 'taonga Maori' for sale to the Department of Tourist and Health Resorts (14 September 1904 ANZ TO 1, 1901/162/19). Henry Uru ran an emporium in Christchurch where he sold a bewildering range of 'Maori curios'; everything from traditional cloaks to woven tea cosies and carved pipes (*Souvenir* 1907: 85). One photograph of a curio display (possibly Uru's shop) shows a great variety of items displayed as they would be in any auction room (ATL G215461/1). There was ironically greater room for Māori agency in retail businesses than in the tightly circumscribed sphere of the museum. The few instances of Pakeha adopting this Māori category are found in the sale of curios. A catalogue for the Butterworth collection in New Plymouth carries the title 'Taonga tawhito (possessions of olden times): Catalogue of Maori curios'. This contains Māori words for the items on sale, in contrast to museum publications, which generally employed English titles (ATL PAM 016.704; Day 2005). T.E. Donne, New Zealand Agent-General in London and an enthusiastic Māori collector, sometimes used the word *taonga* in personal letters (Donne 4 November 1909 TPA MU 152, box 3/3).

What do the words in *te reo Māori* for museums and exhibitions reveal about Māori responses to Western technologies of display? Museums were referred to variously as: the 'house' for seeing or looking at 'taonga', 'lore' or 'expertise'; the 'house for heaping/leaving/laying out things'; or the 'store house of marvellous things'. International exhibitions were referred to with phrases such as 'the great displays to the world' or 'displays of taonga'.[6] The words denoting placing, laying, or leaving suggest Māori saw these Pakeha buildings as spaces where things were left or perhaps neglected. The use of *taonga* in Māori texts of the time suggests that the Māori objects in museums were still regarded as such though they were no longer in Māori hands. Other museum objects such as natural wonders, historical relics and decorative arts were considered *taonga* in their own way and were equally the object of Māori curiosity (Blackley 1997: 5). The words '*mātakitaki*' (look at, watch, inspect, peer, pry), or '*whakakitekite*' (reveal, disclose, display) highlight what Polynesian people thought was the peculiar importance of vision amongst Westerners. But Māori people were not passive objects of the gaze, nor was it confined to Western eyes only. Two Māori from the Waikato region visiting Europe in the 1850s remarked on the way that a crowd of people in Vienna, like a 'swarm of midges', followed them around staring at them. They refer to themselves being 'on display' but the way people 'marvelled' at them seems almost to be a source of pride. The highlight of their sightseeing in the Austrian capital was the lion in the zoo, a creature that they observed with the fascinated attention of amateur naturalists (Hogan 2003: 24–5).

Different cultural attitudes to display did not deter Māori from attending museums, however. There is circumstantial evidence of Māori visitation at most New Zealand museums in the nineteenth and twentieth centuries and a number of fascinating accounts of Māori going to exhibitions abroad (Mackrell 1985; Hogan 1997; Butts 2003; McCarthy 2004). In 1855 for example, Hoani Wiremu Hipango of Whanganui visited the Crystal Palace and the British Museum where he saw Māori exhibits and marvelled at the Egyptian coffins (Hipango 1969: 27, 29; Owens 2004: 195–6). Māori visitors were not always so enthusiastic. After his visit to an Australian art gallery in 1874, Ropata Wahawaha was astonished by the hypocrisy of Victorian decorum:

> Really the pakehas are a most extraordinary people. They are shocked if a button falls from a man's shirt collar ... and yet they manufacture naked images of stone and exhibit them to strangers! (*Te Waka Maori* 10.16, 11 August 1874)

From the time the Colonial Museum opened in Wellington, it attracted a steady trickle of Māori visitors. On their way out after their visit they wrote their names and where they came from in the visitors' books, or had an attendant sign for them. Though fragmentary – Māori with English names may not have been identified and not all visitors signed the book – it has been possible to build up a crude picture of Māori visitation.[7] These signatures prove that Māori made up a small but consistent audience for the institution up to the turn of the century. By 1900, however, the proportion of Māori visitors may have increased as Pakeha numbers remained about the same or even declined. Although the Māori population of Wellington was not large, visitors patronized the Colonial Museum fairly regularly not only from the city but also the adjacent suburbs of Petone, Heretaunga (the Hutt Valley) and further afield from Porirua and the Kapiti coast. Wī Tako Ngātata and Te Puni of Te Āti Awa, Porutu (son of Wiremu Kīngi Te Rangitāke) of Taranaki, and Tamihana Te Rauparaha of Ngāti Toa are examples of notable visitors from the wider region. The names of Māori politicians, who sat in the House of Representatives from 1868, appear several times a year: Wī Parata, Mōkena Kōhere, Wī Pere, Paikea and Hōri Kerei Taiaroa. There were numerous out-of-town visitors, as might be expected from the museum's location conveniently close to Parliament and government offices where they were likely to have had business in the capital. The names of prominent tribal leaders such as Paora Tūhaere of Ngāti Whātua, Paratene Ngata of Ngāti Porou and Waata Hipango of Whanganui can be found, along with people like Tuta Nihoniho who were later to play a very active role within the museum itself.

Just as the museum attracted the Wellington social elite, these signatures demonstrate the presence of influential Māori from powerful *kūpapa* (loyalist) tribes. Pro-government leaders like Tāreha Te Moananui, who Belich calls the 'Maori winners of the New Zealand wars' (1996: 265), were the most likely to engage with Pakeha society in the form of museum activities. Like indigenous peoples elsewhere, the actions of Māori patrons in assembling collections, donating things to museums and giving gifts to distinguished visitors can be seen as 'direct evidence of active self-positioning' (Phillips 2005: 117). For example, Metekingi and other local Māori donated things to the museum in Whanganui (Butts 2003: 140). In 1866 Metekingi deposited a 'pare' at the Colonial Museum 'said by him to be called *Te Whakangoto*' (anonymous note 27 November 1866, TPA MU 147, 1/276). The fact that he referred to this object in Māori terms, shows that winning the fruits of collaboration did not mean abandoning his own values. Yet for rebel tribes, whose material culture had became the spoils of war, the relationship with this repository of government 'booty' was more difficult. In petitions by Rukupō in 1867 and Wī Pere in 1878, Rongowhakaata tried to gain redress for the loss of *Te Hau ki Tūranga*. This does nevertheless confirm that Māori from Gisborne continued to visit their house in Wellington and were familiar with how it was displayed (*AJHR* 1867 G-12; *AJHR* 1878 I-3: 23). In Rukupō's obituary in 1873 for example, the Reverend Mohi Tūrei wrote that *Te Hau ki Tūranga* was 'used for exhibiting the curiosities of the world' (*Te Waka Maori* 9.19, 10 December 1873).

There are clues that *Te Hau ki Tūranga* was a considerable attraction for Māori people as well as Pakeha. After its installation in early 1868 there was a noticeable increase in the number of Māori signatures in the visitors' books at the Colonial Museum. Over 40 Māori visited in June and July, several of them more than once. At the end of June, a group of twenty-four Te Arawa and Whanganui people went to the museum, among them notable loyalist chiefs Kēpa Te Rangihiwinui (Major Kemp) and Metekingi, who took a seat in Parliament that year. One 'G. Aperaniko' from Whanganui visited no less than six times between July and September.

Evidence of specific Māori responses to museum exhibits is rare but a letter from a Māori visitor has survived. This man, who identified himself as 'a New Zealand chief', visited the museum on 9 June 1874 (TPA MU 147/4). He wrote to James Hector the same day, saying that he liked the museum 'and the things in it'. The good thing about the museum, he said, was there were things to see 'for Maori and for Pakeha'. He was obviously impressed with what he saw, perhaps most of all by the foreign displays, because he praises the Pakeha for achieving these 'worldly works'. He ends by asking for God's guidance 'in your important work'. But despite these positive comments, he sounds a more sombre note in his criticism of 'the display of dead things' (TPA MU 147/4). Whether he was referring to human remains or merely stuffed animals is not clear. The public display of *tapu* material such as *mokamokai* (preserved tattooed heads) or *kōiwi tangata* (human bones) may have created the impression that the museum was a charnel house and made Māori visitors feel uncomfortable.[8] It is also possible however that Māori at this time had rather more complex responses to this matter than the blanket condemnation that greeted this issue in the late twentieth century (Mackrell 1985: 73). Note Hector's observation of Māori fascination with the Egyptian mummy:

> As an exhibit it has excited the greatest interest and crowds of visitors daily come specially to inspect this new attraction. To the Maories [sic] in particular it is an object of wonderful interest. (Hector 17 September 1885, in O'Rourke 1996)

OBJECTS OF EMPIRE? NEW ZEALAND COURTS AT WORLD'S FAIRS

At the Great Exhibition of 1851, the small New Zealand presentation contained a diverse range of produce: Māori carvings, Māori-made products (such as flax *kete*), samples of flour ground in Māori mills and various woods sent by a Māori exhibitor (Henare 2005: 149–50). In the first New Zealand exhibition of 1865, there was a section devoted to 'articles of Maori manufacture, and specimens illustrative of the arts and customs of the Maori race' (*New Zealand Exhibition* 1866: 321). A surprising variety of display categories were at work here. Māori objects were sometimes described as 'curious' or 'rude' but also received praise for their ingenuous construction, grace and beauty. As well as specimens, they were often referred to as 'manufactures,' 'productions' or 'implements' and were viewed as skilfully made objects that demonstrated specific processes or the potential of raw materials. Māori things could be seen as old, but their antiquity was not considered, at this stage, an impediment to Māori potential for technological advancement. The catalogue commented on objects 'of bygone days' contrasting these with the current adoption by Māori of European clothing and customs. It noted that Māori were 'one of the finest and most intelligent of aboriginal races' who had thrown off the 'barbarism of their forefathers' and earned the 'respect of the Colonists' (*New Zealand Exhibition* 1866: 321–32). Colonists saw Māori as capable of the progress that defined the colony, compared to the more racist rhetoric later in the century, which erased them from modern history. Their inclusion in the exhibition implied their participation in national life.

The Vienna Universal Exhibition of 1873 provides another example of the indeterminate status of Māori material. As a colony of Great Britain, New Zealand's court took its place alongside those of India and Australia. Isaac Featherston, then Agent-General in London and exhibition commissioner, saw the venture as an opportunity to advertise New Zealand in Europe (*AJHR* 1873 H-5). James Hector thought the exhibits would encourage immigration and promote local exports and suggested the inclusion of raw materials like minerals, ores, timber, wool and flax (Hector 18 September 1872 ANZ IA 25/4). The New Zealand court contained a wide range of objects: coal, gold and flax from the Colonial Museum, 250 mounted birds from Walter Buller's collection and a *moa* skeleton from the Canterbury Museum. The 'Fine Arts' section contained 'scenic views of New Zealand' in the form of photographs commissioned from D.L. Mundy. Featherston contributed his own collection of carving and weaving in addition to a 'rebel' Māori flag (*Reports* 1874; 'Descriptive catalogue' 1873 ANZ IA 25/4).[9] The court included a 'fancy mat' in the 'manufactured flax' section made by 'Tarahora' (*New Zealand Messenger*, 1 November 1873).

For Hector, the display had to be simple as well as commercially effective. He argued that 'in these exhibitions the best effect is produced by objects of considerable size, labelled and arranged in an imposing and intelligible manner' (Hector 18 September 1872 ANZ IA 25/4). He wanted the *moa* skeletons to form 'a striking centre piece for the New Zealand court'. Other items were placed in glass show cases, and photographs were mounted under glass on stands, with the principal objects explained to visitors through 'large size explanatory tickets' (*AJHR* 1873 H-R: 4–5). The Austrian geologist Ferdinand Hochstetter, a keen student of New Zealand fauna, arranged the moa into a tableau with some stuffed *kiwi*. Viewers reported that the *moa* was a 'magnificent sight' (Von Haast 1948: 674) and it 'excited much attention from its enormous proportions' (*AJHR* 1873 H-5: 13). In addition to being presented as products and specimens, Māori objects were simultaneously displayed as decorative exotica. Mundy's landscapes included Māori scenes, obviously meant to portray the Pacific peopled by colourful natives, including the photograph (Figure 1.4) of a 'carved panel from the Maori House, Colonial Museum' ('Descriptive catalogue' 1873 ANZ IA 25/4). This image is described on the caption as a 'fine specimen' but the artfully haphazard composition echoed the scenes of wild bush and skeletons of gigantic birds. A curiosity, it was not meant to convey any idea of the function of these objects, but to exaggerate their strangeness and difference.

Exhibitions were far from a clear-cut affair but a compromise between the scientific order of carefully arranged specimens, the romantic allure of foreign peoples and the commercial spectacle of material possessions. They were subject to competing claims from ambitious collectors, local officials and the lofty ideals of exhibition commissioners back in New Zealand. The visual technologies used at world's fairs – trophies, glass show cases, picture galleries and photographs and above all the exhibits piled up on tables in the barnlike interiors of the halls – have obvious connections with urban spaces such as shopping arcades where things were laid out in particular ways for consumers to look at (Armstrong 1993: 21–3). Exhibition design was a messy affair, as much the result of practical opportunism as policy or politics. In contrast to theories of social control, the resulting chaotic jumble of sights, sounds and experiences could be exhilarating and liberating for visitors (Greenhalgh 1989; Armstrong 1993; Witcomb 2003: 19–21). Māori culture was simultaneously displayed within a number of categories – souvenirs, commodities, specimens, curios – in ways which made the exotic more familiar than was otherwise the case. The contingent nature of these fluid categories shows that colonial cultures of display were susceptible to intervention and as the archive suggests, Māori agency was a key, if often hidden, part of this enterprise.

Three years later, the contents of the New Zealand court at Philadelphia reflected the values of Māori exhibitors (Figure 1.9). As part of the Colonial Museum contribution, Resident Magistrate R.W. Woon from Whanganui organized a collection of 'garments, ornaments, weapons etc' on behalf of several prominent chiefs. Woon's description of these objects, obviously obtained from the owners themselves, reflected a Māori value system in contrast to Hector's 'instructive ethnological series' arranged in an upright show case (TPA MU 147, 4/298). The tribal heirlooms were referred to in labels and catalogue by name, and their connection to *whakapapa* and historical events was intimately associated with the *mana* of the individual donor:

> *Haimona Te Ao o te Rangi*, chief of the Ngatipanioaua tribe – a patuparaoa, whalebone weapon, called 'Pai a te Rangi,' handed down from ancestor named Kahunui, four generations back. Has been used in many battles, in which several chiefs 'were made to lick the dust'. (*Philadelphia International Exhibition* 1876: 335)

Woon's correspondence reveals that some Māori had a pragmatic attitude to exhibiting their culture. It seems that they regarded the exercise as a form of exchange and expected

Figure 1.9   New Zealand court at Philadelphia International Exhibition, 1876
(The Free Library of Philadelphia, Print and Picture Collection C.021438).

the Americans to 'take the hint' and reciprocate in kind (*AJHR* 1876 G-1: 32). Woon told Hector that local Māori expected 'some acknowledgement' from the US government, and that 'a tardy response' might risk Māori cooperation if 'demands for exhibits' were made in the future. In particular a response was sought from the US President who had been gifted a magnificent *kākahu kura* by Captain Wirihana Puna (TPA MU 147, 4/172; *Philadelphia International Exhibition* 1876: 335). When commissioners tried to buy the collection, which was regarded as an extremely fine one, Māori refused to sell as 'they expect articles to be returned except those given as presents' (TPA MU 147, 4/250).

Māori involvement in the New Zealand court was in stark contrast to the display of Native Americans at Philadelphia, which was intended to 'create the impression of Indians as an antithesis to the forces of progress' (Rydell 1984: 25). But if ethnographic displays were designed to condemn colonized peoples to evolutionary oblivion, then Māori clearly saw themselves as fit for survival. Māori newspapers often praised the inclusion of Māori exhibits in foreign expositions as a sign of 'progress'. Indeed, exhibition publications some-times gave Māori a *de facto* European status 'superior' to that of other indigenous groups (*Intercolonial Exhibition of Australia* 1867: 532). A series of photographs of Māori in the New Zealand court at Philadelphia, commissioned from the photographer Herbert Deverill, can be seen in the same light. Images of Te Rangitāhau and his wife, recently deconstructed as imperializing images (Maxwell 1999: 133–64), may be interpreted as displays of chiefly property rather than resignation and defeat (Figure 1.10). Te Rangitāhau's artificial pose may reflect the choreography of the photographer, but the image is similar to other photographs in the exhibition depicting richly attired groups of people in front of their carved meeting houses who 'show off' their heirlooms, brandish weapons and strike poses of cheeky defiance (ATL PA1-f-173-20). Nor did Māori necessarily feel they were positioned in subservient roles even in live displays. An Australian Commissioner offered to pay for the passage of a Māori so visitors could see 'a live descendent of a cannibal race' (Rice 2003: 55). Talk of sending a Māori to Philadelphia prompted a ready volunteer – but only if the price was right (Kahoe *Weekly News*, 16 June 1876).

We have another glimpse of Māori agency with the display of the meeting house *Mataatua* at the Sydney International Exhibition in 1879. This exhibition featured an ethno-logical court for the first time in Australasia, apparently at Hector's suggestion (*AJHR* H-5: 2; *Sydney International Exhibition* 1880). Government officials approached Ngāti Awa in the Bay of Plenty with the plan to 'show to the world the work which the Maori people were doing in the erection of carved dwellings…' (ANZ MA 5, 6/18). George Preece, the Opotiki magistrate who negotiated the deal, reported that 'they were very much pleased with the idea' and at a meeting in Whakatāne agreed to 'present' *Mataatua* to the government for display (*AJHR* 1880 G-4: 10). Ngāti Awa's expectations of involvement did not stop at sending their *wharenui*. Preece wrote to Hector with the proposal that a group of knowledgeable people 'should proceed to Sydney with the house and assist to erect it there in order that it might be put up in proper Maori style' (TPA MU 188, 1/122). This unfortunately did not

Figure 1.10 Te Rangitāhau in his *wharepuni*, C.1875 (Alexander Turnbull Library Deverill G-4706-½).

happen and the final installation was anything but sympathetic. Hector had the *whare* set up inside out because it cost too much to erect 'in the ordinary manner as a Maori house' (*AJHR* 1880 H-5: 2). Standing in the exhibition grounds, with a New Zealand flag pole outside, the house was a rather bizarre sight with its *poupou* and *tukutuku* exposed to the weather and the roof covered with Chinese matting (Figure 1.11). The only concession to its Māori owners appears to have been the history of *Mataatua* recounted by the carver Wepiha Apanui, which was placed in the porch. The gravity of this tribal history, with its detailed genealogical analysis of the carvings, contrasts with the official description of the house as 'grotesque' and 'novel' (*AJHR* 1879 G-4: 1–2).

For the first time, Māori people were literally 'on display' at Sydney but this living exhibit was a private commercial venture rather than a strictly ethnological exercise. Māori were no strangers to performing abroad. Several groups had taken part in lecture tours, 'exhibitions' and concerts in England, and in 1862 one group had visited Sydney (Mackrell 1985). At the Sydney exhibition a concert party from Ngāti Maru was housed in the garden palace near the *whare*, along with some Fijians, although they were not happy with their lodgings and decamped to the harbour foreshore (*New Zealand Messenger,* 17 January 1880). By

Figure 1.11   *Mataatua* at the Sydney International Exhibition, 1879
(Museum of New Zealand Te Papa Tongarewa Archives MU 14, 5
(13/27/127)).

most accounts the show was not a success. Officials wrote that the native performers were disappointing as 'types' of their race and were, moreover, 'far from ease' in their 'war paint and feathers...' (*Official Record* 1879: 365).

The literature on world's fairs in the Victorian age emphasizes how they served the interests of imperialism through the subjugation of native peoples (Rydell 1984; Greenhalgh 1988; Karp and Lavine 1991; Benedict 1994). As with Timothy Mitchell's work on Egypt (1991), New Zealand courts complicate this picture. Just as the idea of museums as an exclusively European domain is incomplete, the impression that exhibitions were solely the product of colonization is misleading. The examples discussed above reveal that before Māori objects were inscribed as art or ethnographic artefacts in early twentieth-century museums, they appeared in a variety of forms that were subject to a range of interpretations. Different modes of display prompted different responses to Māori things, some of which were similar to indigenous values: tribal *mana*, personal heirlooms, gift exchange, and trade. By participating in local and international fairs, Māori saw themselves as partners in colonial development rather than as subjects of it.

RECOLONIZATION AND DISPLAY, 1880s TO 1900s

When the Duke of Cornwall and York visited Wellington in 1901, loyal subjects constructed a series of arches to welcome him. This photograph captures the moment when the royal party passed through the government arch (Figure 1.12), an extraordinary structure made up entirely of native foliage, Māori painted designs and carvings borrowed from the Colonial Museum (Hodgson 1990: 169). The distinguished visitor was welcomed with the Māori words *'Nau mai haere mai'*. This is one of the many examples of how the self-fashioning of Pakeha was framed by Māori symbols. The changing economic, political and social context of the late nineteenth century, which Belich calls 'recolonization', explains this shift in the culture of display. After the initial explosive development, the colony's natural resources began to run out and as boom turned to bust there was a crisis of identity. The export of refrigerated meat and dairy products to Britain became New Zealand's economic lifeline and the relationship between the metropolitan centre and the colonial periphery of the British empire was renewed and strengthened. Although half way round the world from what many thought of as 'Home', New Zealand operated like a town supply, sending goods to Mother England. Formerly a relatively independent colony, the country became a loyal neocolonial outpost, the 'better Britain of the South Pacific' (Belich 2001: 11–12, 29–30).

Ethnic relations were also reconfigured. When Māori refused to expire as predicted, the policy of 'smoothing the pillow' of a dying race (Galbreath 1989: 76–77) switched to

Figure 1.12   Government Arch, royal tour, Wellington, 1901
(Alexander Turnbull Library F-79242-1/2).

rehabilitation and assimilation. Ideas of 'brown' Britons' and 'white Maori' were fuelled by the 'Aryan' philosophy of linguist and writer, Edward Tregear (1885). He accounted for Māori abilities by assigning them a pseudo-Caucasian ancestry, a useful tool for colonial administrators and gentleman scholars (Byrnes 1990; Ballantyne 2001). In this period Māori culture was 'collected, laundered and embalmed by Pakeha savants' in order 'posthumously' to provide New Zealand with 'a rich past, runes and ruins'. The only problem was that in the midst of this process of entombment 'the mummy woke up' (Belich 2001: 124). Māori responded in two ways. There was the straight-out resistance of independent leaders like Te Whiti, who led a campaign of peaceful non-cooperation. On the other hand, there was the engagement with the Pakeha state, seen in the *Kotahitanga* (unity movement), which ran its own Māori parliament, or disengagement, like the *Kingitanga* (King movement), the Māori monarchy, which withdrew into its own territory (the 'King country') after the wars. For those Māori who worked within the system, such as the parliamentarians referred to as the Young Māori Party, utilizing the white Māori discourse gave them political leverage (Belich 2001: 210–15).

From the 1880s, the social transformation from colonization to recolonization produced a series of important changes in the exhibitionary apparatus. On the one hand, world's fairs adopted a more scientific classification of nature and natives. There were more extensive and defined ethnological courts, often utilizing contemporary racial theories, which were more imperialistic in tone than previously. Convinced that the indigenous people were doomed, museums frantically embarked on a scramble for remnants of the Māori past (Belich 2001: 83). With the advance of colonization, which tied the colony even more closely to Britain, every corner of the land with its plants, animals and people were studied and categorized – constituting 'an empire of nature' (Griffiths 1996: 12). On the other hand, romantic representations of Māori were more prominent and what had once appeared to nervous colonists as curious or grotesque came to be seen by collectors and Pakeha enthusiasts as exotic and colourful. Before migrants were lured by scenes of an empty land from which local people were erased, now images of picturesque 'Maoriland' became popular with an audience made up of settlers and tourists.

Categories of museum display were reshuffled in the late nineteenth century in response to changing audience perceptions. 'Curio,' with its associations of rarity rather than wonder, became more common in the auction house than the museum. 'Specimen' became the dominant category, moving from a looser version based on the biological sciences to a tighter one constructed around ethnographic theories. Māori people and their culture, now safely within the orbit of empire, became the object of intense study, the process of analysis, dissection, comparison and classification that were part of the colonial project. But to many Pakeha, those Europeans now firmly settled or born in New Zealand, softer views of Māori reflected the fact that they were no longer a threat but a source of distinctive symbols for the colony. Towards the end of the century, disappearing Māori culture, like native birds and forests, rose in Pakeha estimation, as reflected in the use of terms such as 'relic' or 'antique'. These ambiguous words, applied to things which were seen as part of recolonial New Zealand's cultural heritage as the Britain of the south seas, were related to a developing Māori notion of heritage, itself spurred by increasing concerns over cultural loss (Werry 2001).

At the same time, another category of visual display had appeared. A very influential group of amateur ethnographers associated with the Polynesian Society, nursing 'lofty ambitions of intellectual acknowledgement', constructed a Europeanized version of Māori culture, complete with a hero-explorer, a great fleet, a supreme being, and a school of higher learning (Byrnes 1990: 20–2, 59–60; Belich 2001: 213–15). Another prerequisite for a noble race of honorary whites was visual art. A restricted usage of the word 'art' began to be applied by Pakeha collectors in the late nineteenth century to selected examples of Māori material culture. This sense of native 'art handicraft,' although still secondary to fine art made by Europeans, offered a more elevated position for Māori culture within recolonizing discourse, a kind of *de facto* European status within the dominant culture. It was a convenient way of making Māori part of recolonial New Zealand – they, and their art, were now considered almost, but not quite, as good as Europeans.

ETHNOGRAPHY AND ART: 'MAORILAND' THROUGH PAKEHA EYES

Barbara Kirshenblatt-Gimblett argues that museum objects are 'artifacts of our disciplines', so that ethnographic objects, for example, are 'objects of ethnography' (1998: 2, 17). The travels of *Te Tākinga* illustrate the way that Māori carvings became ethnographic specimens but also acquired the status of a symbol of recolonial New Zealand. Prior to entering the museum domain, *Te Tākinga* was a famous *pātaka* (food storehouse), which stood in the marae gardens near Rotoiti (Rotorua), the whales depicted on its *maihi* (bargeboards) representing the prosperity of the Ngāti Pikiao people. *Pātaka* were pre-eminent symbols of tribal *mana* in the early nineteenth century, but from the 1870s large meeting houses (*whare rūnanga*) became fashionable, and some *pātaka* found their way into museums and private collections. *Te Tākinga* was acquired by the collector Walter Buller in 1886 and became a prime specimen in his ethnological collection. The complex provenance of this building, among Māori and between Māori and Pakeha (Neich 2001: 388–9), reinforces the interpretation of *taonga* as property.

Soon after its purchase in 1886, detached carvings from *Te Tākinga* were on display at the Colonial and Indian (Colinderies) Exhibition in London. Julius von Haast, the director of the Canterbury Museum, designed the New Zealand court to 'picture the development of New Zealand's civilisation by contrasting it with the primitive condition of the Maori' (Von Haast 1948: 908). Visitors responded as he had hoped, judging by the reporter from *The Times*, who wrote that he had been led from 'Old New Zealand', exemplified by the Māori exhibits, to 'the present high standard of civilisation' (26 July 1886). Buller was a lawyer and amateur naturalist whose illustrated book on New Zealand birds was considered the authoritative work on the subject. A disciple of Darwin, he believed that native people, like native animal species, were inevitably dying out, and his duty was to collect specimens of a vanishing culture for posterity (Galbreath 1990). Buller displayed his birds, *moa* bones, portraits of Māori by Lindauer and a number of carvings (including from *Te Takinga*) and other items comprising 'Ethnological Collections, illustrating the history, arts, customs and habits of the Maori race' (*Colonial and Indian Exhibition* 1886: 271).

Although some New Zealand critics thought there were too many Māori exhibits, the English press were enchanted by the exotic setting of a carved tomb amongst the 'charming fernery', which brought to mind the 'melancholy saying of the Maoris' about their disappearing before the white man 'as foreign clover is killing our ferns…' (*Illustrated London News,* 2 October 1886: 226). *Te Tākinga* functioned as a remnant salvaged from a disappearing race. A contemporary engraving showed how the front of the *pātaka* was set up (Figure 1.13), completed with stray carvings which were themselves fragments. Having failed to display a living exhibit at Philadelphia, this New Zealand court employed wax figures that made quite an impression on British viewers. A couple wearing cloaks holding weapons and *kete* stood alongside the *pātaka* and another figure crouched in the porch. One writer commented on the 'comely Maori damsel' which brought the tableau to life (Cundall 1886: 68). Just as the makeshift building was a fabricated 'example' of a storehouse, so these figures reflect the intention of Haast and Buller to 'illustrate' Māori customs (Rice 2002: 58). The same group was exhibited at Paris in 1889, and their 'typical faces' and 'national costume' were said to 'give a very fair idea of Maori life' (*Universal International Exhibition at Paris* 1889: 7).

The Colinderies exhibition included several groups of living native people from around the Empire (Benedict 1983: 46). Similarly, wax figures have a long association with public display and with the representation of the Other (Atlick 1978: 333–49; Jacknis 2002). Suggestive of corpses, they are 'equiposed between the animate and the inanimate, the living and the dead' (Kirshenblat-Gimblett in Karp and Lavine 1991: 398). However, they do not have a large part in this genealogy, eventually appearing in New Zealand museums in the late nineteenth century. When real Māori proved to be too much of a handful or refused to live up to their ethnic stereotype, wax models were found to be a much more malleable substitute, their mortuary pallour signifying their fate in a much more acquiescent way.

Two years after its London showing, *Te Tākinga* was sent to an industrial exhibition in Melbourne. Here it was set amongst native plants (Figure 1.14), functioning as a picturesque centrepiece for a New Zealand court containing everything from pictures to perambulators (*New Zealand Court Catalogue* 1888: 17). Feature displays employing spectacular Māori objects were by now a common element of New Zealand courts as officials sought to distinguish themselves from their colonial neighbours, attract overseas visitors and appeal to a domestic audience (Johnston 1999: 234). On Buller's return to the colony, *Te Tākinga* was set up next to Lake Papaitonga on his estate in the Horowhenua. In this outdoor setting it was preserved as a picturesque ruin amid the remnants of native bush, which often featured in the photographs of Pakeha tourists. By the time Buller's son donated it

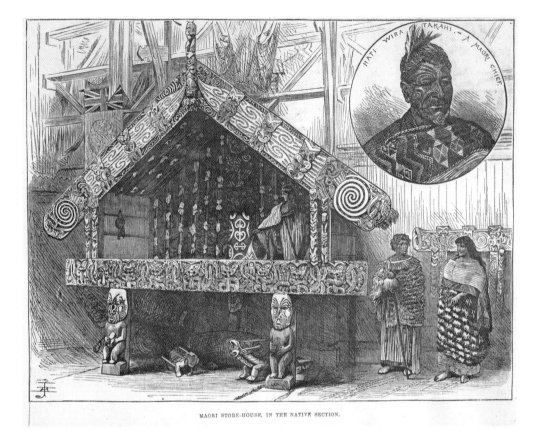

Figure 1.13 *Te Tākinga* at the Colinderies Exhibition, London, 1886
(*Illustrated London News*, 2 October 1886, 365).

to the Dominion Museum in 1911 it was regarded as being of national importance (Park in Erikson, Neumann and Thomas 1999). The reception of *Te Tākinga* demonstrates how Pakeha attitudes moved from disdain to a kind of proprietorial fascination, as old Māori carving became a relic, something to be protected for the nation rather than sold to tourists as a curio. It is also important to see these shifts in the wider context of European visual culture. The close relationship between exhibiting and leisure, tourism and travel suggests that native objects made the exotic familiar (Werry 2001) or appealed to a liberating sense of mystery and irrationality beyond Occidental control (Witcomb 2003: 23–4).

Meanwhile, at the Colonial Museum, the growing emphasis on *ethnographica* made little impact on an institution more and more inured to outside influences. Photographs of the interior of the Colonial Museum dating from the 1880s and 1890s reinforce the impression that, despite Hector's best intentions, it was a cabinet of curiosities rather than a scientific showcase (ATL PAColl 3114-2). The main hall was crammed with an array of disparate items: plaster casts of Greek statues, stuffed birds on shelves, suspended marine

Figure 1.14   *Te Tākinga* at Centennial International Exhibition,
Melbourne, 1888 (Museum of New Zealand Te Papa Tongarewa B.15245).

mammal skeletons, the wall above the doorway bristling with antlers and horns. The only Māori object in view was a single *tauihu* (canoe prow) on top of a case. Unlike Thomas Cheeseman at the Auckland Museum, the ageing Hector had failed to keep up with current British practice, which by this time emphasized the 'new museum idea', the educational use of museum display through the scientific classification of objects (Cameron 2000: 147; Bennett 2004: 33–5). In 1890 Hector complained that he was unable to achieve this goal due to the 'overcrowded condition of the exhibition halls' (AR 1890). When Rudyard Kipling visited Wellington in 1891, he found the contents of the Colonial Museum monotonously familiar. 'Ah, here I am at home again', he told a local reporter, 'amongst the dead bones and the ancient stones' (Wilkens 2002: 7). A visiting geologist from the British Museums Association was extremely critical of the labelling and arrangement of specimens, concluding that the Museum was probably 'the worst managed institution of the kind in the whole of the Southern hemisphere' (Bather 1894: 208). In this regard, the Colonial Museum was by no means exceptional and merely reflected the general situation in Europe and North America, where ethnologists were unable to get their huge collections in order, and came under pressure to replace their packed cases with clearer didactic displays (Glenn Penny 2002: 187–204).

Apart from the collections in the meeting house, there was no attempt to set up a Māori ethnographic hall like those at Auckland and Canterbury Museums, which had followed developments in Britain and North America. Fiona Cameron suggests that Cheeseman's separate Māori exhibit at Auckland was a response to the innovations of anthropologist Franz Boas in American museums (2000: 176). There, large feature objects and dedicated ethnographic displays were popular with local visitors and tourists, reflecting the rising value placed on Māori culture. Back in Wellington however, *Te Hau ki Tūranga* was the Colonial Museum's only major attraction by the end of the nineteenth century. *The Cyclopedia of New Zealand* (1897: 337) noted that the Museum 'is seldom thronged with visitors' although the *whare* was 'particularly attractive to tourists and others who take an interest in the arts and wonders of aboriginals'. Although more of the Māori collection found its way into the public halls, the display of Māori objects as art was still to come.

In *Reinventing Africa* Annie Coombes (1994: 5) has shown how public debate around 'aesthetic criteria and the artistic categories of art and design' in museums contributed to the formation of cultural identities – both the racialized identity of Africa and the national ideology of the British Empire. At the time when Māori became 'whitened' as part of better British society in late Victorian and Edwardian New Zealand, their 'art' was assimilated into a nascent form of colonial settler identity (Thomas 1999: 95–109; Belich 2001: 206–10). One of the first signs of this change came in the 1880s when Auckland art students became interested in Māori carving and weaving. Their annual exhibitions gathered a range of Māori objects from local collectors and mounted them alongside greenery, paintings and *objets d'art* (Blackley 1987). When newspapers criticized their show for lowering itself 'into a sort of Maori curiosity shop', the artist Alfred Sharpe replied that 'We do not call them curios; we call them Maori works of art; and they are so in every sense of the word' (*Herald*, 27 October 1885: 6). This small group of students, artists, collectors and enthusiasts began to revalue Māori carving, under the influence of Ruskin, Morris and the arts and crafts movement, which in England had brought about a greater appreciation of a broader range of domestic products in relation to fine art.[10] In an 1889 address to the Auckland Institute, S. Percy Smith, the editor of the *Journal of the Polynesian Society*, referred to *waka* and *pātaka* in the museum as 'works of art – if I may so term them'. This apologetic reference to what in the same paper he also calls 'relics' shows how their status as art was still fluid and provisional (TPA MU 206, 2/9).

These same objects were regarded very differently by their Māori producers and audiences. There was no word for 'art' in the Māori language, no corresponding concept of beauty or aesthetic form within Māori culture or tradition, nor was '*taonga*', despite Mead's retrospective definition, a synonym for art.[11] The various 'arts' of the meeting house – *whakairo*, *tukutuku*, and *kōwhaiwhai* – were essentially a statement of group identity and were valued as for their communicative qualities rather than for their own sake (Neich 2001: 127). Rather than being discovered, Māori 'art' was produced through the colonial culture of display.

The best known Pakeha advocate of the artistic qualities of Māori culture was Augustus Hamilton, an amateur naturalist and ethnologist, an avid collector, and a keen photographer (Dell 1993). He gathered an impressive collection of Māori carving at the Hawkes Bay Philosophical Institute in Napier and, along with Dr T.M. Hocken, was closely involved in the Māori court at the 1889–1890 New Zealand and South Seas Exhibition in Dunedin. This display demonstrated the 'artistic' abilities of the Māori 'artist' (*New Zealand and South Seas Exhibition* 1889: 177), although judging by newspaper reports not everybody shared the tastes of these collectors. Hamilton became synonymous with a large illustrated book (Hamilton 1901a) which became known as *Maori Art* (originally titled *The Art Workmanship of the Maori Race*). This influential publication established the popular status of Māori visual culture as art, and can be seen as the culmination of the contemporary arts and crafts aesthetic. In his introduction, Hamilton wrote that 'Maori Art'– note the capital *A* – had reached a 'very high level' among the native people (1901a: 5). Though a surprise to many colonists, Hamilton's exploration of Māori 'ornament' reflected intellectual currents in Europe. By the early twentieth century, many varieties of domestic arts and crafts, and even the work of non-European people, were considered a form of art in their own right (Coombes 1991: 209).

When he became director of the Colonial Museum in December 1903, Hamilton noted in his diary that his main objective was to 'get a representative collection of Maori art' (Pischief 1998: 124). He launched a concerted buying campaign, and pressured the government to make good its promises of a new building in order that he may collect 'the pick of the finest art of the Maori artist' (TPA MU 206 1). In a public lecture on Māori 'art workmanship' in 1904 he recommended that the basic patterns of 'Maori decorative art' be applied to architecture and everyday objects so that it became 'a national characteristic' and a 'memorial to the race who created and developed it' (ANZ TO 1, 1901, 162/20). Māori art, as a 'national' tradition, was appropriated by Pakeha while Māori were consigned to endlessly copying 'traditional' forms. Along with other Pakeha patrons of Māori carving, Hamilton was somewhat notorious for constraining Māori experimentation and encouraging a traditional orthodoxy. However this was the result of a self-conscious indigenous historicism as much as European-imposed orthodoxy. When the carver Te Rāhui borrowed Hamilton's *Maori Art,* he praised 'the work of the ancestors' and said that he 'promised to try and produce carvings of that quality' (cited in Neich 2001: 195). Nor was the condemnation of artistic innovation confined to Pakeha experts – witness Canon Wī Repa's comment in 1913 that the new carvings on the Manutūke church near Gisborne were a 'vile parody' of the 'old treasures' (cited in O'Rourke 1994).

The layout of the Colonial Museum under Hamilton relegated natural history to the north wing, and geological exhibits to the south wing 'so as to leave the main hall entirely for specimens of Maori art'. The displays at the Museum from 1903–13 reflect the growing admiration for customary Māori carving as the decorative art form closest to European sculpture (Figure 1.15). Hamilton sought to display wooden carvings in a way that drew attention to their 'sculptural' qualities. A *tekoteko*, dubbed a 'Maori Venus de Medici', was set up as a free-standing figure in front of a backdrop of *poupou* and *tukutuku*. *Te Hau ki Tūranga* featured prominently in Hamilton's campaign to raise carving to the status of art. Hamilton augmented and updated the *whare* as a 'Maori Art room' (Pischief 1998: 127). The Museum's new focus on Māori art was apparent to colleagues and visitors. Nevertheless, although it was considered capable of aesthetic beauty, Māori art was not necessarily the equal of fine art. It provided props to be incorporated into the portraits and historical paintings of Pakeha artists such as Linley Richardson, Goldie, Lindauer and others.

Hamilton commonly referred to Māori objects as 'specimens', reflecting the fact that, although he may have thought Māori carving 'artistic', it was ethnology which determined the arrangement of objects on display. This mixture of typological and aesthetic approaches was also evident at other New Zealand museums.[12] Citing English geologist Thomas Huxley, Hamilton defined a museum as a 'consultative library of objects' (Hamilton 1902a). He aimed to replace Hector's 'chaotic' arrangements with structured displays. Hamilton distinguished his institution from what he saw as heterogenous collections of curiosities, such as Petherick's Museum in the Wellington suburb of Newtown. Through the scientific order of its displays, the museum had a 'definite aim' in that 'each specimen should teach or illustrate something' (TPA MU 157 1, 2/14). Despite the lack of space Hamilton and his staff attempted to impose order by introducing a systematic series of printed labels (Figure 1.16). Pounders, sinkers, adzes, necklaces and clothing were laid out in table cases in an orderly fashion as 'proof' of primitive Māori life, like specimen trays of rocks or insects. House carvings were arranged together so that they suggested whole architectural features: windows, doors and facades.

Figure 1.15   Main hall of Dominion Museum showing *Te Heke Rangatira*, 1907 (Museum of New Zealand Te Papa Tongarewa Hamilton C.1048).

We know little of how audiences responded to what were seen as realistic forms of museum display in the Victorian and Edwardian periods, but it appears that visitors liked the verisimilitude of photographs, taxidermied specimens, models and dioramas – techniques which had developed at the same time as the new disciplines of natural history and ethnography (Hill 2005: 107). Donald Jenkins has argued that museum layout, in which exhibits were flattened, bordered, and covered in glass like photographs, was configured for the gaze of visitors who 'looked like a camera at snap shots of the world' (1994: 246–7). Hamilton

Figure 1.16   Main hall of Dominion Museum showing *Rahurahu*, 1907
(Museum of New Zealand Te Papa Tongarewa Hamilton C.1047).

employed these new technologies in the service of ethnology. Through photographs and models, he tried to attract the attention of the public, constructing naturalistic pictures of Māori life for Pakeha. James McDonald, the artist-technician on the museum staff (Dennis 1996), constructed a model *pā* which was one of the most popular exhibits for several decades. The fanciful arrangement of the fortified hill top village, like McDonald's historical paintings, seem to be based on romanticized early European images. As well as a statue group at the Christchurch exhibition in 1906, McDonald also made a life-size figure of a chief to model *kākahu*, an idealized man in dramatic pose modelled on figures at the Smithsonian Institution in Washington.

Hamilton tried to acquire portraits of Māori by Charles Goldie, and commissioned sculptor Nelson Illingworth to make busts of Māori 'types' modelled after those of Native Americans exhibited at the American Museum of Natural History in New York (TPA MU 157, 1/2). The director was unhappy with the results but a number of these busts were exhibited in the entrance hall. Though stereotypical representations of ennobled savages, the circumstances of their production makes us wonder who exactly was in charge and how they were received. This photograph (Figure 1.17) shows Illingworth with the model Te Wharekauri at Galatea surrounded by his family and playful children, an image richly suggestive of Māori agendas, with the women in the foreground staring back at the camera. Was this venerable chief merely the object of the gaze, or did he seek to have his *mana* enhanced by being immortalized in bronze?

The results of Hamilton's work were seen in what was now called the 'Maori hall' of the Dominion Museum. The war canoe *Te Heke Rangatira* took pride of place, positioned north to south along the length of the hall (Figure 1.18). Though it may originally have been a fishing canoe, it was displayed as a complete *waka taua*, with *tauihu* and *taurapa* from other areas added to the existing hull, and new carvings on the *rauawa*. It was painted red, like most other carvings that came into museum collections at this time, according to the ethnographic orthodoxy that Māori coloured their *tapu* carvings with red ochre (Hamilton diary 29 April 1910 TPA MU 144). Hamilton went to considerable trouble to embellish the *waka* with appropriate decorations, and, although later museum staff were critical of the result, this was the first time the museum had displayed a large Māori object in anything approximating its 'original' state (TPA MU 206, 2/2). The rest of the floor space was taken up with glass table cases containing garments, small carved objects, weapons, pounders and other stone tools (Figure 1.19). Carvings were everywhere: *whakawae* and *tekoteko* were fastened to columns, *pou* stood upright on the floor, and *paepae*, *poupou*, *pare* and other house carvings were attached to the gallery. At the south end of the hall we can see what looks like a whole house (Figure 1.18), but on closer inspection it is only the *amo*, *kōruru*, *maihi* and a shallow porch creating the impression of a house façade. Overcrowding is plainly evident. Table cases and carvings were crammed around the *waka*, with McDonald's model figure, a *tauihu* and other loose carvings placed anywhere there is room (Figure 1.19). Like his predecessor, Hamilton's ambitions may in the end have been defeated by the sheer volume of the collection.

ANTIQUITIES AND *TAONGA*: MĀORI AND SALVAGE

One day about the turn of the century, a Māori veteran of the New Zealand wars walked in to the Colonial Museum and gave his sword to the staff. In a speech he explained that he was donating it:

> …so that it may not be lost, but may be preserved forever in your *whare-matakitaki*, your great gazing house, for future generations to see… It may be our young people in time to come may wish to see it, and I will tell my story too, so that it may not be lost…
> (Cowan in *Canterbury Times*, TPA MU 157 1/1)

Figure 1.17   Illingworth and his model Te Wharekauri and
family, Galatea, c.1910 (Museum of New Zealand Te Papa
Tongarewa B.012619).

At this time Māori contact with the European culture of display increased dramatically.
Parallel to a growing sense among Pakeha of Māori things as antiquities, the early years of
the twentieth century saw changes in Māori thinking about preserving their past. Māori
participation in museums and exhibitions reflected a congruence of the concepts of salvage
and *taonga*. Māori began to claim a place within the recolonial project of modern New
Zealand.

Figure 1.18   Main hall of Dominion Museum, 1907 (Museum of New Zealand Te Papa Tongarewa Hamilton C.1049).

Figure 1.19   Main hall of Dominion Museum, 1910 (Museum of New
Zealand Te Papa Tongarewa Hamilton C.1050).

When Māori tribes welcomed visiting British royalty at Rotorua in 1901, Pakeha viewers
were astonished at their generous presentation of gifts (Hamilton 1901b). This incident
added to the growing concern that Māori carvings were leaving the country at an alarming
rate. James Carroll, the Native Minister in Premier Richard Seddon's Liberal government,
announced in July that legislation would be drafted with the aim of 'preserving all Maori
works of art' (*New Zealand Parliamentary Debates* 9 July 1901: 195) In October, Carroll
presented the Māori Antiquities Act to Parliament. It was one of the first examples of
legislation in the world preventing the export of cultural property (Carroll cited in *Herald*,
5 October 1901).[13] The elevated status of Māori carving was reflected in changes to the
wording of the bill, where 'antiquity' was substituted for 'relic,' and 'curiosities' was replaced
by the phrase 'articles manufactured with ancient Maori tools' (*NZPD* 9 October 1901:
278–9). Antiquities, which had been among the first categories of display in Renaissance
proto-museums, by this time referred not just to objects from classical antiquity but
embraced a range of material evidence of the past, natural and cultural, oral and written
(Pevsner 1976: 111–17; Griffiths 1996: 21).

The Antiquities Act was not motivated merely by Pakeha salvage, but overlapped with a Māori desire to protect what was left of their customary culture. The Māori version of the bill translated antiquities as '*taonga Maori o namata*' ('treasures of ancient times') (ATL P Box q 499M). The Māori newspaper *Te Puke ki Hikurangi* welcomed a Bill intended to 'care for ancient treasures' (15 November 1901). Another paper *Te Pipiwharauroa* joined in the criticism of gifts lavished on royalty and pointed out that Pakeha now had more *taonga* than Māori themselves (1 September 1901; 1 May 1902). When the Te Arawa house *Rauru* was reported to have been sold to a German museum in 1900, the editor of *Te Pipiwharauroa*, Pārākau Maika, called for Māori to hang on to the keepsakes of their ancestors because they were 'chiefly symbols' of the Māori. Rather than selling them off to just any Pakeha and ending up 'hidden in their houses' he urged that they be 'given or sold to the government alone' so that they can be 'preserved as taonga for the whole tribe' ('He whare whakairo' 1 June 1900). Like other settler colonies, indigenous collusion with official preservation projects was the result of changing attitudes about the relationship between tradition and modernity (Phillips 2005). Putting old things in museums was a marker of modernity because it recognized that they were no longer present, but the Māori consciousness of ancestral culture was not a return to the past but a 're-imagination of the future' (Sissons 2005: 11).

The active involvement of a strong Māori advocate was crucial to the antiquities legislation. The bilingual James Carroll, born of a Pakeha father and Māori mother, was a pragmatic politician who worked tirelessly within the government to advance Māori causes (Ward 1993). When Augustus Hamilton circulated proposals for a Māori Museum in response to the public debate about the loss of Māori antiquities, Carroll took up the cause with great zeal. He was instrumental in having Hamilton appointed as director of the Colonial Museum, and supported his efforts to enlarge the Māori collection and get a new building. Carroll hoped that Māori would deposit family heirlooms and tribal history in this new Māori Museum as a 'constant reminder to the coming generations of the capabilities and taste of the Maori race' (AM Ms 131, vol 11, 1/5).

The ideas for the 'National Maori Museum' that Hamilton and S Percy Smith presented to Carroll in 1902 are remarkable for the singular focus on 'the antiquities of the Maori race', as well as the representation of Māori on the proposed board (Hamilton and Percy Smith 1902b). This separate museum dedicated to Māori culture was meant to be a 'Valhalla for the Maori, a place in which the memories of their great ones can be enshrined and perpetuated' (Hamilton 1902a). Although the Māori Museum was not built, something of the ideal survived in the singular focus on Māori culture after Hector's long neglect while in charge of what was essentially a museum of geology. To Hamilton, a museum was 'an agency for the instruction of the people of the whole Colony in that which is at once her pride and peculiar heritage' (AM Ms 131, vol.11, 1/2). The establishment of a 'State Storehouse for the remaining ancestral possessions of the native race', wrote Hamilton, would heal the wounds of the past and show their 'fellow subjects' (Māori) that the 'pakeha rat' should not drive out the *kiore* (Māori rat) (Hamilton 1902a). Hamilton's commentary, despite the patronizing tone, reflects the importance given to Māori culture within postsettler nationhood in this period.

The 'National Maori Museum' also received encouragement from Māori leaders, who tried to steer a Pakeha project towards Māori ends. Carroll felt sure that Māori supported the proposal and claimed many had offered to deposit their own 'treasures' if a suitable museum was built (*NZPD* 9 July 1902: 167–8). The Wairarapa leader Tamahau Mahupuku's presentation to the government of the house *Tākitimu* was a major boost for the campaign. Mahupuku's letter to Carroll containing this offer is an important articulation of Māori views about preserving the past. Far from salvaging the vestiges of a dying race, the metaphor of *Hine-ahu-one* ('the earth formed maiden' created by forest god *Tāne*) evokes renewal and rebirth. Indeed Mahupuku's comments suggest that Māori had come to see museums as worthwhile places where the works of their ancestors might be displayed in a way that maintained a link to present and future generations:

> Therefore proceed with your work, preserve it in your preserving-chamber, fashion it with the earth of Kurawaka, so that another Hineahuone may arise … in the new building-up and collecting-together of our ancient lore, our history, our treasures … and everything that can be preserved of us as a people. (ANZ MA 1, 1906/1413)

It appears that *Tākitimu* was intended to be set up next to parliament 'as a taonga for the whole colony', a statement of bicultural nationhood that reflected Mahupuku's accommodation of Māori self determination and Pakeha power (*Te Pipiwharauroa* No. 71 January 1904; TPA MU 152, 9/3). Mahupuku was both a wealthy landowner who supported the Seddon government, while at the same time hosting major Kotahitanga *hui* at Pāpāwai *pā* near Greytown (Ballara 1993). This modern cultural centre was the venue for development projects including a *whare wānanga* (tribal university) and 'museum' established by the Tāne-nui-ā-Rangi committee which set out to collect and record Māori tribal history and *whakapapa* ('Reserve Papawai' TPA MU 152, 4/3). Despite Hamilton's at times ethnocentric attitude toward the *tangata whenua*, his work earned him the respect of Māori. He acted as trustee, supported the publication of traditional Māori history and was given the name 'Tupai-whakarongo-wānanga' [a counsellor of the tribal university]. Tūnuiārangi (Major Brown) bestowed this honour on Hamilton after he attended a large *hui* where he told the assembled leaders 'let not the knowledge of your ancestors die away' (*The Advocate* 19 July 1907). On his gravestone the Māori inscription described him as 'someone who cared for the treasures of the past' (TP B.10555).

In 1910 Elsdon Best, New Zealand's best known ethnologist, was appointed to the staff. Best was to remain at the Dominion Museum for over twenty years producing a huge volume of literature on Māori subjects (Sissons 1993). His knowledge of the Māori language facilitated Hamilton's contacts with Māori elders and raised the profile of the Museum in Māori circles. Best was sent to interview a number of knowledgeable *kaumātua* who had some dealings with the museum, such as Te Whatahoro. Although this work was undeniably part of the colonial campaign to salvage indigenous information before it was 'lost', Māori were usually willing partners in this research, despite the fact that their notions of history were different. The manuscripts compiled by the Tāne-nui-ā-rangi committee, and later translated and published, are an example of this cultural collaboration (Hilliard 2000). Tūwharetoa paramount chief Tureiti Te Heuheu Tukino (Figure 1.20) had a friendly relationship with Hamilton which dated back some years. Te Heuheu had a copy of *Maori Art,* and was a supporter of Hamilton's work at the Museum, donating carvings to the collection on more than one occasion. When he knew the *rangatira* was visiting, Hamilton made sure Te Heuheu's portrait was hanging (Diary 29 April 1910 in O'Rourke 2001). In the same way, the Ngāti Porou leader Tuta Nihoniho formed close working relationships with Best and Hamilton. His work went beyond being merely an informant for their ethnographic archive, a common role among Māori connected with the colonial administration. In a letter to Pōmare, critical of Pakeha mistakes in the museum, Nihoniho wrote that it was important that 'corrections' were made 'so as to make plain to the white peoples of the world the true and real language of the Māori people, the meaning and history of each word, name or thing' (TPA MU 147 10/7). The museum displays were often the product of careful negotiation with Māori indivduals and communities. For example, the tree stump from the Bay of Plenty, which Hamilton thought a 'fine exhibit' next to the model *pā,* was procured only after lengthy discussions with Māori politicians and local *iwi.* As the following letter from Tai Mitchell suggests, this enigmatic object was just as interesting for Māori as for Pakeha visitors:

> The relic is well worthy of every effort to procure. Nothing I have ever seen brought more vividly to my mind the extraordinary patience exercised by our old kaumatuas in this sphere of their life than the silent and eloquent testimony of this old Totara Tree. (18 August 1909, in O'Rourke 2001)

At this time *taonga* encompassed a diverse range of things, including manufactured Western products. An example of this was the donation of Hongi Hika's armour, which Hamilton put on display in the museum 'where it will form an interesting relic' (TPA MU 152 2/6). This European suit of armour, acquired by the Ngā Puhi warrior from King George III in England in the 1820s and rediscovered in 1909, may have been considered merely a 'historic trophy' by Pakeha, but it was referred to as a 'taonga' by Tainui and Whanganui leaders who thought it should be placed in the 'heaping house of venerable treasures for ever more' (TPA MU 152 4/6). Waata Hipango in particular seems to have approved of museum collections which would preserve 'the relics/keepsakes of my ancestors.' When Hamilton offered to buy the war canoe *Te Mata o Hoturoa,* then lying neglected on the banks of the Whanganui river, Hipango wrote that it was better to show respect to the *waka* and care for it so that it will 'live long' rather than being 'gnawed by the sun, wind and rain' (TPA MU 152 ½). The Māori category of *taonga* was thus enlarged and augmented in a similar way to Hawaian chiefs who 'stretched' traditional concepts of *tapu* (sacredness) to incorporate

Figure 1.20   Tureiti Te Heuheu Tukino at the Dominion
Museum, Wellington, c.1910 (with the permission of Te
Heuheu Tukino VIII/Museum of New Zealand Te Papa
Tongarewa Hamilton B.1797).

new classes of trade goods (Appadurai 1986: 26). Rather than assuming that *taonga tuku iho* (treasures handed down from the ancestors) was a 'traditional' pre-European concept, it may in fact have been a response to colonization.

With the passing of the Antiquities Act, Māori began to see museums as places where *taonga* might be preserved and displayed in ways that benefited Māori people as well. Yet, at times, museum collecting and display prescribed an orthodoxy of 'traditional' Māori life in the face of ongoing cultural practices which brought the staff into conflict with contemporary Māori ideas. In 1909 Hamilton commissioned Anaha Te Rāhui of Ngāti Tarāwhai to carve motifs for a museum display. Mead claims that Hamilton underpaid the impoverished elderly carver (Mead 1986b: 168–72), while Neich accuses Hamilton of forcing the carver to systematize his stylistic vocabulary and even censoring designs that did not conform to his own ideas (Neich 2001: 226–9). But Hamilton did not always get things his own way. Mere Whāriki, a Ngāti Kahungunu weaver who was hired to produce work for exhibitions, was quite capable of defending herself from accusations that she used 'Pākehā colours' on her *kete*. In a letter she insisted on the quality and authenticity of her work, the blunt tone of her reply making it very clear that she was not about to be told by an upstart Pakeha how to make *taonga Māori* (TPA MU 206, 2/9).

Māori were plainly capable of distinguishing between the preservation of the past and the romantic Pakeha notion of living in the past, which stifled their own development. They certainly did not hesitate to object if they and their culture were represented as 'backward'. According to a letter in a Māori newspaper of 1911, a concert party in London were not amused when their English audience seemed to treat their performance as an exercise in primitivism, turning off the theatre lights in case the natives took fright. The suggestion that Māori had never seen electricity before was too much for the editor, whose sarcastic comment appears at the end of the letter. 'Friends, that's just like the Pākehā,' he wrote, 'to think we are living in the ancient world' (*Te Māreikura* cited in Simpson 1994: 44).

The New Zealand International Exhibition in Christchurch of 1906–7 offers further proof exhibitions were ambiguous spaces which sometimes allowed for a degree of interaction and dialogue between spectators and spectacle which undercut ethnographic 'othering' (Ames 2004: 314–15; Henare 2005: 225–6). Despite the formally staged images (Figure 1.21) archival evidence suggests that Māori were closely involved in the construction and running of the *pā* and had a distinctive and enthusiastic response to the experience (McCarthy 2004). The accounts of contemporary observers show that visitors recognized the 'poetry and illusion' of the exhibition, and understood that just because Māori wore historical costumes did not mean they lived in the past. When English visitor John Gorst met some young educated Māori dandies, he was left with no illusions about their future aspirations:

> ... there were one or two young men, not of the 'haka,' who wore English dress and spoke in English fashion, and wished us to know that there was a race of young Maories [sic] now springing up who were ... ambitious of seeing their race become in every respect the equals of the Europeans, and of taking part in the government and administration of the country. (Gorst 1908: 66)

Heritage is, ironically, a sign of modernity not only because it recognizes the past as past but recycles it as a regenerative resource (Kirshenblatt-Gimblett 1998: 149–50). The

Figure 1.21   Group photograph, Māori *pā*, New Zealand International Exhibition, Christchurch, 1906–7 (Museum of New Zealand Te Papa Tongarewa McDonald C.1686).

clearest expression of a Māori agenda of cultural revival at the Christchurch exhibition were the speeches on the *marae,* which were recorded by observers. When James Carroll was welcomed with a large *pōwhiri* in April 1906, the Minister complimented the Māori on their work:

> We the Maoris have little left … but it is much to have a fortified *pa.* Remember the proverb of your ancestors, 'The house built out in the open is food for the flames, but the carved house in a fortified *pa* is the sign of a chief.' (Cowan in *Dominion Museum Bulletin* 1911: 40)[14]

The *pā*, intended as the last remnant of a dying race, was in practice a display of Māori *taonga* as well as Pakeha salvage. It symbolized Māori strength and identity at a time of change, and illuminates the way that the colonial culture of display sometimes included opposition to colonialism's culture. Exhibiting was implicated in the loss or effacing of what was shown; the rare, the obsolete, the extinct. In this chapter I have shown that what Māori exhibited was the continued strength and vitality of their customary culture. Pakeha and Māori approaches to preservation converged around related values of cultural heritage. By collaborating with the sanctioned revival of tradition, the indigenous people celebrated the past as heritage and thereby signalled that they too were now modern.

NOTES

1. The Canterbury Museum designed by Benjamin Mountfort (1870) shows the same variety of objects in a central hall (ATL Barker PAI-q-166-052). In 1876, the Auckland Museum in Princes Street had a similar arrangement in a two-storey central hall with gallery (Powell 1967: Figure 17).

2. Though often used interchangeably in the nineteenth century, ethnology was the scientific comparison of different ethnic groups (usually concerned with racial origins and classification) whereas ethnography was the systematic description of a single group, which in the twentieth century became synonymous with fieldwork (Barfield 1997: 158).

3. To Āpirana Ngata the Māori portraits of artist Gottfried Lindauer were 'shadow carving', which were valued as 'treasures' in their own right (Graham 1965: 17–18).

4. 'The ahistoric essentialism behind the traditional concept of the norm of reciprocity conceals the particular cultural configurations in and through which inalienable possessions are empowered to act as the source of difference and hierarchy' (Weiner 1992: 48).

5. Though Hedley criticizes dictionary definitions because their precise Western categories do not capture the fuzzy edges of this culturally imbedded concept (Hedley 2004: 56), the value of this genealogy lies in historicizing a category which is usually naturalized.

6. All Māori examples are taken from nineteenth-century newspapers. See: Digital Library Niupepa Māori Project, University of Waikato: www.nzdl.org/cgi-bin/niupepalibrary/.

7. From December 1865 to August 1866, there were 28 recognizably Māori names in the visitor's book out of a total of 1,600. In 1868, there were aproximately 74 Māori visitors from a total of 2,260. Obviously this represents a very small proportion of overall visitors to the museum and of the total Māori population – aproximately 3 per cent of the museum audience when Māori made up over 10 per cent of the total population in the 1860s (Belich 1996: 249–50). However, it is surprising that Māori were present at all, given that very few lived in the cities. All information about museum visitation, unless otherwise stated, comes from the Colonial Museum visitors' books 1865–1903 (TPA MU 130 boxes 1–10).

8. At the Canterbury Museum in 1873, Von Haast had a *mokamokai* covered with a cloth 'out of consideration for Maori susceptibilities' (Von Haast 1948: 633).

9. Flags made by anti-government leaders like Te Kooti, exhibited at several exhibitions, may have been intended as war trophies but inadvertently represented Māori resistance and adaptive creativity (Rice 2002; Binney 1995).

10. Arts and crafts sprang up in the 1880s and 1890s and sought a return to the natural forms and materials of medieval and folk traditions in response to industrialization (Hamilton 1978: 131; Williams 2004:159–66).

11. Māori words currently used in English for art, such as '*toi*' or '*whakairo*', were previously adjectives or verbs rather than nouns. '*Whakairo*' for example denoted design or pattern and not an object itself – '*whakairo*' was not carving but *anything* that was decorated such as weaving, clothing, etc. (Mead 1984a: 21; Neich 2001: 123–37).

12. At Auckland, Cheeseman organized his growing collection typologically in standing cases, while the larger carvings were aestheticized to some extent, displayed as free standing forms against the plain walls (Powell 1967: 17; ATL PA1-f-179-79-3).

13. The Liberal government pioneered old age pensions and was the first country to grant women the vote.

14. This *pepeha* (see xv) is a well-known statement of chiefly *mana* (Mead and Grove 2001: 137–8).

2 'OUR NATION'S STORY', 1914–42

While settler self-fashioning is energized by an uncertain and/or relationship between the native and the national connotations of objects like boomerangs, the merging of these associations is never complete or final.

(Thomas 1999)

In Figure 2.1 two Māori men are bent over a lattice work *tukutuku* panel intent on their work. They carefully weave the dried strands of *pingao* through the board, constructing the zig-zag pattern known as *poutama*. The photograph was taken on a Dominion Museum

Figure 2.1 Āpirana Ngata and Peter Buck at *tukutuku* work, Waiomatatini, 1923 (Museum of New Zealand Te Papa Tongarewa McDonald A.4046).

'ethnographic expedition' to New Zealand's east coast in April 1923. Captured on film, the object of the men's efforts has been salvaged, rescued from imminent oblivion. We see the unknown craftsmen, their materials laid out for our inspection, and the process of its manufacture, all recorded faithfully for posterity. The picture constitutes *tukutuku* as an artefact of the 'old time Maori.'

James McDonald, then acting director of the Dominion Museum, who filmed customary Māori practices on the trip to the Waiapu valley near Ruatoria, was behind the camera. He was accompanied by his colleague Elsdon Best, the museum's ethnologist, and author Johannes Andersen, both of whom were also engaged in ethnographic field work. The collection and display of these vestiges of the past in archives, libraries and museums in this period reveals the social construction of what Best (1924) called 'the Maori as he was'. Exhibiting Māori in the interwar years reconstituted Māori culture as an artefact within the emerging discipline of anthropology. No longer considered a dying race, Māori people were to be assimilated into modern New Zealand. It was their 'traditional' culture that was thought to be disappearing and thus had to be collected for the museum.

Another photograph tells quite a different story (Figure 2.2). The two men now stand and turn to the camera. These successful Māori face the viewer confidently, leaning on the *tukutuku* panel as if to claim it not as an artefact but as their own handiwork. Far from being clad in traditional 'costume' such as we might see in a museum reconstruction, they are well dressed: ankle length boots, suits, fashionable trilbys and bow ties. Their features are immediately familiar, and their impressive *curriculum vitae* dispel any idea that they are innocent objects of the ethnographer's gaze. On the right is Peter Buck, known as Te Rangihīroa in Māori circles, a doctor who was to become a world-famous anthropologist. On the left is his friend Āpirana Ngata, lawyer and Member of Parliament, who was instrumental in securing government support for the Dominion Museum, the Polynesian Society and other research projects. In their view, Māori people could be 'partners' in the project of anthropology (Ngata cited in Sorrenson 1987, vol. 2: 126).

Though Ngata and Buck encouraged and participated in ethnographic research, they did not want to display *tukutuku* as a museum memorial but as a stimulus for a living tradition (Ngata 1929). Like their Pakeha collaborators they wished to preserve Māori culture but with the ultimate goal of reviving it. In their actions, another discourse is at work, at times overlapping with the dominant one of ethnography/anthropology and at times in opposition to it. Māori intellectuals, while collaborating in the staging of a Māori golden age, simultaneously advanced a reconstructed Māori identity independent of Pakeha society. This was 'Maoritanga', an indigenous project of cultural development that was inspired by James Carroll's call for Māori to 'hold fast' to their identity (Walker 2001: 353).[1]

This chapter examines further shifts in the culture of display in the inter-war period – specimen to artefact, 'art' to arts and crafts – through exhibits at the Dominion Museum in Museum Street, international exhibitions, and the new Dominion Museum in Buckle Street

Figure 2.2   Ngata and Buck standing by *tukutuku,* Waiomatatini, 1923
(Museum of New Zealand Te Papa Tongarewa McDonald A.4043).

from 1936. Māori objects were constituted first as 'artefacts' within the emerging discipline of anthropology, a project that was actually a collaborative enterprise between Pakeha staff and key Māori supporters. At the same time they became 'Maori arts and crafts', a new category of decorative arts that had considerable Māori support and a strong social and political agenda. The chapter ends with an examination of the National Art Gallery and its distinctive display of fine art, examined in terms of Bourdieu's concept of symbolic capital – a form of high culture that reinforced the social position of the Pakeha elite in isolation from Māori patrons and their customary culture.

'OUR MAORIS': DOMINIONISM, ASSIMILATION AND THE MUSEUM

The discourses of dominionism and assimilation shaped New Zealand's development between the wars. Māori and Pakeha relations were worked out against the backdrop of a tightening recolonization.

With gratitude for the past and confidence in the future we range ourselves without fear beside Britain. Where she goes, we go; where she stands, we stand. (Savage cited in Belich 2001: 269)

With these words, Prime Minister Michael Savage announced New Zealand's entry into the Second World War. Before the 1880s, as a relatively independent colony, New Zealand did not become involved in Britain's foreign conflicts. From the late nineteenth and early twentieth century, however, as a 'better Britain', it was increasingly dependent on the mother country as a market for frozen meat, cheese and butter, and went to tragic lengths to demonstrate its loyalty on the battlefield, especially in the First World War. Closer economic ties produced a country that was more British than the British.

If the period from the 1880s to the 1960s was one of 'recolonization', then New Zealand cultural history between the wars displayed a determined 'dominionism' (Belich 2001: 108–18). The former Colony of New Zealand had became a Dominion in 1907 (and the Colonial Museum changed its name to the Dominion Museum). This new status also occurred in the white settler colonies of Australia, Canada and South Africa 'where British models of gentility and hierarchy were energetically replicated and enthusiastically reproduced' (Cannadine 2001: 28–9). Ironically, the Dominion of New Zealand was even more closely allied to the Empire than the Colony had ever been. There was an official preference for high-brow British models, and, although a distinctive local character eventually emerged, this culture never amounted to what later writers claimed was an independent nationalism (Curnow 1960; Brown and Keith 1969). As politician and diplomat Sir James Allen put it in 1924, New Zealand was thought of as a 'part of England set in the southern seas' (quoted in Johnston 1999: 283). Most European New Zealanders thought of themselves as British (Gibbons 1992). The 'nation' referred to in the school textbook *Our Nation's Story* was Britain not New Zealand (Belich 2001: 118).

It is a truism that war was the crucible of New Zealand identity (King 2003: 291–303). After the carnage of 1914–18, the government built monuments to the fallen dead decorated with an iconography of civic duty, which were the centre of ANZAC ceremonies (Australia New Zealand Army Corps), a kind of sacred day when crowds gathered to affirm the loyal *British* identity of the Dominion (Martin and Phillips 1990). This state-endorsed cult of 'dominionism' (Belich 2001: 249) had as strong an influence on New Zealand museums in the early twentieth century as the private societies had in the nineteenth century. When the Auckland War Memorial Museum was opened in 1929, its hill top site and neoclassical architecture reflected the patriotic militarism of the period (Stead 2001: 14–15). In 1934 the same mood pervaded the laying of the foundation stone at the National Art Gallery and Dominion Museum in Wellington, with uniformed soldiers standing to attention and Union Jacks fluttering. Together with the War Memorial Carillon, this new national institution, which opened in 1936, commemorated the 'martyrs' who had sacrificed their lives for their country. The museum will be a 'national shrine', announced the Mayor T. Hislop at the opening ceremony, that should inspire citizens to work for the 'ennoblement of our national life'. The austere, colonnaded façade had a 'solemnity' that 'cannot be divorced in sentiment from the slender tower whose voice is a persistent reminder of the men who did not return...' (*Dom*, 3 August 1936: 10).

The memorial atmosphere that infused New Zealand museums reflected their function as Pakeha mausoleums of the Māori past. In a society that developed myths of racial harmony to smooth over the violence of its colonial birth, it was telling that Māori Halls with their model villages were the feature displays of New Zealand museums. The postsettler identity constructed within dominionism, a natural and social paradise that was better than Britain but otherwise interchangeable with it, was built through a tightly controlled uniformity that necessitated the assimilation of Māori people and the entombment of their history (Belich 2001: 209). Ideal race relations amounted to Māori becoming brown Pakeha. 'I look forward for the next hundred years or so, to a time when we shall have no Maoris at all,' said Native Minister William Herries, 'but a white race with a slight dash of the finest coloured race in the world' (cited in Belich 2001: 190).

Most Māori politicians and leaders cooperated with the government policy of assimilation despite continuing socio-economic disadvantage. Simultaneously, they created segregated organizations that retained some degree of Māori independence, such as trust boards, land schemes, native schools, concert parties and sports teams. The achievements of the *Rātana* church, the pan-tribal movement that initiated a successful partnership with the Labour Party in the 1935 national election, is an example of this strategy. Even those Māori who worked largely outside the state, such as Te Puea Herangi in the Waikato where land had been confiscated, engaged with Pakeha society to win support for re-establishing the independent Kingitanga (King movement) on its new *marae* at Tūrangawaewae. Many Māori even went along with the Pakeha appropriation of Māori symbols. The Ngāti Toa *haka* 'Ka mate' was adopted by the All Black rugby team; *kōwhaiwhai* pattern was used as a decorative border on everything from public buildings to stamps; and large scale Māori ceremonial and ritual were employed to give national events a distinctive Polynesian tinge (Belich 2001: 213–15). This was dramatically illustrated at the 1940 Centennial celebrations at Waitangi (Figure 2.3) where Āpirana Ngata led the *haka* on the *marae* in front of the new meeting house.

Exhibitions were a public arena where the discourse of recolonial integration competed with Māori aspirations. In contrast to the fluidity that characterized the colonial culture of display, in early twentieth-century New Zealand visual categories were increasingly formalized as cultural institutions became an important apparatus of the modern state. The National Art Gallery and Dominion Museum were the products of a young nation but not of nationalism. Their exhibitions produced a sense of cultural heritage for a settler society but this was ultimately a local chapter in an essentially British story. In 1931 New Zealand deferred the Westminster declaration, deciding to remain a dominion rather than become independent and in 1939 joined the mother country in defence of the British Empire. Despite the relative status 'our Maoris' achieved, they were assimilated along with

Figure 2.3   Ngata leading the *haka* in front of the meeting house *Te Tiriti o Waitangi* at the Centennial celebrations, Waitangi, 1940 (Alexander Turnbull Library PAColl-3060 (F-2746-1/2-MNZ)).

other minorities into the homogenous Anglo-Protestant majority who fought for King and Country.

FROM SPECIMEN TO ARTEFACT

Following Hamilton's death, James Alan Thomson became the new director of the Dominion Museum in 1914. A Rhodes scholar and a brilliant scientist, he was more interested in the natural history collections somewhat neglected by his predecessor (Hornibrook 1996). Thomson declared that museums were primarily 'storehouses for the rare and the beautiful, and for the history of man' but he acknowledged that 'public galleries serve a portion of the public not otherwise catered for' (AR 1917). His emphasis on education was to set the agenda for the institution for the next twenty years. Thomson thought that a museum, a place where collections were exhibited, was different to an exhibition because it was for learning and not commerce. The Dominion Museum should cater for the general public in carefully arranged popular sections, whereas the student and collector could study the displays in specialist areas (Thomson 1915). This was a significant change in museum lay-out: the separation of permanent displays of the collection for the visiting public from the storage areas 'out the back'. It was a division that was in line with international trends towards more instructive exhibits for public consumption in contrast to specialized research collections (Glenn Penny 2002: 148).

Although he was familiar with anthropology, Thomson allowed staff to pursue their own interests, as Best did with ethnography. He favoured comparative displays of Poly-nesian objects 'grouped together to show the evolution of civilisation' (Thomson 1915: 13). This broadly scientific approach to the display of specimens at the Dominion Museum was maintained for the next two decades. As has already been noted, museums in Britain were descended from international exhibitions and department stores but they distanced themselves from their popular and commercial roots by the late nineteenth century. This resulted in the separation of education and entertainment, of museums from circuses, which persisted to the late twentieth century. British cultural institutions and their colonial descendants, unlike French equivalents, adopted didactic display techniques because they felt audiences should learn something and improve themselves (Greenhalgh 1989). In Melbourne, the 'austere presentation' of exhibits at the National Museum of Victoria was an attempt to set themselves apart from popular forms of entertainment (Goodman 1999). In the early twentieth century American museums also grew away from world's fairs and became isolated both from ongoing experiments in commercial design and consumer spectacle and from advanced scientific research, which gradually shifted from museums to universities (Conn 1998). These developments were quickly disseminated to New Zealand's museums.

At about the same time, a new category appeared, which was to shape the display of Māori culture at the Dominion Museum beyond the life of 'specimen'. 'Artefact', referring to anything that was the artificial product of human workmanship as opposed to natural processes, was a term that had appeared in archaeological terminology in the late nineteenth century, but only came into current usage in the 1920s (OED 1989: 660; Barfield 1997: 17–18). The first reference in Dominion Museum documents appears in 1921 (AR 1921), but by the mid 1930s 'artefact' was the term most commonly applied to Māori objects in museums.[2] The term was employed within the developing discipline of anthropology which gradually subsumed amateur ethnography. Anthropology was introduced to New Zealand in 1920 by H.D. Skinner, the first academically trained anthropologist, when he established courses at Otago University and became curator at the Otago Museum (Carolyn Thomas 1995: 88–101). During that decade self-described 'home grown anthropologist' Peter Buck became a leading international light in this profession (Sorrenson 1982). The Dominion Museum ethnographic expeditions to various regions from 1919 to 1923 can be compared to the famous 1898 expedition to the Torres Strait Islands in which W.H.R. Pitt Rivers pioneered the field work technique which was to become such an important aspect of anthropology (Henare 2005: 227–38).

Elsdon Best was the key figure in this discursive shift. He became increasingly interested in professional anthropology at the same time that international anthropologists discovered the Māori. Though officially only a clerk and essentially self-taught, Best drew on indigenous sources to publish a torrent of articles and books in an effort to establish his reputation as a scholar. He was more interested in writing than setting up exhibits, yet his body of literature, which constituted 'traditional' Māori culture as an object of knowledge, constructed the underlying principles on which display practices were based. An example is the way that the Te Arawa storehouse *Te Tākinga* was inscribed within ethnographic discourse in Best's (1916) *Museum Bulletin No.5: Maori Storehouses and Kindred Structures*. His aim was to lay out a detailed description and classification of this building type which would illuminate the 'social life and customs of the natives' because *pātaka* were 'now becoming a thing of the past' (1916: 18–19).

The anthropological turn can be detected in the increasing specialization of language, which made the new discourse visible by delineating a domain of objects on display. Under Best's influence, Māori words became more widely used than with Hamilton, whose grasp of the language was rudimentary. By the 1920s, most Māori items in the collection were referred to by their specific Māori names. Annual Reports refer to *toki, waka huia, wahaika, māripi*, whereas previously such items were simply called adze, feather box, club and knife (AR 1915–30). Anachronistic words such as 'mats', which nonsensically referred to clothing as floor coverings, vanished from the lexicon of museum registration and labels. Noting critically that little was known of the Māori names for 'the museum exhibits pertaining to ethnology' (AR 1918: 4–5), Best made painstaking notes on 'technological nomenclature,' and compiled exhaustive lists of Māori terms from his informants (ATL Ms 199). The vocabularies looked impressive but were always incomplete; Best's research was intended to convince government officials of the scientific rigour of the project and persuade them of the urgency of salvage.

Best left the work of display to James McDonald. His notebooks compiled from visits to museums suggest he regarded their displays simply as a 3D system of reference like a library with objects, its artefacts like an appendix to one of his ethnographic monographs (ATL Mss 188, 189, 197). His labels show how the reconstitution of otherwise meaningless objects into artefacts was carried out through the process of archival systematizing and labelling. For example, the label for *Te Heke Rangatira* was longer and more precise than Hamilton's original, with tribal history added to clarify the significance of the name:

> This canoe was made in the Wai-rarapa District and named 'Te Heke Rangatira,' after one of several vessels in which Te Rangi-tawhanga and others of the Rakai-whakairi clan migrated from the Napier District to Wai-rarapa seven generations ago. (TPA MU 206 2/2)

It is important not to overstate the colonizing dimension of Best's painstakingly assembled archive of Māori tradition, as his work ironically provided raw material for the twentieth-century cultural renaissance (Sissons 1993). His research was not only supported by Māori contemporaries, but Māori sources funded his publications (Condliffe 1971: 147–9). The Tūhoe *tohunga* Paitini Wī Tapeka of Maungapōhatu, far from being exploited by his Pakeha friend, actually offered his services as a paid advisor (Craig 1964: 82–5). *Kaumātua* were anxious to preserve Māori knowledge, and may have contributed to the anthropological construction of Māoritanga for the same reason they donated *taonga* to museums. In a letter to Best, carver Hurae Puketapu addressed him in terms of great respect as a 'retainer' of the 'works of the ancestors' who have passed on, an 'elder' who has been left behind for the Māori people (TPA MU 47 1/26).

Current interpretations of anthropological museums charge them with freezing indigenous cultures in the past, denying contemporary development (Karp and Lavine 1991). According to Fiona Cameron, the Māori displays set up at the new Auckland War Memorial Museum took little notice of Māori values and attracted little Māori interest, despite the involvement of individuals like George Graham, with his strong Māori connections, who founded the Museum's Anthropology and Maori Race Section in 1922 (Curnow and Graham 1998). Yet in the late 1920s the Māori King Te Rata responded positively to a museum request for donations, saying he would help to 'preserve and perpetuate the traditions of our ancestors' (Cameron 2000: 219–20). A readiness to give objects to museums did not necessarily endorse the project of salvage, nor was the preservation of their historical culture a denial of coevalness (Fabian 1983: 31) but may simply have been an attempt to keep the past alive in the present as a source of identity and strength. This awareness of heritage, although based on an appreciation of the past, was orientated towards the future. Indeed, displaying historical *taonga* may have been a way of negotiating modernity, of claiming a place in the present on the strength of past glories. When McDonald filmed a *kaumātua* making an eel trap on the east coast in 1923, the old man adressed the whirring camera with the words: 'Speak on, speak on ... I shall go with the pictures to London, to Japan...' (Gibbons 1992: 211). Māori were engaged in dialogue with anthropology, and these indigenous interlocutors saw it as a means of gathering the seeds for further growth.[3]

There were a number of different styles of presentation at the Dominion Museum at this time. Much of the Māori collection had already been moved out to the iron shed on the corner of Museum Street and Sydney Street and the remaining items were 'restored' and rearranged in the main hall during the First World War. The main hall was in much the same state as it had been in for fifty years, with the exception of the Māori objects which had been removed to another building. In their place were Pacific artefacts, spears on the wall and *vaka* (canoes) on top of the display cases. Many Pacific Island objects came into the museum, but there is little evidence of a comparative Māori/Polynesian collection although it was referred to from time to time. In the 1920s, museum staff referred to 'the Maori collection' as a distinct entity, and for the first time, a distinction was made between foreign ethnology and Māori ethnology (AR 1920-36). By this time ethnographic exhibits presented a detailed description of a single culture, whereas the more old fashioned ethnological exhibits placed items in a comparative global framework. The staff at the Dominion Museum, who preferred the term ethnology and resisted revisionist theories of New Zealand prehistory, moved gradually to the latter position by the 1950s.

The provision of a new space in a department store in nearby Featherston Street in 1924 allowed for the consolidation of the anthropological approach to the museum display of things Māori. Objects were separated out from the miscellaneous collections and shown on their own for the first time in the history of the institution when the Māori collection was moved to the Dominion Farmers' Institute Building. An apartment on the fifth floor was fitted out as 'a temporary museum', which, Thomson reported, allowed 'a 'better classification of exhibits' (AR 1925). Māori objects were exhibited in a dedicated space divided up into sections based on function and use: weapons, weaving, cooking and agriculture, fishing, personal adornment, religion, as well as games and toys. Best's version of anthropology underpinned these displays which were set up by his disciple, W.J. Phillipps, who was a key figure in the setting up and running of the Farmers' branch, and later in overseeing the installation of Māori exhibits at the new building. His own ideas of Māori culture were very much part of the prevailing recolonial vision of Māori 'absorbed' into mainstream New Zealand society, their material culture representing the treasures of the past (ATL Ms papers 4316). Judging by a reporter's response, Phillipps's arrangement conveyed an aesthetic reverie submerged in the Pakeha present:

> The Maori was a true poet. His song may not be heard amid the rush and bustle of the white man's New Zealand, but the poem ... may still be read in the sweep and counter sweep of Maori decorative art applied lavishly on every article he used and valued. (*EP*, 21 June 1924)

The growing artistic appreciation of Māori carving among Pakeha in the 1920s was matched by more Māori interest in the public display of their culture. In the absence of visitor's books, there is little quantitative evidence of Māori visitation to the Dominion Museum, but the files suggest that Māori often came into the museum and frequently interacted with the staff (TPA MU 1, 16/66 (10/1/18)). Best maintained an extensive correspondence with tribal authorities from around the country which certainly points to regular Māori visitors to the museum after 1910. The speech of one elderly visitor was recorded, and expresses support for Best's work at the museum:

> I have closely watched your procedure and noticed your innumerable questions anent [sic] my ancestors, their deeds and acts and achievements in the world of life ... I sit here and listen to your endless questions from early morn until the sun sinks to rest. Then I go home, and, as I lie on my couch, I reflect on the benefits that your work will bring to me and my people. Hence I come here daily to greet you and to observe this great work. (Craig 1964: 141)

'ANTHROPOLOGY'S INTERLOCUTORS'

New Zealand museum staff were engaged in a dialogue about the meaning of Māori objects, a conversation with Māori people and between Māori and the discipline of anthropology (Said 1989). For evidence of Māori interaction and response to the culture of display, we have to look inside the Dominion Museum and beyond it. In this section I examine the New Zealand court at the British Empire Exhibition at Wembley in 1924, and the work of Māori carver Thomas Heberley at the Sydney Street shed next door to the Museum.

As world's fairs after St Louis in 1904 focused more on the future than the past, with new technologies replacing historical and ethnographic courts, they were seen as occupying a mercantile realm that was more and more distinct from museums (Schrenk 2005; Rydell 1993). Because Māori objects were now seen as historical artefacts rather than mercantile produce, Pakeha were unwilling to include Māori exhibits in New Zealand exhibitions that were meant to demonstrate the country's progress. When Gilbert Archey of the Auckland Museum suggested displaying the 'past handicrafts of the Maori race' at Wembley, the committee disagreed on the grounds that the exhibition was not 'historical' and that English people would not be interested in 'anthropological collections' (*Herald,* 24 January 1923). Others were concerned that if Māori people were sent to the exhibition it would undermine 'the idea of the Dominion being "up-to-date"' and give the 'impression that New Zealand is mostly populated by them to the disadvantage of the Dominion' (TPA MU 1, 26/15).

The British were more enthusiastic about Māori exhibits, however. When the meeting house *Mataatua* was rediscovered in the basement of the Victoria and Albert Museum, it was British officials who urged its inclusion (TPA MU 1, 26/15). Set up in the Wembley exhibition grounds, the old *whare* was a striking contrast to the classical façade of the New Zealand pavilion. The New Zealand court hosted a Māori troupe, which included the famous guide Maggie Papakura from Rotorua. Māori were divided over support for this troupe and the exhibition generally (McCarthy 2005). Something of this ambivalence is captured in a photograph of two young women from Whanganui who were members of the Rātana concert party setting out on an overseas tour that included the exhibition (Figure 2.4). Their 'traditional' dress and heirlooms, on closer inspection, reveal political agendas. Note the head band with the reference to the 1840 Treaty of Waitangi, and the *whāriki* backdrop, which speaks simultaneously of loyalty to the Empire (the Union Jack), the Old Testament (the crescent moon) and oppression (the star of David, through which Māori identified with the Jewish people).[4]

This is also evident in recorded responses of Māori who visited Wembley. T.W. Rātana, the prophet who had founded a large religious and political movement intent on raising Māori fortunes, led a delegation to London to present a petition to the King seeking to honour the Treaty of Waitangi (Ballara 1996). Rātana and his party complained to the press that they refused to enter the New Zealand pavilion because it suggested to the public that 'we are low down in the scale of native races'. Rātana's secretary Moka told reporters that, 'Our party

Figure 2.4   Martha and Piki-te-ora Rātana, Whanganui, 1924
(Alexander Turnbull Library PAColl-5932-40).

is disgusted with the Māori hut at Wembley because it is only half of Maori workmanship and the carvings are a poor example of Maori art' (*Dom*, 23 June 1924). This reaction to the display, perhaps heightened by the Rātana movement's modernizing philosophy and its explicit rejection of tradition, is nevertheless a sign that many Māori at this time would not put up with images perceived to be condescending. It also reveals that they did not so much oppose the imperial ethos of the exhibition as demand their proper place within it. Māori objects on display were not simply the objects of empire. The agency of display shows that they were objects of Māori negotiation with that empire. Māori exhibitions were likewise complex events that did not just create subjects *of* empire, natives subsumed within nations, but subjects *within* empire.

Despite this example of the Māori reception of Māori exhibitions, there is little evidence of Māori involvement in their production. Back at the Dominion Museum in Wellington, by contrast, there was a Māori presence. From about 1926, Thomas Heberley, nephew and pupil of the Te Āti Awa carver Jacob Heberley, was the first Māori to work full-time on the museum staff (Neich 1991). His duties were described as 'the preparation of Maori exhibits for the new museum' (TPA MU 14 5 (13/27/164)) but he actually had a much wider brief and was closely involved with Phillipps in collecting and display. He undertook several successful field trips on his own, largely because of the way he was able to operate independently within Māori communities. In 1929 on a visit to Pūtiki *pā* in Whanganui he initiated the successful negotiations over the acquisition of the war canoe *Teremoe*, a complex transaction which involved the Hīpango *whānau*, local carver Hōri Pukehika and the local Alexander Museum (Butts 2003: 143).[5] In 1932 he ventured into the remote Urewera region, where he persuaded the Tūhoe people at Ruatāhuna to donate *Te Whai a te Motu*, a house closely associated with the *Ringatū* faith and its leader Te Kooti. Heberley was able to mediate between Māori and the museum, showing an inclination for the ethnographic values of his colleagues, as well as sympathy for the beliefs and aspirations of local people:

> I explained to them, that my visit was to take away the carvings of Te Kooti, which had been lying about for many years, to the Tapu House at Wellington, so that their ancestors would not be forgotten. Meetings lasting for three days, were then held in the different hapus, to deal with this question. The natives then decided that I was the proper person to take the carvings, Chief Tewhenuanui [sic] giving the order for their removal to Wellington… (TPA MU 14, 7 (13/27/270))

Heberley set up his workshop in the corrugated iron shed in Sydney Street, just down the street from the Museum, where he carried out the repair, 'restoration' and reconstruction of the large objects that would form the centrepiece of the Māori Hall planned for the new building. He assembled complete artefacts from different fragments and portions that were newly carved as well as producing replicas based on other museum collections, and was closely involved in the reconstruction of *Te Hau ki Tūranga* and *Teremoe*. Heberley visited the Auckland Museum to inspect *Hotunui*, the recently acquired *whare whakairo* from Thames which was being displayed as the centrepiece of the Māori court in its new building (TPA MU 14, 5). Details of its construction, such as the thatching of the roof and the overall village layout, provided the model for the new Dominion Museum's Māori Hall a few years later.

Thomas Heberley's working space contrasted with the more strictly classified exhibits in the Farmers' Institute. Heberley's workshop resembled a curio auction house of the nineteenth century, in which ethnographic categories had been abandoned and chaos ruled (Figure 2.5). Called a 'treasure house' by a visiting reporter (*Dom*, 26 October 1929), it was described in tones of hushed wonder as the 'secret horde' lying 'hidden from the eyes of men' (*Dom*, 29 April 1931). In 1932 the 'Maori workshop' was open to the public one day a week and it created so much interest that from 1933 it was open five days a week (AR 1932, 1933). Aside from the visual appeal, crowds flocked to it to see Heberley himself, in his white coat, working away at his carving and showing people around. This working carving school, with its energy and communal bustle, presented a different notion of display to the funereal exhibits of the old Dominion Museum next door. This 'living' display, with the carver demonstrating the continuing vitality of Māori cultural traditions, made quite

Figure 2.5   Sydney Street shed with Māori collection, Dominion Museum, c.1932 (Alexander Turnbull Library EP-2217-1/2-G).

Figure 2.6   Māori carvers in the Sydney Street shed, Dominion Museum,
1936 (Museum of New Zealand Te Papa Tongarewa Hall-Raine B.13045).

an impression on a Wellington public that thought such practices were dying out. With the arrival in 1936 of a large group from the Maori School of Arts and Crafts in Rotorua, the workshop became such a popular attraction that access had to be limited (Figure 2.6).[6] The *Evening Post* described the busy scene as the group of Ngāti Raukawa women from Ōtaki worked on the *tukutuku* panels:

> At the work they sing Maori songs, with occasional relaxing interludes provided by gramophone, and many visitors passing the Maori workshop in Sydney Street have collected at the open door to watch fascinated. ('An Ancient Art', *EP* n.d. in O'Rouke 1994)

A 'NATIONAL TREASURE HOUSE': THE NEW DOMINION MUSEUM, 1936

On 1 August 1936, the National Art Gallery and Dominion Museum opened in Buckle Street. The ideology of dominionism found expression in the sober design and historical European style of the building's architecture (Figure 2.7). The stripped classicism of the elevated façade of 'Wellington's Acropolis' was a visual link to the civilization of antiquity (*Dom*, 1 August 1936). This was 'an Antipodean Parthenon', built as 'a memorial to fallen

Figure 2.7   National Art Gallery and Dominion Museum, with the
Carillon and National War Memorial, Buckle Street, Wellington, 1936
(Alexander Turnbull Library PAColl-5932-21).

New Zealanders', which epitomized the 'end of the struggle that left the Empire once more fearless and free and proud' (Irvine-Smith 1948: 199). The emblematic shields on the cornice were inscribed with the names of disciplines: geology, ethnology (with the profile head of a Māori warrior), technology, botany, zoology, architecture, sculpture and painting. The Minister of Education lauded the new institution as a 'noble building for a noble purpose' (Fraser cited in *EP*, 31 July 1936). This purpose, public education, was integral to the recolonial discourse that shaped the dominion of New Zealand.

For the Museum's exterior, architects Gummer and Ford deployed a stripped neoclassical style in keeping with its sober function. Internally, the design was influenced by consulting architect Samuel Hurst Seager, who had recently worked on Tate Britain. At this time, the best models were considered to be American rather than British (Bennett 2004: 120), as the British Museum's typological displays were now considered old fashioned (Bledisloe 1934: 14). In the American Museum of Natural History in New York, for example, the realistic settings of life group and habitat dioramas were designed to attract the public. It also adopted didactic exhibits as a way to educate visitors by setting objects within the discursive framework of explanatory text, images, diagrams and other graphic elements (Dias 1994: 170–2; Jenkins 1994: 267–8).

The new director W.R.B. Oliver was an exponent of the educational approach. A botanist and ornithologist, Oliver had taken over as director after Thomson's death in 1928, and he continued the campaign to modernize display techniques. The aim 'should be to teach something', through displays that will 'explain the structure of different groups of plants and animals ... or ethnological materials and methods' (TPA MU 208, 2/1). He was generally critical of crowded permanent exhibits in New Zealand museums, and particularly lamented the lack of 'technological displays' showing the manufacture of Māori objects, which have 'distinct educational value' (Markham and Oliver 1933: 93). The Governor-General Lord Bledisloe expanded on the theme of education in his speech at the laying of the foundation stone in 1934. He claimed that the new institutions should become 'not a storehouse of fusty and ill-assorted curios and a farrago of artistic mediocrity, but a source of intellectual and aesthetic enlightenment which will vitalise every sphere of educational effort...' (Bledisloe 1934: 2).

Within this new 'educational' approach, the anthropological construction of Māori objects as artefacts of a distant past was perpetuated through the 1930s and 1940s. The US Carnegie Corporation supported the establishment of a schools service in New Zealand museums, and new ideas in display technique were disseminated from 1936 to 1941 (McQueen 1942). These new strategies, typified by the Field Museum's 'Plains Indians Hall' opened in 1936, used commercial techniques showcased at Chicago's Century of Progress exposition in 1933 (Belovari 1997: 413). Dominion Museum staff attended a workshop run by an American 'preparator', who introduced a new style of highly constructed display, incorporating models, habitats and painted backdrops (*EP*, 30 January 1938). Education officers showed 'typical Maori artifacts' to children, and the Museum's Māori club discussed 'primitive peoples of the present day' (AR 1939: 42).

Despite these experiments in museum education, the new 'exhibition halls' suffered from a transitional approach to exhibit design that contained a mix of older and more up-to-date methods (Oliver 1944). Reviews observed that they had been 'laid out and will be run on the most modern lines and in accordance with the most advanced museum principles' (*EP*, 31 July 1936). Although the case layout was in fact relatively conventional, there was a degree of novelty in the spatial configuration for Wellington audiences. Visitors liked the change from the 'old traditional idea' of rows and rows of specimens to 'modern' methods such as clear labels that were said to be 'attractive' and 'instructive' (*EP*, 31 July 1936). The spacious halls clearly distinguished exhibitions from collections, a demarcation that had been professed but not implemented in the cramped quarters at Museum Street. In continental European museums since the turn of the century, exhibitions were distinguished from expanding collections, often through livelier display techniques, which began to mark them off as being for public consumption, in contrast to the 'sober' storage of specimens behind the scenes (Bouquet 2000: 186; Hudson 1987: 75).

Figure 2.8   The Maori Ethnology Gallery, Dominion Museum, 1936
(Museum of New Zealand Te Papa Tongarewa B.5622).

The 'Maori Ethnology Gallery', which occupied the entire north east wing next to foreign ethnology, was strictly ethnographic in orientation (Figure 2.8), and followed the lead of H.D. Skinner's Maori Gallery at Otago and Gilbert Archey's Anthropology Hall at Auckland. Its objects were now classified separately from other collections and displayed with a clear regimentation and lack of clutter that struck contemporary viewers (*Dom*, 24 July 1936). Tall glass pier cases and 'Carnegie' table cases were arranged alternately down the centre of the space, leaving the side walls, apart from one or two wall cases, free for the display of pictures and maps intended to portray Māori life. Artefacts, devoid of their contextual history, were placed on glass shelves, functioning as illustrations of the extended labels beside them. As in many museums at this time, display was a by-product of the archive, the collections and texts were the ethnologist's primary interest, with the public halls being treated like an excerpt from a research monograph (Jenkins 1994: 267–8). Generally, ethnographic museums had moved from the old typological layout, where numerous objects were arranged in typical series, to culture areas, where a few selected artefacts illustrated the way of life of a people in a particular geographical environment (Jacknis 1985; Jenkins 1994).[7]

Oliver concluded that each department should have a separate 'exhibition hall' with a distinct architectural treatment suited to the objects being exhibited. 'Moreover, the hall can be arranged as a unit', he wrote, 'with pictures, diagrams or flat exhibits on the walls to amplify the exhibits on the floor, the object being to tell in the best way the story of the exhibits' (Oliver 1944: 20). With the innovation of the storied exhibit, a narrative told through objects, it is obvious that museums once again borrowed a technique used earlier in world's fairs, a theatrical element that belied their commitment to scientific discipline. The message people at the time probably took away with them is suggested by L.B. Inch who wrote in 1937 with reference to this Gallery that the 'the development of human society' was 'epitomized' in the Māori people's development from 'neolithic simplicity to civilisation' (ATL Ms 1070).

But the Māori Ethnology Gallery was not the centrepiece of the new museum. This was without doubt the 'Maori Hall' in the middle of the building (Figure 2.9). When visitors

Figure 2.9   General view of Māori Hall, Dominion Museum, 1936, showing *Teremoe* (left), *Te Tākinga* (centre) and *Te Hau Ki Tūranga* (right) (Alexander Turnbull Library PAColl 3959 G 3855 1/1).

walked in the front door of the museum they entered an impressive foyer, leading them to the large hall, which ran east to west along almost the entire length of the building. Inspired by the newly completed 'Maori court' at the Auckland Museum, with its *marae* centred on the porch of a recessed meeting house, the Māori Hall contained four *waka*: the two war canoes *Teremoe* and *Te Heke Rangatira* and two *waka tiwai*. Flanking *Te Hau ki Tūranga*, which was embedded into the south wall inside a concrete shell, were the two storehouses, *Te Tākinga* on the left and a smaller composite structure on the right (Figure 2.10). These buildings were 'completed' by Heberley's carving, fresh red paint and newly thatched roofs. At either end of the hall, Neke Kapua's *waharoa* and several 'canoe tombs' and palisade posts were positioned up against the walls, suggesting the profile of a Māori *pā* which was far from overawed by the European architecture.

Contemporary reports praised the imposing dimensions of the Māori Hall, enjoying the celebratory atmosphere lacking in the ordered regime of the adjoining ethnographic halls (*EP*, 31 July 1936; *Dom*, 29 March 1936). It was an expansive, naturally lit open

Figure 2.10   Māori Hall, Dominion Museum, 1936 (Museum of New Zealand Te Papa Tongarewa Hall-Raine C.1978).

space, contrasting with the enclosed exhibition halls, and made a deep impression on viewers (Figure 2.10). With its lofty proportions and large, free-standing objects, it was the 'central shrine' of the whole museum, holding the nation's 'priceless treasures'. Preserved here were some of 'the finest examples' of the 'unique' and 'advanced' culture of the Māori, treasures that were 'inseparable from the story of early New Zealand' and 'woven into the very fabric of the colony's pioneer communities' (*Dom*, 1 August 1936). The meeting house displayed inside the museum symbolized the essence of Māori culture and its place within the nation. 'The white man, in designing his national treasure house', declared a journalist, 'has certainly given pride of place to the storied history of a proud race' (*Dom*, 1 August 1936). Reports of high attendances suggested that New Zealanders liked their new national museum, which must have buoyed the director's hopes that the institution would become a source of national pride. It's jewel was *Te Hau ki Tūranga*, 'a wonderful carved house that is a prized exhibit' (*Dom*, 31 July 1937). Recolonial New Zealand responded to the museum display of Māori culture with possessive pride:

> Out from the past there is bequeathed to us a heritage – an art of abiding beauty peculiarly our own... It is for us to-day to see to it that in our national life all that is best in Maori art will be revivified to live again in a new and better age. (Phillipps 1943: 24)

Benedict Anderson (1991: 164) has suggested that 'political museumizing' in late colonial societies profoundly shaped the way that they imagined their domain and the legitimacy of their settler ancestry. Museums recycled precolonial cultures as regalia for the secular state, allowing them to pose as guardians of a generalized local tradition (Anderson 1991: 181–3). As the formalized display of artefacts superseded specimens in museums, Māori material culture was taken out of the nature story and inserted into the national story, acting as a prehistoric foil to European history in New Zealand. The culture of display enshrined a Māori past as a prelude to its Pakeha present.

The number of Māori visitors to the Māori Hall was not recorded, nor were their reactions to it, but some at least joined in this celebration of their past. A short Movietone film of the early 1940s shows a smartly dressed, well-groomed young Māori man walking around the *tauihu* of *Teremoe* and pausing to look at Kupe's famed anchor stone *Te Punga a Matahourua*. 'Today a modern Maori surveys one of the oldest and most cherished relics of his race', declares the narrator, implying that Māori culture belonged to the past and assimilated Māori to the present. Yet the term 'relics' is ambivalent and suggests the display elicits a celebratory response from our model Māori. 'One of the most advanced races of the Pacific', the narrator continues, 'the Maori adorned with intricate carvings their dwellings and their canoes' ('Dominion Museum', 1940s). This episode reveals the role that museums played in the construction of the modern Māori subject. Though it was in the Māori Hall that the assimilationist discourse of the period was most clearly expressed in the way a '*marae*' was built into the museum, this space was also the site for a Māori attempt to insert themselves into 'our nation's story'.

'NGA TAONGA O TE MAORITANGA': MĀORI ARTS AND CRAFTS

From the second decade of the twentieth century, the category of arts and crafts became synonymous among Pakeha New Zealanders with Māori cultural activities such as carving, weaving, *tāniko*, *tukutuku* and the other 'traditional' decorative arts of the meeting house. But to Māori, more was at stake than simply the revival of traditional crafts. Through an analysis of Āpirana Ngata's cultural programmes, this section examines the politics of Māoritanga and how they advanced the 'indigenisation of modernity' (Sahlins 1993).

The School of Maori Arts and Crafts was established in Rotorua in 1927 by an alliance of Māori MPs, a sympathetic Prime Minister, the Board of Maori Ethnological Research, the Dominion Museum and the Te Arawa Trust Board. Like the antiquities legislation, it was the result of Māori iniatives supported by well meaning Pakeha (Ngata cited in Sorrenson 1987, vol. 2: 193). The initial proposal by Āpirana Ngata and Herbert Williams argued that the best patron for a school of Māori art was the Māori race (TPA MU 14 7 (13/38/2)). At the first meeting of the Board, Te Arawa representatives duly insisted that its projects should be tribally based (Ngata 1940: 323). At the same time the chairman of the Board of Māori Arts, Māui Pōmare, choosing his words carefully for a Pakeha audience, positioned their work within the discourse of Dominionism. 'I think we can fairly claim to have the public with us in preserving the art of our Maoris', Pōmare told a reporter after a Board meeting in 1928. 'Every country should try to preserve the original arts of its pioneers' (*EP*, 21 September 1928). The term 'pioneer' is here used not in its usual sense to refer to Pakeha founding fathers but to Māori, reflecting a growing historical consciousness that was to come to a head in the 1940s.

Amidst the favourable press reaction to the establishment of the School of Arts and Crafts during 1926/7, the phrase 'arts and crafts' appeared frequently among similar form-ulations like 'Maori artcraft,' or 'native art', all of which suggest a higher status than the earlier 'art handiwork' (TPA MU 157, book 3; TPA MU 14, 7). Distinct from the more precise scientific categories of specimen/artefact, these words allowed some slippage towards a pseudo-art status. The word 'art' in these constructions was always qualified by non-formal or mechanical overtones, and preserved the distinction between European 'fine art' and Māori craft. For example, during the First World War when busts and sketches by Illingworth were placed at the entrance to the museum's main hall, it was commented that '…they make an effective artistic contrast to the many fine examples of Maori arts and crafts around them' (AR 1916, 1926).

Alfred Gell's (1999) anthropological approach to art, which moves beyond the considerations of aesthetics, is useful for understanding the designation of Māori art amongst Pakeha. Certain groups of objects (the genres of painting and sculpture) became fine art by categorizing them as such within a *genre*; other objects are art by *intention*, while others are art by *reception* (quite apart from the question of what is considered good art or bad art in terms of a judgement of quality); still other objects, though not art by genre or intention/reception, are considered 'artistic'. European painting is art because it belongs to a genre of fine art within a recognized art world (Becker 1982). The issue for this study is how non-European objects produced outside the European art world are subsumed into it – by being reclassified as art – in spite of their original purpose or the intentions of their makers. New Zealand museums and art galleries in this period provide a detailed case study of how things 'become' art through the culture of display, how things exterior to the art-culture system are revalued by virtue of their outsider status; how Māori art in the sense of its perceived artistic qualities was seen by Pakeha viewers.

As the arts and crafts movement in New Zealand became an accepted field in its own right, it created an environment that made possible the elevation of Māori decorative arts, that indigenous form closest to Western ideas of craft that had also raised its profile within the art world (Calhoun 2000: 72–5). At the ethnographic end Best saw Māori objects as advanced examples of neolithic technology. He wrote that the Māori was 'more than an artisan, he was an artist … [who] combined the useful and the ornamental wherever it was possible' (Best in G.E. Thomson 1927: 83). Buck used the term 'decorative art' in his articles on *tukutuku* and weaving (Buck 1921, 1924). Anthropologists like Raymond Firth referred to Māori art as a social expression, explaining that he preferred not to study Māori art in museums where it is 'dead and set apart' but in its social context where it is 'full of life and character' (Firth 1925). The English artist and teacher W. Page-Rowe, closely involved with the School of Maori Arts and Crafts, analysed Māori art in aesthetic terms, although he specified that it was an applied rather than pictorial art. He concluded that a *tauihu* was 'something very much more than an interesting ethnological specimen. It is a work of art' (Page-Rowe 1928: 37).

Nowhere was the rise in status demonstrated more clearly than in the positioning of Māori arts and crafts at the heart of the capital's new Dominion Museum. In 1934, Governor-General Lord Bledisloe welcomed the 'perpetual reminder that this Dominion is the natural centre for the display of the finest specimens of Maori art and handicraft' (Bledisloe 1934: 12). Ngata noted that formerly interest in 'Maori art objects' was ethnographic or commercial, but now with the School the aim was 'the renaissance of the national art of the Maori, and not merely the craftsmanship' (cited in Page-Rowe 1928: v). There is considerable debate about the extent to which the School imposed a 'traditional' orthodoxy (Ellis 1998; Neich 2001). Initial ideas were surprisingly open to contemporary influences and even envisaged that, though it would follow 'old time models and traditions' preserved in museums, Māori art would eventually develop in new directions (TPA MU 14 7 (13/38/2)). Buck wrote later that the 'creation of a new brand of tohunga whakairo' was a 'cultural phenomenon of no mean importance,' but his dream that Māori artists would carry on where their ancestors left off and 'command the attention of the artistic world' had to wait another thirty years (cited in Sorrenson 1987, vol. 2: 153).

In the end, the social achievements of the School of Maori Arts and Crafts were more important than its artistic ones. Even when they acquiesced in Pakeha representations of 'Maoriland' at tourist resorts such as Rotorua, Māori people were always concerned about current welfare needs (McClure 2004: 41–8, 109–11). Māori MP and health reformer Dr Māui Pōmare responded caustically to Pakeha criticism that new housing at the Māori village at Whakarewarewa was less picturesque than the old shanties. '[I] would rather have my Maoris live', he said, 'than that they should satisfy the curiosity of the passer by and die' (cited in McClure 2004: 43). Ngata's social agenda for the School was clear. Almost thirty meeting houses or halls were built in twenty-five years. The opening of each one was accompanied by ceremony, cultural festivals, sports tournaments and other activities. Regenerated *marae* with their new meeting houses became focal points for strengthening *iwi*, an essential part of Ngata's strategy of wresting from the state a form of benign segregation for his people (Walker 2001: 214–16). He was heartened by the revival of cultural practices and the growing pride in Māori identity that these projects fostered. After the opening of *Raukawa* at Ōtaki in 1936 (Figure 2.11), Ngata explained the social value of this '*taonga*' to the Ngāti Raukawa people:

> They now possess a taonga which their hearts can embrace, which will help them to recall
> the spirit of their ancestors, and a common meeting place for the hopes and aspirations
> of the young people in the Pakeha world. (cited in Sorrenson 1987, vol. 2: 215)

Figure 2.11   Opening of *Raukawa* meeting house, Ōtaki, 1936
(Alexander Turnbull Library PAColl-5584-35).

By embodying communal identity, meeting houses created communities (Henare 2005: 252; Neich 1995: 21–41; Thomas 1995a: 60–1). This was not simply what Western scholars call the 'invention of tradition' (Hobsbawn and Ranger 1983). It is better understood, taking indigenous agency into account, as the construction of the future. As Gell puts it, the perspectival flux of tradition and innovation in Māori houses show that while as artefacts they are *retrospective*, as political gestures they are *prospective* – they express the promise of the future (1998: 256–8). The social conditions for the formation of arts and crafts included contemporary politics bound up with an historical aesthetics. Indeed, with the Māori category of *taonga* operating outside the museum sphere, politics and aesthetics were never divorced. What Ngata called *'nga taonga o te Maoritanga'* were the building blocks of a discourse which resisted the assimilation of Māori identity (Kaa and Kaa 1996: 352). Put simply, through the display of *taonga* young people could identify themselves as Māori. Far from its former usage in the prosaic world of business, as discussed in the previous chapter, *taonga* were now more precisely defined as a range of tribal treasures in the service of the younger generation. In a political pamphlet distributed to Ngāti Porou before the 1935 election, the member for Eastern Māori told his constituents that he had worn himself out 'reviving the true works of our ancestors as taonga for this generation' (Ngata cited in Kaa and Kaa 1996: 393). The list of those *taonga* – visual and performing arts, language and literature (*kōrero*), house building and marae customs, mana and political independence (*rangatiratanga*) – provides us with a prewar inventory of Māori cultural aspirations which were linked with 'the maintenance of the mana and rangatiratanga of the Maori people' (Kaa and Kaa 1996: 393).

Through Āpirana Ngata's involvement in the restoration of *Te Hau ki Tūranga* at the Dominion Museum, the communal category of Māori arts and crafts and the dominant museum category of artefact briefly came together. Despite the unsatisfactory outcome, this was the first Māori attempt to conceive, design and install an exhibit in a New Zealand museum.[8] Oliver planned to install the projecting porch of the *wharenui* as a central feature of the Māori Hall along the lines of the Auckland Museum. In August 1935, one year from the opening, Ngata approached the Dominion Museum, and told Oliver he was 'desirous of having the Meeting House erected in true Māori style according to the customs of the East Cape district' (Oliver cited in O'Rourke 1994). From that point on, the Museum seems to have effectively handed over the work to Ngata and his team of carvers and weavers from The School of Arts and Crafts (Figure 2.6). They were based in the museum workshop in Sydney Street East to allow Ngata easy access from his office in the nearby Parliament buildings. Apart from the involvement of Heberley, the museum provided the resources and materials, their staff becoming bystanders as Ngata and his team took charge.

Ngata's own research, concurrent with his work at the Dominion Museum, convinced him that the surviving portions of *Te Hau ki Tūranga* were the best extant examples of Māori carving (1958a, 1958b). The house figured prominently in his plans to reinvigorate the carved meeting house in communities around the country (Ngata 1940). The carving style established by famed carver Raharuhi Rukupō in Tūranganui-ā-Kiwa (Gisborne), became a model for the School's carvers who made the most of the opportunity to study the *whare* at close quarters (Ngata cited in Sorrenson 1987, vol. 2: 216). While based at the Dominion Museum, they reproduced *poupou* in the Gisborne style for new structures that memorialized modern leaders: Pōmare in *Te Ika roa ā Māui* at Manukōrihi marae in Waitara, and Carroll in *Tākitimu* community hall at Wairoa (Walker 2001: 319–20, 322–3). Rather than endorsing museum anthropology and its display of Māori objects as artefacts, museums were seen as a spring board for cultural maintenance and display as a means of uplifting Māori pride and unity.

At the same time, therefore, as they served assimilationist forces, museum collections provided the base for a counter-hegemonic discourse of tribal identity. Ngata envisaged 'students of Maori art attached to museums', who would eventually take over from the School of Arts and Crafts (Ngata in Sorrenson 1987, vol. 2: 137–8). As early as 1930 Ngata had envisaged 'the local museum carving branch under Heberley' playing a role in resuscitating Te Āti Awa carving (cited in Sorrenson 1987, vol. 2: 56). The school's carvers spent some time at the Auckland Museum with ethnologist Gilbert Archey studying northern carving styles to use on the new house at Waitangi in the Bay of Islands. This house *Te Tiriti o Waitangi*, named after the Treaty which had been signed nearby in 1840, was the Māori equivalent to the nearby cottage or 'Treaty house' which was restored to mark the nation's birthplace. With its spacious interior and pan tribal iconography, the *whare* was designed as a monument or museum (Ngata in Skinner 2005: 65). At the 1940 centennial celebrations, when Ngata led a dramatic *haka* in front of the new meeting house (Figure 2.3), it was clearly meant to remind Pakeha that their Treaty partners were not going away.

Back in Wellington, Ngata forged close connections between *Te Hau ki Tūranga* and the small Maori community by forming a concert party to perform at cultural competitions held in conjunction with the opening of new *whare*. Called Ngati Poneke Young Māori Club, they were drawn from the men and women working in Sydney Street, but were soon joined by local Māori (McEwan in Dennis, Grace and Ramsden 2001: 71). One photograph captures the group, dressed in their costumes, gathered around the piano in the unfinished interior of the meeting house (Figure 2.12). Their first concert in the Wellington Town Hall incorporated the carvings intended for Waitara. 'For a background and "wings"', wrote the reviewer for the *Dominion*, 'eight great seven-foot pieces of totara enriched with carvings from the Sydney Street School, grotesque with lolling tongues and slant eyes of paua shell, were effectively disposed between fronds of artistically woven reeds' (*Dom*, 28 May 1936).

The reinstallation of *Te Hau ki Tūranga* at the new Dominion Museum in Buckle Street clearly indicates the difference between conventional museum display and Ngata's active social programme. The initial preparations, carried out by Heberley and Phillipps, suggested an ethnographic approach. This was reflected in the faithful reconstruction of the *maihi* which were modelled on the bargeboards of the Gisborne house *Te Poho o Rawiri* (TPA MU

Figure 2.12   Ngati Poneke Young Maori Club in *Te Hau ki Tūranga*,
Dominion Museum, 1936 (with the permission of Ngāti Pōneke/
Museum of New Zealand Te Papa Tongarewa Hall-Raine B.13061).

208, 2/1). Ngata did not think much of Heberley's shallow chisel work, albeit historically 'correct' and preferred the sculptural Te Arawa style which the school had adopted after reviving the use of the long handled adze (Ngata in Sorrenson 1987, vol. 2: 88). Less restricted by historical precedent, the pragmatic Ngata sanctioned the inclusion of external elements not part of the original carvings, added extra *poupou* and altered the dimensions of replacement *tukutuku* panels. He had no hesitation in changing the length and proportions of the house in order to make it fit the allocated space, thus retrospectively constructing a spacious *whare rūnanga* on modern lines and not the squat chief's house it had probably been (Letter Ngata to Oliver, 29 October 1935 in O'Rouke 1994). It is possible that this generous internal space, unimpeded by display cases or extraneous objects as it had been in the Colonial Museum, was created because Ngata conceived the house as performing a social role that went beyond simply being a passive museum exhibit. Although there is no written record of the house actually being used for *hui* or other Māori ceremonies or events, certainly Ngāti Pōneke continued to regard it with some propriety, as their posters and stage scenery attest (Dennis, Grace and Ramsden 2001: 151). One private photograph of the group in costume posed in the interior of *Te Hau ki Tūranga* is titled: 'A reminder of the glories of their heritage' (ATL Utiku collection, photo album F180916 ½ p.12).

When visitors walked into the new Dominion Museum in late 1936, they saw the profile of what appeared to be a complete *whare whakairo* facing the main entrance (Figure 2.12). When they moved through the foyer they found themselves in the grand interior of the Māori Hall, with *Te Hau ki Tūranga* at the centre, flanked by *pātaka* and *waka*. The composite exterior and reconstructed interior, in which the original *heke*, *poupou*, *poutahu* and *epa*, combined with the new *tukutuku* panels, and two *poutokomanawa* from Ngāti Kahungunu, equated with an idealized concept of 'classical' Māori culture. Overlooking the substantial modifications, the *Evening Post* commented: 'As at present erected, the interior of the carved house presents as nearly as possible the original character which its designers intended' (*EP*, 31 July 1936). The *Dominion* called it a 'national icon of Maori artistry' (*Dom*, 1 August 1936), while another Pakeha critic recounted:

> The first fleeting glimpse through the archways conveys the impression that here lies the heart of sentiment in New Zealand; the culture and romance – arrogance perhaps – of a race steeped in tradition; possibly westering a little under modern influences, but rich in the legacy of ancestors … That Maori house … is one of the greatest treasures. A cursory view is impressive, but the full wealth and intricacy of ornament cannot be absorbed casually … The dim interior literally breathes the past of the Maori, its romance and legend. (National Art Gallery and Museum 1936)

Though the display of *Te Hau ki Tūranga* was successful in winning a place for Māori within New Zealand's national museum, it did not meet all the objectives of its Māori designers. A shortage of materials meant the *whare* was left unfinished at the opening, and Āpirana Ngata, unhappy with the results, was too embarrassed to attend the ceremonies (*NZPD* 31 July 1936: 225–6). As a member of the Board, Ngata was still able to exert influence on the Dominion Museum's display of its Māori collection, and there are subtle signs that the staff's first-hand interaction with the Māori arts revival had a lasting influence. After Heberley's death in 1937, attempts to replace him at least acknowledged the need for a Māori carver on the staff (AR 1937). The standing of *Te Hau ki Tūranga* certainly seems to have been enhanced. Rather than 'Maori house,' staff now generally referred to it as the 'meeting house', the term that became current usage among Pakeha in the postwar period (Phillipps 1943: 3). It once again assumed its status as one of the museum's most popular attractions. Phillipps published several illustrated articles about the house (Phillipps 1938, 1940, 1946), which made it better known outside the museum field. Perhaps as a result of his contact with the carvers, his research subsequently turned away from a preoccupation with precontact classical culture to focus on the modern meeting house as it currently existed on *marae* around the North Island (AR 1939).

The Māori section of the 1940 Centennial Exhibition in the Wellington suburb of Rongotai had even more Māori involvement and a correspondingly better Māori response.

To an extent, it shared the ideology of national progress seen at earlier fairs, celebrating the 100 years since the signing of the Treaty of Waitangi. There was a great deal of emphasis on the paternal role of the modern state, which provided for the lives of its citizens 'from the cradle to the grave', including the improvement of Māori social conditions through 'race uplift' (Labrum 2002; Martin in Renwick 2004: 54–64). The new Labour government's state welfare agenda was announced through popular displays in departmental courts, where clean art deco lines expressed the streamlined efficiency of modern design. Architect Edward Anscombe's futuristic designs, incorporating decorative elements such as the *koru* fern frond, suggested more progressive possibilities for Māori culture within modernist aesthetics, in contrast to the anti-modern aesthetic of the arts and crafts movement. But, despite the geometric simplicity of its *kōwhaiwhai* border, the official exhibition logo maintained a dichotomy between past and present. The 'Māori' side (1840), with the cloaked chief and *whare*, clearly represented the past, divided by a stylized *nikau* palm from the Pakeha side (1940) with its scenes of industrial modernity (*Official Guide to the Government Court* 1939, n.p.).

Yet Māori were able to present a counter view to assimilation, one which resisted their being consigned to the past or barred from the present. Māori MPs were extremely critical in Parliament of the exhibition's inadequate representation of Māori people. The organizers defended themselves, pointing out that the Dominion Museum already had Māori exhibits, but Ngata evidently did not consider them an adequate substitute. Nor was he impressed with plans for depicting Māori today, asking sarcastically if a Māori dressed in plus fours playing golf would be an acceptable image of civilized Māori? (*NZPD* 25 July 1939: 725–6). Having gained control of the project, the wily old politician set out to portray a modern vision of Māori New Zealanders. With artefacts borrowed from the collection of the Dominion Museum, carvings from The School of Arts and Crafts, and innovative *tukutuku* panels, a *whare rūnanga* was constructed in the centre of the Māori court. The 'blend of a beautiful ancient form with modern adaptations' was said to reflect the 'Maori renaissance'. Houses like this, claimed the souvenir booklet, were regarded by Māori themselves not as 'curiosities' or 'relics' but as 'symbols of their social life' (*New Zealand Centennial Exhibition* 1940: 4–5). Inside the rich decorative arts of neotraditional meeting houses – *tukutuku*, *kōwhaiwhai*, *whakairo* – adorned what otherwise looked like a modern hall (Figure 2.13). In fact the very form of the house, with its raised stage for performances in the form of 'a house within a house' showed that 'the Maori people still retain after one hundred years an individuality of its own' (*New Zealand Centennial Exhibition* 1940: 11). In Māori hands, display became a cultural means to a political end.

The large Māori audience for the popular Centennial Exhibition contrasted markedly with the Dominion Museum. In comparison to the fun of the fair at Rongotai, the dry pedagogy of museum display cases and the refined aura of rooms full of painting seems to have had little appeal. The exhibition was a more successful part of Ngata's social programmes for urban Māori than the Dominion Museum. Along with *kapa haka* (concert parties) and

Figure 2.13   Interior of Māori court, Centennial Exhibition, Wellington,
1940 (Museum of New Zealand Te Papa Tongarewa A000626).

demonstrations of arts and crafts, Rotorua carver Tuhaka Kapua sold his work from a stall
– 'see him at work' announced the sign – a display of 'living' arts that would never have
been sanctioned by museum ethnographers (Figure 2.14). The huge crowds visiting the
exhibitions included many Māori who apparently found the side shows and rides more
interesting than the government courts. The 'jovial Maori temperament accorded well
with the Exhibition gaiety', reported the *Dominion*. After the opening 'there were many
visiting Maori still in Wellington, and the Exhibition was filled with elders wearing valuable
kiwi-feather cloaks over their garments, walking around staring at the exhibits' (*Dom*, 16
December 1939). Oral histories, snapshots and souvenirs confirm that the Māori court
was a magnet for young urban Māori. With the outbreak of war, the Māori population in
the city had been bolstered with the people brought to the region as part of the manpower
regulations (Dennis, Grace and Ramsden 2001). Ngāti Pōneke, who provided most of the
entertainment at the exhibition, subsequently became very busy with concerts for fund
raising and other patriotic activities.

The most enduring image of the 1940 exhibition was the photograph of Prime Minister
Savage and the Māori warrior shaking hands, the mural that faced viewers as they entered

Figure 2.14   Carver Tuhaka Kapua at 1940 exhibition, Wellington
(Alexander Turnbull Library PAColl-0765 (½-036996-F)).

the Government Court (Figure 2.15). The date 1840 appears above the warrior, and 1940 above Savage, suggesting, like the logo, that Māori represented the past and Pakeha the present and future. It is rather too easy to dismiss the exhibition, like the picture, as another patronizing example of Pakeha portraying 'their Māoris' as grass-skirted primitives. In fact the exhibition was a complex product of the changing relationship between the Crown and Māori in the mid-twentieth century. Māori wanted parity with Pakeha, and though they had to settle for something less, their social and economic advancement was now on the agenda. Māori were newly enfranchised after the 1935 election, in which Rātana candidates in league with the Labour Party swept into all four seats specifically designated for Māori. New MPs like Paraire Paikea were prepared to celebrate nationhood in 1940 as long as their claims to equality were advanced (Walker 2001: 339). At the closing ceremony, Eruera Tirakātene of Kai Tahu, the leading Rātana MP, said the exhibition proved that Māori were not dying out, but were 'adapting' to modern life. The best exhibits were the 'arts and crafts', said Tirakātene, 'which the Maori has been able to retain over the tidal wave of progress in this country' (Tirakātene cited in Palethorpe 1940: 123).

The myth of racial homogeneity expressed in the image of Savage and the 'savage' could be interpreted as either patronage or partnership. Yet the Centennial Exhibition was another forum where views of successful Māori adaptation to modernity confounded Pakeha notions of a people consigned to living in the past. One encounter recalled by Jock McEwan gives us

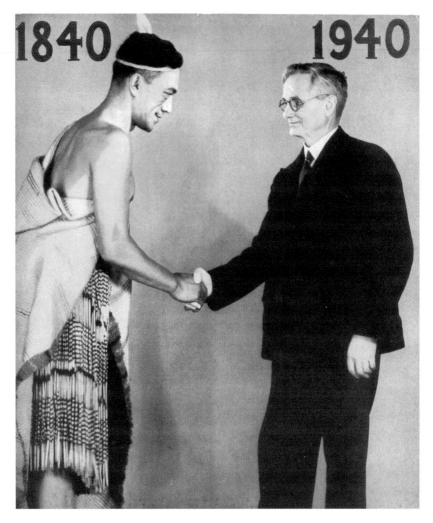

Figure 2.15   Entrance mural, Government Court, New
Zealand Centennial Exhibition, Wellington, 1940
(frontispiece, *Official Guide*, 1940, n.p.).

a glimpse of the kinds of informal interactions that were probably common. As the carver
Kapua worked at his stall, a Pakeha visitor aggressively pushed his way through the crowd
around, and stood with a 'disapproving' look on his face, hands on hips. 'Your ancestors
didn't do that with a steel adze', he declared. 'No', Kapua responded, 'and you didn't come
here in a stage coach' (Hocken Misc Ms 0423).

OBJECTS OF ART HISTORY: FINE ART AT THE NATIONAL ART GALLERY

One sphere of Pakeha culture remained impervious to Māori arts and crafts and isolated
from Māori people, however: the National Art Gallery. Though it was domiciled in the same

building from 1936, there was little contact between it and the Dominion Museum. In the interwar period, the culture of art was differentiated from other branches of visual culture which were more accessible to Māori audiences. This was not simply because Māori people chose not to visit art galleries, but was related to 'the social production of aesthetic space' (Prior 2002: 171). Whereas the Māori Hall presented a vision of national heritage that sought to assimilate Māori, the display of art in the galleries upstairs marked off this space as an exclusively Pakeha domain.

Art exists in an art world (Becker 1982). Like the objects of ethnography discussed in Chapter 1, art works can be thought of as objects of art history. The 'fine arts' of painting and sculpture were created only in the eighteenth and early nineteenth century (Staniszewski 1995; Preziosi 1997; Shiner 2001). A new academic discipline (art history), and a new institution (the art museum) accompanied the appearance of 'Art' and provided the social conditions necessary for its reception (Mansfield 2002: 4). Pictures were 'skied' up to the late nineteenth-century at the French Salon, hung frame to frame several rows deep in a manner that appeared chaotic to later viewers. Patricia Mainardi has shown how a new spare style of exhibition installation replaced the Salon hang from the 1880s, a form of aesthetic purity appropriate to the 'the moral order of fine art' engendered by the capitalist marketplace (Mainardi 1993: 108–9). By the early twentieth century, public art museums generally displayed painting and sculpture by themselves (Bann 1998: 233–4). Works were arranged into chronological surveys illustrating the 'triumphant evolution of styles and schools' (Duncan 1995: 22–6). These conventions of display served to separate art from other branches of visual culture, providing the upper classes with an ideal means of maintaining social distinctions between themselves and the lower classes though the display of cultural capital (Bourdieu and Darbel 1991). It was a case of what Prior has called the 'high within and the low without' (2002: 51–7). Brandon Taylor's history of art exhibitions in London notes a consistent tension between class and ideals of public improvement (Taylor 1999). It is important to acknowledge, however, that while the culture of art was socially stratified, the elite control of art galleries did not go unchallenged by working class visitors (Witcomb 2003; Whitehead 2005).

Art's genealogy of display was replicated around the globe in the wake of European colonization and the relations of power and social distinction that attended its display were similarly reproduced and contested in the colonies. In New Zealand, art was cultivated through a network of institutions supported by an audience, comprised almost exclusively of Pakeha, who wanted to reproduce familiar cultural practices from 'Home.' In the British Empire 'art galleries' were distinguished from other types of museums.[9] Art societies and art schools were established in the major cities in the 1870s and 1880s and the first permanent art gallery was opened in Auckland in 1888 (Thomson 1981: 16; Maclennan in McLintock 1966: 97). In these exhibitions painting and sculpture were generally singled out from other decorative or industrial 'arts' by the early twentieth century. Though Pakeha viewers may have accorded it aesthetic merit, Māori 'art' was rarely displayed next to painting or sculpture in an art gallery context. As we saw in Chapter 1, individual paintings and sculptures were displayed amidst other collections at the Colonial Museum, due to the lack of space rather than as a result of the more relaxed taxonomy of the period. In most cases, however, indigenous arts were not considered the equal of fine art. The Māori appeared as the subject of paintings – the Māori *in* European art – just as Māori people were assimilated into the wider society.

The prehistory of New Zealand's National Art Gallery goes back to the 1880s, when the Fine Arts Association of New Zealand was founded at the Colonial Museum by Wellington painter C.D. Barraud and a group of local painters in 1882. It changed its name to the Academy of Fine Arts in 1889 (Eden and Kay 1983) and built a gallery in Whitmore Street in 1892 which staged one or two exhibitions annually (Maclennan in McLintock 1966: 97). In nineteenth-century Britain, public art exhibitions were displays of social refinement as well as of art (Fyfe 2000: 53–76) and in the colonial context this form of cultural capital had a specific inflexion. Māori attendance at art exhibitions was the exception rather than the rule (Blackley 1987, 1997).

Though the Colonial and Dominion Museum did display works of art, generally painting and sculpture in Wellington remained the domain of the Academy, which maintained a separate building and distinctive display conventions. Even when the plans for the proposed art gallery and museum became entwined in the years before the First World War, the positioning of the pictures by themselves on the top floor of the planned new building implied fine art had a superior cultural status. Some members of the Academy wanted to remain aloof from the museum (Eden and Kay 1983: 80) and there appears to have been some tension in the 1920s and 1930s over different approaches to exhibitions in the proposed new building at Buckle Street. Because of his educational agenda, Oliver did not like the minimal art gallery labels then coming into fashion because people unfamiliar with art would not learn from them (Oliver and Markham 1933: 90). At most, it was believed art galleries should aim to raise the level of public taste by showing people the best of British, avoiding foreign influences and aberrations such as abstract art in the pursuit of what historian Keith Sinclair called 'compulsory loyalism' (Sinclair 1959: 240). In contrast to natural history museums with their mandate for popular instruction, art galleries tended to exclude those social groups without the educated taste required to understand and appreciate fine art (Prior 2002: 52). By the 1920s art institutions in Britain no longer reached out to broad audiences (Taylor 1999: xiv–xv) while in America the new aestheticism gradually swamped the progressive tradition of public art museums (McClellan 2003:17–24).

The development of modern art in the early twentieth century was complicit with its formalized display in art museums, where the new aestheticized form of installation design favoured the contemplation of the isolated art object (Staniszewski 1998: 62–3). It took longer to arrive in New Zealand. The 'white cube' style of exhibitions design associated with international modernism did not appear until the postwar period, as the next chapter shows. Meanwhile, the taste for what came to be called Māori art encompassed a broader range of society than the tiny elite who fostered or practised modern art. The wide appreciation of Māori art in New Zealand in the 1920s predated the new aestheticized installations of indigenous objects in French and American museums of the 1930s and 1940s that had flowed on from modernist primitivism (Staniszewski 1998: 98–9). A whole issue of *Art in New Zealand* was devoted to 'Maori art' in 1929. 'There was a time,' remembered Cowan, when Māori art was associated with 'the grotesque and the barbaric'. Now the 'art culture' of the Māori was attracting the 'sympathetic study' of artists, architects, and designers who saw in the 'whakairo of old New Zealand' a 'rich store' for 'national art ideals' (1929: 121).

In the early twentieth century a new generation of museums, designed in a Neoclassical or Beaux Artes style, were built in leafy parks on the edges of US cities such as New York's Metropolitan Museum of Art. These palaces of art replaced earlier industrial museums established along the lines of the South Kensington Museum (Conn 1998). The physical isolation of art galleries underlined their symbolic removal from everyday life and the transcendent nature of the visitor's encounter with art (McLellan in Mansfield 2002; Mainardi 1993). If the new National Art Gallery and Dominion Museum building in Wellington was a temple on a hill, with the entrance road sweeping up past the Carillon and its gardens to the broad steps and stone columns of the Museum, then the Gallery on the first floor was the inner sanctum sanctorum. 'From left and right broad stairways lead to upper light and freshness', wrote one reporter, 'large frosted window spaces giving the maximum of daylight while preserving the sense of seclusion that seems so necessary in a treasure-house of art' ('National Art Gallery and Museum' 1936: 24). With little craft or decorative art on display in the National Art Gallery, there was no opportunity for Māori arts and crafts to be considered fine art even by proxy. The two institutions were differentiated by the manner in which their displays divided up visual culture between them, the architecture preserving a clear distinction between the artefacts on the ground floor in the Museum and the art in the Gallery on the first floor. The art/culture hierarchy rested on the assumption that only art was philosophically capable of disinterested aesthetic appreciation, while the creations of more primitive peoples were viewed for their scientific interest, not their pure form (Duncan 1995: 12).

Visitors to the National Art Gallery were presented with views through the elegant, naturally lit galleries (Figure 2.16). The only decoration was the fluted pilasters marking the entrance to each room. The style of installation then current in Britain and North America, in which paintings were hung in a single line along neutral walls rather than being skied, was a novelty for local critics and visitors. Reviews called attention to other 'modern' design features (*EP*, 30 July 1936). Labels on the frames were the only concession to education. One reviewer praised the 'ample space for display', adding that 'each and every picture has full justice done to it', in contrast to the former 'confusing jumble' (*EP*, 30 July 1936). The Academy's close association with the gallery was reflected in their virtually indistinguishable exhibitions – indeed many visitors to the 'national group' found it hard to distinguish one from the other (Maclennan in McLintock 1966 vol. 1: 93).

Figure 2.16   View through Western galleries, National Art Gallery, Wellington, October 1936 (Museum of New Zealand Te Papa Tongarewa B.5611).

Early exhibitions at the National Art Gallery reflected the prevailing dominionism, and functioned to remind New Zealanders of their dominion status within the British Empire. In addition to colonial landscapes and a handful of twentieth century works, the 'best British art' was borrowed through the Empire Art Scheme, including 'masterpieces' by famous artists like Reynolds, Gainsborough, Constable and Turner. These works were displayed to 'educate public taste', creating a British base for New Zealand art by providing models for local artists (*EP*, 30 July 1936). Critic Roland Hipkins commented that the public enthusiasm for British art was more a result of 'patriotic fervour' than an interest in art, because New Zealanders were 'so much a part of the Motherland' ('National Art Gallery and Museum' 1936: 11). 'Quite appropriately', wrote another reviewer, 'pride of place has been give to the large and dignified portrait of his late majesty, King George V' (*Dom*, 1 August 1936). This huge painting was hung on the end wall as the focal point of a stately vista through a succession of galleries (Figure 2.17), showing how 'civilizing rituals' were enacted in public spaces (Duncan 1995). The National Centennial Art Exhibition staged in 1939/40 attracted 57,000 visitors. It furnished another example of neo-British cultural patriotism heightened by the wartime mood (Mackle 1984; Blackley 2004).

Figure 2.17 View through sculpture hall to portrait of King George V, National Art Gallery, October 1936 (Museum of New Zealand Te Papa Tongarewa B.5617).

When it opened, the only Māori elements on the entire first floor of the National Art Gallery were a handful of portraits and Māori subjects by Charles Goldie, Marcus King and Linley Richardson (*National Art Gallery: Souvenir Catalogue* 1936: n.p.). Richardson's *Taihuri* hung in the Academy's annual exhibition (*Dom*, 1 August 1936). Aside from these images of noble Māori from a romanticized past, Māori people themselves played little part in the institution. If any Māori visitors found their way up the grand staircase to the hallowed halls above, there was certainly nothing produced by Māori artists for them to see. Perhaps they were simply not interested in art and art galleries. However, as the dramatic events of the postwar period show, Māori would become more interested in art when art served Māori interests.

If display was constitutive of audiences (Fyfe 2000: 160), then an elite Pakeha art public was created at the National Art Gallery in the 1930s. With Māori culture downstairs and Pakeha art (minus craft) upstairs, the key elements of New Zealand society were now on display in the national institutions. Through its display as artifacts and arts and crafts, Māori culture was elevated to the status of national heritage in recolonial New Zealand, the reforged paradise of British stock, albeit with a garnish of Polynesian flavour. As often happens in this genealogy, there was a sudden break as history intervened. With the advent of the Second World War, the building was closed down in 1942, when it was commandeered by the Air Force. The next chapter shows how during and after the war, Māori flooded into the cities and eventually infiltrated every sphere of Pakeha cultural life, including the symbol of its cultural capital, the National Art Gallery.

NOTES

1. Although the word Māoritanga was certainly used in the nineteenth century to mean 'native custom' it adopts its modern English meaning of 'Maoriness' in the early twentieth century (Van Meijl 1996) and occurs frequently in English after the Second World War (Orsman 1997: 481).
2. The first published usage of the word was in a report on a trip up the Whanganui river, when Best, McDonald and Buck were accompanied by the British anthropologist W.H.R. Pitt Rivers (Pitt Rivers 1924).
3. The Māori view of time is fundamentally different: the past is situated in front of speakers (*ki mua*), whereas the future (*ki muri*) is behind them (Williams 1971: 213–14).
4. These symbols were first used in the folk art of the Ringatū church established by Te Kooti (Binney 1995). In the Rātana church, the Treaty and the Bible were the guarantees of modern day Māori rights (Binney in Binney, Bassett and Olssen 1990: 224–5).
5. *Teremoe* was another example of Māori participation in the museum display of tribal *taonga*. The famous *waka*, considered of 'high value' to Te Āti Haunui-ā-Pāpārangi, was donated on the condition that a photograph of Waata and Ema Hipango was displayed with it. A history of *Teremoe* was provided by Pukehika which expresses support for the work of 'collecting those relics which are left for the coming generations to see' (TPA MU 1, 18/59).
6. In this photograph, Tom Heberley can be seen in the background sitting with the women.
7. Culture areas were pioneered by American anthropologist Franz Boas at the Field Museum in Chicago (Belovari 1997: 409–10). By the 1920s displays at the Auckland Museum conveyed the use and function of objects, often employing photographs to suggest context, as Boas had done in the US (Cameron 2000: 213–14).

8. The *whare Hotunui* had been opened with a Māori ceremony at the Auckland Museum in 1929 but Ngāti Maru had no input into the display (Powell 1967).
9. This distinction survives in current usage, whereas in North America the term 'museum' applies universally to institutions of art and/or history, natural history and so forth.

3 'ART APART', 1949–79

The museum, as it isolates and separates (*frames apart*), is undoubtedly the site *par excellence* of that act of *constitution* … through which both the status of the sacred conferred on works of art and the sacralizing disposition they call for are affirmed and continually reproduced.

(Bourdieu 1995)

Te wehenga o Rangi raua ko Papa [The separation of Rangi and Papa] by Cliff Whiting (Figure 3.1) was exhibited at the National Art Gallery in 1978. It tells the Māori story of creation that parallels the birth of Māori art and the rebirth of Māori culture in modern New Zealand. In indigenous cosmology the sky father and earth mother were joined together in the darkness before being separated by their children. Here *Ranginui* can be seen in the sky blue and star patterns above while *Papatūānuku*, mother earth, is represented by the dark mountainous shapes below. Between them are their sons, six stylized figures in floating circles, associated with the elements and natural domains: sea, wind, earthquakes, cultivated food etc. In the centre right we see the god of the forest *Tāne Māhuta*, depicted upside down pushing his father away from his mother like the trees which stand between the earth and the sky.

Whiting's modern account of the creation of the Māori world is a scene of energy and dynamism, told in bright colours and new materials for the young generation living in

Figure 3.1   Cliff Whiting *Te wehenga o Rangi raua ko Papa* [The separation of Rangi and Papa] (1969–74), mixed media, National Library, Wellington (with the permission of Cliff Whiting/Alexander Turnbull Library).

the cities. His reinterpretation of Tāne's heroic feats, in which a 'world of light' is wrested from the darkness, expresses the struggle for an independent Māori identity in postwar New Zealand. The work contained recognizable motifs from customary carving, but the decorative exuberance of the design was no longer restricted by the width of a tree trunk, or the structural iconography of the meeting house (O'Regan 1984). *Te wehenga* was an example of 'contemporary' Māori art, in contrast to what was called 'traditional' Māori art, the customary styles of carving usually displayed in the museum. In terms of the terminology introduced in the last chapter, the works of Whiting and other modernist Māori artists were not objects produced outside the art world that were seen as art by those in it. These paintings and sculptures were produced within the category of fine art from the start – even if they were not always regarded as very good art. Though its style and content were insistently Māori, *Te wehenga* drew from modernism and showed an enthusiastic engagement with the Western art world. Part of a discourse of nationalist independence, this art movement clamoured for a place within the field of New Zealand art, and for space within the art gallery. Despite the concessions signalled by this exhibition however, Pakeha aesthetics resisted Māori politics.

In this chapter I trace the history of Māori exhibitions from the reopening of the National Art Gallery and Dominion Museum in 1949 up to 1979, when key temporary exhibitions broke new ground and presaged the changes of the following decade. The continuing recolonial vision of a harmoniously integrated society produced displays of Māori objects as artefacts and primitive art at the Dominion Museum. Once again, Māori were far from absent and acquiescent in a period of conformity and conservatism. In the 1960s and 1970s, as a new discursive formation – decolonization – reconfigured Māori relations with the Pakeha state, Dominion Museum exhibits reflected a new Pakeha concern for national identity, and a renewed Māori concern for national self-determination. 'Māori exhibitions', now a form of display in their own right, increasingly showed the influence of Māori audiences, and reflected the dynamism of Māori society in a time of rapid social change.

RECOLONIZATION AND INTEGRATION, 1950s TO 1960s

> A spectacular ceremony of address to the meeting house, Te Hau ki Turanga, performed by the Hon. E T Tirikatene, member of the Executive representing the Maori Race, was the highlight of the reopening of the Dominion Museum in Wellington last night. (*EP*, 30 September 1949)

When the Museum finally opened its doors to the public again in September 1949, after a seven-year closure, Māori played a more prominent part than they had in 1936 when the inaugural ceremonies excluded Māori people and ceremonial. The *pōwhiri* led by Ngāti Pōneke, and the *whaikōrero* by Cabinet Minister Eruera Tirikātene (the pre-eminent Māori politician of his day) were part of the first official welcome performed on the *marae ātea* in front of the house, which now functioned as a space with its own cultural integrity rather than merely as a showpiece (AR 1949). The Second World War, which had forced the closure of the museum in 1942, provided the leverage for Māori to improve their position in New Zealand society. The Māori war effort was rewarded by social and political advances pursued vigorously by a new generation of Labour-Rātana politicians such as Tirikātene. Supported by Peter Fraser, Prime Minister and a committed Minister of 'Māori' Affairs (the word 'Native' was dropped from government terminology in 1947), Māori people now enjoyed improved incomes, and greater access to healthcare, welfare and housing. Broadcaster Wiremu Parker expressed something of this sentiment in *Towards Tomorrow*, a film commissioned by the Department of Education:

> Our Maori people are not content to be left behind in the rush to New Zealand progress.
> We want to be prosperous and secure, we want the same things as pakehas: a good home,
> comfort, a good life. (*Towards Tomorrow* 1956)

Māori hopes for a brighter and more equitable future were only partially met. Just after the museum reopened, a National government took power and ushered in a period of conservative retrenchment as Māori gains were rolled back. Demographic changes could not be repressed, however. A Māori population explosion accelerated a 'new migration' to the towns and cities, which had enormous social consequences (Metge 1964). Postwar government policy advocated 'integration' of Māori into wider society (Walker 1992: 503). Some Māori leaders cooperated with this state ideology while others defended their newly won place in national life and resisted the surrender of a separate Māori identity. In 1955 Dr Maha Winiata dismissed the idea that 'the Maori should become a pocket edition of the pakeha'. He insisted that 'the Maori wants to retain his identity within the New Zealand framework.' Against the refrain, 'We are all New Zealanders' he advocated the bicultural equation: 'Two peoples, one nation' (*New Zealand Listener*, 25 March 1955: 24–5).

New Zealand still saw itself as 'God's own country', a Pacific paradise. Although its influence was considerably weakened by the growth of American political and economic power in the region after the war, diplomatic and trade ties to the mother country remained. When New Zealand adopted the statute of Westminister in 1947 and joined the British Commonwealth as an independent nation, it was still 'better Britain'. The new Queen received a right royal reception when she visited the country in 1953 – crowds flocked to see her waving the Union Jack and singing *God Save the Queen* (which remained the national anthem until 1977). Maintained by a long economic boom from the 1940s to the early 1970s, based as before on the export of agricultural produce to a guaranteed British market, New Zealand society was largely conformist, monocultural and 'British' (Belich 2001: 320).

Māori people in the cities were encouraged to become modern New Zealanders, 'brown skinned Pakehas' who effaced their own identity, their past memorialized in displays of 'classic' culture. Like schools and other state institutions, museums were infused with the recolonial discourse of integration. In a 1951 newsreel, a group of student teachers follows a man in a white coat up the steps of the Dominion Museum and into the Māori Hall. The ethnologist carefully takes a *hei tiki* from a glass case, and gives it to the students so that, the voiceover tells us, 'they can examine the workmanship of the old time Maori.' In the next shot we see the *tiki* in the hands of a well-groomed young Māori man dressed in a blazer. He puts it against his chest, where it would have sat, and smiles as he poses for his classmates. 'A precious museum piece now', says the narrator, 'it will no longer be worn as a pendant but will be here to be admired and studied for all time' (*Maori Art Treasures* 1951).

FROM ARTEFACT TO ART

With the tacit approval of older Māori, and little opposition as yet from politicized youth, New Zealand museums basked in the praise of overseas visitors whose approval of Māori exhibits confirmed the recolonial myth of racial harmony. Olive Royston wrote in the *Museums Journal* that Māori exhibitions 'have a considerable value for Maori and Pakeha alike, in stressing the cultural heritage of the Maori people, which is now an accepted part of New Zealand culture' (Royston 1956: 231). The Dominion Museum's ethnographic vision of an idealized Māori past reduced racial difference to a generalized heritage available to all. The new director Dr R.A. Falla carried on the scientific and educational mission pioneered by Oliver, emphasizing the social value of its renovated exhibits including the traditional Māori culture enshrined in the renovated Māori Hall (Falla 1950: 41–2). Dr R.K. Dell, director from 1967, stated that Māori and Pakeha were one people: 'New Zealanders'. 'Our biggest hope is the increasing integration of Maori and pakeha', he said, 'and if we all end up coffee coloured, the quicker the better' (Guiney in O'Rourke 1994).

Didactic display cases in the Māori Hall and the published work of ethnologists W.J. Phillipps and his successor Terence Barrow presented objects as evidence of pre-European Māori material culture. The collection was known as 'Maori ethnology' and things in it as 'artefacts', which was the word commonly used by the general public. Within the Museum, English terms were preferred for Māori objects, so that *waka* reverted to 'canoe', *kākahu* to 'cloak' and *pātaka* to 'storehouse'. Despite Phillipps' research into meeting houses, the broad direction of museum displays was even more scientific than the prewar methods of self-taught enthusiasts like Best or McDonald and sometimes lacked their intimate association with Māori people, language and culture. Now professionally trained in social anthropology and archaeology (subjects taught at Auckland University from the 1950s) museum ethnologists were exposed to current Anglo-American museology through journals, trips abroad and visiting scholars. Ethnologist Terry Barrow, for example, a student of Skinner at Otago, went on to obtain a PhD at Cambridge.[1]

The exhibits in the Māori Hall in the 1950s and 1960s were more artefact than art. The space was, if anything, more crammed than in 1936, because the additional collections formerly placed in the north gallery had to be relocated to the Māori Hall in order to make way for the expanding foreign ethnology collection (Figure 3.2). Although extra space was freed up when the Te Arawa *pātaka* and one of the war canoes, *Te Heke Rangatira*,

Figure 3.2 Māori Hall, Dominion Museum, 1949 (Museum of
New Zealand Te Papa Tongarewa B.15521).

were given to the Canterbury Museum, the overall impression was of a crowded exhibition hall, except for the '*marae*' space cleared in front of the *whare*. A visiting British collector complained in 1959 that, despite the space in the 'cathedral-like Maori Hall', the collections were now 'sadly cramped' (ATL Ms papers 3522, 14). It was certainly more ethnographic than before, due to the series of thematic glass cases around the walls and table cases out on the floor, which were 'ordered to show different aspects of Māori life and good examples of his workmanship' (Dell 1965b: 191). Falla told a reporter in 1949 how visitors could get the most from a visit by a 'systematic' study of the displays, which were organized in a 'planned sequence' (*Listener*, 7 October 1949: 6–7). The 'newly arranged bays' were the result of moving the island cases, originally designed to stand in the centre of the halls, back against the walls, thus allowing distinct subjects to be grouped together. Starting off with something familiar, the visitor was led 'gently' to more 'classified' information. Those interested in ethnology, for example, should be able to work their way back from the 'ancient civilizations' (represented by the Egyptian material), through 'primitive systems such as those of Polynesia' and on to 'prehistoric man' (*Listener*, 7 October 1949: 6–7).

Following the Carnegie experiments in the early 1940s, design, colour, lighting and labels were designed to situate the object within a scientific narrative which explained to the viewer 'the place of an article in the culture of a people' (McQueen 1942: 52). Clear glass cases were divided up into self-contained units, with backing and shelves, to cut down on the reflection and concentrate on one topic at a time. A small number of 'artefacts' were mounted within these didactic panels in order to 'tell a story which would be comprehensible to young people of normal intelligence, rather than to present rows and rows of similar objects which would have meaning only for specialists' (Dell 1965a: 21). The education officers had an active role in developing exhibits and checked label copy by taking it outside to the gardener to see if he could understand it (Dell 1965b: 189).

A simplified anthropological construction of pre-European Māori culture dominated. For example, the 'Rat trapping' case, with its layers of handwritten text, plus diagrams and photos on cards stuck on to backing, was like a textbook on a wall (Figure 3.3). In the case titled 'The Maori as a fisherman', fish hooks were laid out on sloping shelves, arranged in neat rows against a wash of colour to show the progression from bone to steel. Small handwritten object labels were placed close to the relevant item. The 'Fowling' case used reconstructed models of traps and mounted specimens of birds to show 'stone age' Māori technology (Figure 3.4). A little like a diorama, it created a semi-naturalistic setting of the forest, but rather than a painted scenic backdrop the false wall at the back was left plain and merely painted a light colour to provide contrast for the objects.

Beside 'Fowling,' and placed in a prominent position between the *whare* and the *pātaka*, a case dealt with the sensitive subject of 'Religion, death, burial.' The side panes were covered in with hessian and the back painted a dark colour, which, together with the low fluorescent lighting, suggested the cave in which the 'bone chests' (*waka tūpāpaku*) were found. These objects are highly *tapu* because they are associated with death and today they are generally

Figure 3.3 'Rat-trapping' case, Māori Hall, Dominion Museum, 1949 (Museum of New Zealand Te Papa Tongarewa F.425/4).

not displayed at all or reproduced in photographs. Yet in 1964 they were not only put on public display but in proximity with food items, considered *noa*, on the other side of the very same case, an even greater transgression of customary sanctions. Even more controversially, this case contained, on a centrally positioned shelf, four *mokamokai* (preserved tattooed heads). The press devoted extensive coverage to the 'eye-stopping display of Maori heads' (*EP*, 8 October 1964), which reflected the purient interest common at the time. Even human remains could be considered artefacts of anthropology.

Figure 3.4   'Fowling' case, Māori Hall, Dominion Museum, 1949
(Museum of New Zealand Te Papa Tongarewa F.425/5).

These displays in the 1960s show that the Dominion Museum now had the resources to implement the ideas about museum education introduced in the 1940s. A specialized display department worked together with 'professional' staff, such as the ethnographers, to produce the final exhibit. Nancy Adams designed the first phase of the new Pacific gallery early in the decade, where the whole space was treated as a 'single unit' in which large objects were hung on plain painted walls (AR 1962). The popular Egyptian tomb, designed by Ross O'Rourke in 1963/4, created a realistic enclosed environment for the mummy and associated objects (O'Rourke 2000). In 1969, the bicentennial of Cook's 'discovery' of New

Zealand was celebrated with a large exhibition comprising innovative modular screens and large graphic panels prepared by staff from the Tourist and Publicity Department (O'Rourke 2003). This style of display in which a profusion of objects, graphics and text replaced the simple didacticism of the educational approach, followed developments in US history museums in the 1960s and 1970s where designers, increasingly prominent on the staff, tried to make museums less forbidding and more attractive and accessible (Kulik 1998).

New display techniques did not have a big impact on the Māori Hall, however, because most of its cases had been installed by 1965 (AR 1965). The 'Te Rauparaha' case, set up in 1964 (Figure 3.5), contained portraits of the famous Ngāti Toa warrior, his sword and *taiaha*, the *hei tiki Te Pirau*, and the *mere pounamu Tuhiwai* (AR 1965–6). The following

Figure 3.5 'Te Rauparaha' case, Māori Hall, Dominion Museum, 1964
(Museum of New Zealand Te Papa Tongarewa F.425/9).

year, a special display was set up on 'early Maori families' of the Wellington region, which included 'relics' associated with Te Puni. It seems that nineteenth-century artefacts showing European influence, or European-produced objects owned by Māori, had an ambiguous status. Transcultural objects did not fit anthropological categories because they were 'tainted' by European contact: for example Tamihana Te Rauparaha's cloak with its wool tassels, Hongi Hika's armour, Te Kooti's flag, and Tene Waitere's experimental sculpture were not deemed authentically Māori. Products of a hybrid nature, they were not displayed in museums as 'colonial history' like the European ceramics, textiles and regalia which were increasingly regarded as 'heritage' by European New Zealanders (Henare 2005: 247–256). Yet Māori feelings about tribal or family heirlooms, commonly expressed in the magazine *Te Ao Hou*, were actually very similar to those of Pakeha who celebrated the achievements of their 'early settlers' (*Te Ao Hou* Summer 1953, 3: 28–31).

The most important change in the genealogy of display from the 1940s to the 1960s was a shift in emphasis from artefact to art, the subtle transformation of the dominant category from something that might be described as 'artefact/art' towards 'art/artefact.' Remembering that, in Gell's terms (1992), non-Western objects became art by being reclassified as such, we can see the process through which things produced outside this culture of art gain entry to it by virtue of their exterior qualities. Thus Māori art, like primitive art, folk art, outsider art, and so on, is also an 'object of art history'. In the postwar period, the carving and weaving in the Māori Hall, constituted principally as artefacts, were judged increasingly for their 'artistic' qualities. One of the 'new ideas' tried out by Falla and his staff in the Māori Hall was to emphasize the 'aesthetic' value of some objects that were 'highlighted just as objects of beauty' (Dell 1965b: 191). Certain objects, freed from the didactic confines of the show cases, were isolated as sculptural elements in their own right by being silhouetted against a plain wall or left on the floor as free standing forms, including the palisade figures at either end of the hall and the *taurapa* on top of the canoe cases on the west wall (Figure 3.6).

Although staff generally employed the term 'artefacts' for Māori objects in the collection, they also referred to them in artistic terms. When Barrow started at the museum in 1953, he lost no time in setting up a new permanent exhibit in the ethnographic gallery titled 'Art forms of the Pacific'. The titles of Barrow's publications, culminating in *Maori Art of New Zealand* (1978), show how carving gradually assumed the status of art, one approved of by Māori reviewers (Mataira 1961). *Te Hau ki Tūranga* was unequivocally acclaimed as a 'rare masterpiece', which would 'stand with any world art' (*Gisborne Herald* cited in O'Rourke 1994). Carvings were not displayed with the Museum's fine arts collection, let alone upstairs in the Gallery with equivalent standing to painting and sculpture. The fact that Barrow could describe carving in purely art historical terminology, such as a spiral that is called 'Rococo', is a reminder that 'Maori art' was largely a European construction untroubled by a Māori audience (Barrow 1976: 3). Displayed as art/artefact, Māori carvings became objects of art history as well as anthropology. This transitional category, which heightened the artistic qualities of artefacts, invited Pakeha appreciation of certain Māori objects not

Figure 3.6   Māori Hall, Dominion Museum, May 1969 (Archives New Zealand AAQT 6539, A90627).

actually made as art, but possibly distanced them from appreciating Māori understandings and values.

New display conventions helped to form this new view of Māori art as art. The Cubist 'discovery' of African art in French ethnographic museums led to major changes in the way these objects were displayed in both Europe and North America (Staniszewski 1998: 98–9; Steiner in Mansfield 2002: 137–8). A little later, Oceanic art, well represented in these collections, was rehabilitated by the Expressionists and Surrealists (Clifford 1988: 136). In 1946, at the Museum of Modern Art, innovative Belgian curator Rene d'Harnoncourt staged an influential exhibition called 'Arts of the South Seas.' The catalogue stated that 'many Maori carvings deserve to rank among the art masterpieces of the world' (D'Harnoncourt, Linton and Wingert 1946: 55). Paul Wingert curated 'Art of the South Pacific Islands' at the De Young Museum in San Francisco (Wingert 1953). The Museum of Primitive Art, which opened in New York in 1957, placed objects on spotlit pedestals elegantly arranged in white-walled galleries. This aestheticized design was thereafter institutionalized as the standard display for primitive art. These collections, and the display conventions that went with them, were incorporated into the new Rockefeller Wing at the Metropolitan Museum, which opened in 1971 (Staniszewski 1998: 116–17).

The shift from artefact to art, from natural history museums to modern art museums, certainly validated Pacific art, but, as scholars have argued, it concealed the transformation in meaning that takes place when objects are taken out of one context and reinscribed in another (Conn 1998; Staniszewski 1998). If the Western celebration of non-Western 'art' shows that beauty was in the eye of the beholder, then Māori carvings and other traditional objects became art by reception not by intention. It was a local form of primitive art referred to by contemporaries simply as 'Maori art'. This attitude was related to 'primitivism', the modern West's appropriation of the formal, expressive or magical qualities of the 'primitive' Other (Antliff and Leighton in Nelson and Shiff 1996). In postsettler societies, primitivism in art had strong links with cultural nationalism (Thomas 1999). Experiments among a small group of New Zealand artists in the 1950s and 1960s were part of a discourse of national identity that foreshadowed decolonization (Belich 2001). This primitivist recategorization served to indigenize settler culture by grafting Māori content onto European style, part of the recolonial project of integrating Māori people into Pakeha society.

Most exhibitions of primitive art were actually made up of Pacific Island not Māori objects. The first stage of the new Pacific Gallery, completed in 1961, featured aestheticized displays of monumental sculptural forms like house carvings, masks, and shields. They were greeted as 'rare and beautiful primitive art' (*EP*, 19 September 1961). Similar developments occurred at the same time at the Otago Museum and Auckland Museum (Thomson 1981; Wolfe 1993; Collinge 1999). Therefore, the extent to which primitive art equalled Māori displays in practice is unclear. With Pacific material culture, the geometric simplicity and apparent absence of social meaning made it more accessible to fine arts audiences used to stylized sculpture. The unwillingness to adopt the term in relation to Māori material may have been because New Zealand audiences were too familiar with Māori culture to divest carvings of cultural meaning, or because of fears that increasingly assertive Māori audiences may object to the negative connotations of the word 'primitive'. This cleavage of Māori culture from Pacific art was, possibly, a residue of the historical division of collections between museum (*Naturevoelker*) and art gallery (*Kulturvoelker*) (Bennett 2004: 132).

Pakeha increasingly recognized museum artefacts as art and, like Hamilton's 'art workmanship' and Ngata's 'arts and crafts', the idea if not the meaning of 'primitive art' was employed to raise the status of Māori culture on the national stage and incorporate it into the common heritage of Māori and Pakeha. 'Primitive' Māori art superseded the category of 'arts and crafts', which, after the death of Ngata, slipped out of the museum and into the commercial field of souvenir art. It emerged in the form of 'exhibitions', a mode of art gallery display practice which made visible this new category in museums. In transforming artefact into art, there was a shift in the mode of display from permanent exhibits to temporary exhibitions. Permanent halls or galleries in museums, with the time and resources to provide extra information, were more likely to take the form of didactic displays aimed at educating the public. They were often more elaborate fabrications that contextualized an artefact within a model of Māori culture constructed through images and text like an anthropologist's field report – in line with the anthropological concept of art. With travelling exhibitions, on the other hand, it was technically simpler (and cheaper) to install these same objects as art works against neutral walls with minimal staging, so they could be packed up and taken to the next venue. In this situation, it was easier to stage Māori art as tribal style or beautiful sculpture, a technique that dispensed with the need for wordy explanation or cultural information.

In the 1960s, too, the word 'exhibition' started to appear in connection with temporary installations at or from the Dominion Museum. Used previously for short-term or mobile displays at art societies, dealer galleries or expositions, the term was applied in the immediate postwar period to short-term hangs in art galleries, as distinct from permanent displays in museums. It began to settle into its current meaning, denoting all displays in museums and galleries, temporary or permanent, from this decade. The Dominion Museum, in fact, erected very few temporary displays until the late 1960s, when it established a temporary exhibition gallery with travelling exhibitions sourced from overseas (AR 1968, 1972). In sum, New Zealand museums 'modernized' by adopting an art-gallery style of presentation that was seen as both more prestigious and more 'up to date'.

THE DOMINION MUSEUM AND MĀORI

From the 1940s to the 1960s museums continued to exhibit Māori culture to a predominantly Pakeha audience. The Dominion Museum's displays of 'primitive' Māori art did not tell people much about modern urban Māori and before long young Māori would have something to say about the merits of the label 'primitive'. Māori were certainly present among visitors to the museum, if in small numbers, as they were now in most branches of mainstream New Zealand life. In rugby, for example, due to the exploits of players like Waka Nathan, the All Blacks were rarely 'all white'. But in the 1960s, when 'coloured' players were excluded from New Zealand rugby teams touring South Africa, Māori blew the whistle, objecting to discrimination in a protest campaign dubbed 'No Maoris, No tour.' Annoyance at this exclusion gave rise to a good-natured jibe in a song from the popular Māori musicians The Howard Morrison Quartet: 'Fee fi fo fum, there's no horis in that scrum!'[2] If the gap between the display of Māori in museums and their urban reality became increasingly obvious, it still did not lead to open debate and protest. Their absence on rugby fields received more attention than their absence from museums because sport, for now, was more important in the national life of most New Zealanders.

The myth of postwar New Zealand pictures 'Godzone' as a land of prosperity, conformity and good race relations. The reality for Māori was the struggle to maintain their identity at a time of rapid change. As people moved into the towns, social and cultural traditions were transplanted and transformed in new settings. A contemporary film showed young Māori learning *tukutuku* at Ardmore Teacher's College in Auckland. According to the narrator,

'Arts and crafts are preserved by the older people, learned anew by the young' (*Towards Tomorrow* 1956). In opposition to the recolonial vision of an integrated society held by the majority of the population, Māori articulated a distinct identity through the innovative decoration of community halls and urban *marae* in the cities, for example in the *whare whakairo* at Waiwhetu in Lower Hutt, which opened in 1962. In contrast to the Dominion Museum, where the displays suggested that 'native arts have languished, almost disappeared', the vibrant urban *marae* showed 'a new art form is emerging, less artistic perhaps, but with a clearer social purpose' (*Maori Arts and Culture* 1962).

Of those who were working within the museum culture, Charlie Tuarau was undoubtedly the most important figure. Tuarau was a Cook Island Māori born in Aitutaki, whose language and culture were closely related to New Zealand Māori (Figure 3.7). Tuarau was one of Ngata's team who worked on *Te Hau ki Tūranga* in 1936, who returned to the Museum after the war to prepare the house for reopening, staying on to undertake repairs, maintenance and produce copies of the Māori collection (AR 1978). A respected carver and a popular guide, he often showed visitors around the Māori Hall. As the 'only Maori speaker' on the museum staff, he spoke at the welcome ceremonies that took place from time to time in front of the meeting house. Subject to collegial criticism for his erratic work habits, Tuarau was a law unto himself on the '*marae*' and was regarded by management as a *de facto* 'public relations' and 'protocol' officer when it came to 'Maori affairs' (Yaldwyn in Hobbs 1999).

Although he was not involved with the ethnology department like his predecessor Heberley, Tuarau took an active part in maintaining the permanent exhibits (he can be seen working on the canoe in Figure 3.2). He built a *wharepuni* (sleeping house) which was erected in the Māori Hall between *Teremoe* and *Te Hau ki Tūranga* (AR 1952). Tuarau regarded himself as a 'guardian' of the 'treasures' in the Māori Hall, if not of the 'artefacts' in display cases (O'Rourke 2000). He seems to have ignored Phillipps and Barrow, reminding the latter that he had 'no authority to assign or supervise his work on the Maori collections' (TPA MU 2, 57/7). Barrow may have had reason for complaint on strictly ethnographic grounds (Tuarau decorated the model warrior's ear with a 'greenstone pendant' made from a green plastic toothbrush) but the carver was very popular with overseas visitors and always in demand with school groups. For those Māori who did visit the Museum, Tuarau was a welcome presence. Current employee Tom Ward recalls that as a young man visiting the Museum he often saw Tuarau patrolling the Māori Hall dressed in his white coat, and remembers his hearty welcome: *Tēnā koe e hoa! Nau mai, haere mai!* [Hello friend! Welcome, welcome!] (Ward, personal communication, 27 May 2002).

Apart from Tuarau, and Katarina Ruru who worked for a couple of years in the library (AR 1968), there was a Māori representative on the Board. The men who filled this position were influential figures in Wellington's civil service: Tipi Rōpiha, Michael Rotohiko Jones and W.T. Ngata. These men were part of a generation of Māori civil servants who sought equality of resources within a succession of unsympathetic National governments

Figure 3.7   Charlie Tuarau with an example of his carving, 1960s
(Alexander Turnbull Library 021687).

that dominated the postwar political landscape. There is also evidence of other high-level interaction with prominent Māori in Wellington. In March 1965, a 'Maori evening' took place as part of the museum's centennial celebrations, when local families descended from nineteenth-century leader Te Puni came to see the display devoted to their ancestor in the Māori Hall. On this occasion the Anglican deacon Kingi Ihaka referred to 'the place of the museum as a preserver of traditions' (AR 1965). In a time of change and uncertainty, Māori appealed to things which were regarded as '*taonga tuku iho*', 'treasures' handed down from the past. Indeed many Māori had a reverence for the past not dissimilar to a new national colonial history, increasingly popular among European New Zealanders, which celebrated cultural heritage through early settlers' museums, founders' societies, and the preservation of historic buildings (McLean 2000).

Māori involvement in museums, at the provincial rather than the metropolitan level, was also common in this period. Such indigenous engagement with this form of cultural nationalism, as with Māori involvement in government sponsored events in earlier decades, suggests that Māori sought inclusion – even if, at many levels, they were effectively excluded. There was more going on here than simply revaluing cultural continuities in times of change, as a growing enthusiasm for their own heritage reflects the ongoing Māori project to negotiate modernity on their own terms. If Pakeha had their history, historic places, and cultural treasures, then Māori should too. When the new Māori wing of the Whanganui Regional Museum was opened in 1968 with impressive participation from *iwi*, *kaumātua* Rangi Metekingi of Pūtiki said that the local people 'look upon it as a treasure house' (cited in Butts 2003: 151).

DECOLONIZATION AND NATIONALISM, 1960s TO 70s

When the UK entered the European Economic Community in 1973, New Zealand was left out in the cold, no longer able to sell its butter and lamb to a guaranteed market. After regarding itself as 'Britain's other farm' for almost a century (Belich 2001: 392), the end of recolonial dependence on the mother country came as a rude shock to the orphaned child. The process of disconnection from Britain and opening up to the world, which Belich (2001: 425, 463–5) calls 'decolonization', began in the 1960s and continues into the present. As external relations focused on America rather than Britain and exporters sought new markets across the globe, New Zealand society underwent a major crisis of identity. The romanticized race relations of recolonization were replaced by conflict and difference, as the purportedly homogenous society broke up into diverse sectors and left its imprint on the culture of display.

European New Zealanders became interested in their own local history, art and culture. In 1945 the poet Allen Curnow wrote that 'New Zealand, strictly speaking, does not exist yet' (Curnow in Curnow and Marsh 1945: 2). By the early 1970s, however, cultural nationalists in several fields had roughed out an image of New Zealand that was weaned off its British models. 'New Zealand' was socially constructed through a discourse of cultural languages – literature, painting, architecture, decorative arts, music and popular culture. This discursive break can be seen in a new attitude to Māori culture which was expressed by Pakeha commentators (Schwimmer 1968; O'Reilly 1968). Writer Bill Pearson, citing the artistic achievements of poet Hone Tūwhare and artist Katarina Mataira, rejected integration in favour of allowing 'Maoris to be themselves' (1962). The new mood was reflected in the thinking of Pakeha working in museums. 'Museums had an important national role in encouraging Maori self-respect by exhibiting the culture and treasures of the Maori ancestors', said Roger Duff, 'and in encouraging pakeha respect for the Maori' (*Christchurch Press,* 26 July 1968). Decolonization accelerated both the cultural nationalism which sought a new independent identity for Pakeha, and a Māori nationalism which sought greater political autonomy.

Within Māori society itself, a discourse of nationalist independence was the painful product of social and economic change. Because of wartime and new urban opportunities, the 1940s and 1950s had in fact been a time of prosperity, despite political stagnation. Rapid urbanization and industrialization meant that cultural and political questions were not a priority. The economic recession of the early 1970s had a severe affect on Māori communities and raised political awareness in general (Belich 2001: 477–9). In organizations such as the New Zealand Māori Council, for example, the reins passed to a younger generation. This new cohort of educated urban leaders were acutely aware of injustice and more prepared to speak out than their elders. When social unrest grew, the mood swung towards activism, and groups like *Ngā Tamatoa* led protests that pushed Māori issues into the public domain. Demonstrations disrupted Treaty celebrations at Waitangi in the early 1970s, followed by the nationwide Land March of 1975, and the occupation of Orākei-Bastion Point in the centre of Auckland in 1977–8 (Walker 1992: 512–14). When MP Matiu Rata left the Labour Party in 1979, forming his own Māori political party (*Mana Motuhake*), he introduced the concept of Māori sovereignty to a wider New Zealand public.

A more critical Māori response to museum display also emerged from the late 1960s. If Māori were often flattered by the display of Māori culture as art, there was a cooler attitude towards its display as artefact (Mataira 1961). Unease at the public exhibition of human remains saw the *mokamōkai* from the religion case in the Māori Hall moved to a more discreet location in a dark corner of the vestibule. In the late 1970s they were taken off display altogether, after a complaint from writer Jacqui Baxter (O'Rourke, personal communication 11 October 2001). She probably spoke for many Māori people at this time when she told her friend, the novelist Janet Frame, that the Dominion Museum 'makes her weep because her race is dealt with in the past tense' (Frame cited in King 2000: 351). It was not just Māori who disliked the museum display of Māori culture. Jock McEwen, a Pakeha who was for a time head of the Department of Māori Affairs, probably had the Dominion Museum in mind when he wrote that ethnologists display Māori art 'as if it had come to an abrupt end on the arrival of the European settlers' (in McLintock 1966: 408). 'After all, the signing of the Treaty did not bring an end to Maori cultural activities', he declared on another occasion, 'and what is happening among the Maori of 1972 is more important than the doings of his ancestors in 1672' (Hocken Misc Ms 0423).

There are several examples of Māori disquiet about museum display at this time (Rawiri 1969; Te Punga Somerville 2005). Artist and writer Katarina Mataira expressed her feelings about *Te Hau ki Tūranga* in an illustrated poem, '*Whare whakairo*,' published in the Māori language school journal *Te Wharekura*. Mataira speaks from the point of view of the ancestor house, which describes itself as 'lonely' and forlorn, photographed by curious Pakeha. Its people are lost or dead, and the ancestors inside will never again hear the 'talk or songs of their descendents.' Though ancient and *tapu*, its heart is sick, its spirit fled: 'I am for ever more a house with no purpose' (Mataira 1961: 4–5).

THE NATIONAL MUSEUM AND MĀORI

In 1972, the Dominion Museum finally became the 'National Museum,' twenty-five years after New Zealand gave up Dominion status, and one year after Britain entered the EEC. Pakeha now wanted to explore the question of national identity, to recast their colonial past and their relationship to the land, borrowing from Māori culture to give them a sense of belonging. But attempts to incorporate Māori culture into national life, as part of the decolonizing discourse of nationalism rather than a recolonial discourse of integration, were increasingly challenged by a Māori form of nationalism which sought independence from proprietary Pakeha claims. Compared to the postwar period, Māori audiences in the 1970s were more aware of museums and, though still few in number, began to make their presence felt. The Māori Hall at the National Museum was one of the theatres where the reinterpretation of New Zealand identity was performed. The attempt to bring the ageing permanent exhibitions up to date, particularly in the light of growing criticism of the Māori Hall, was largely unsuccessful, but there were new departures. The decade began and ended with temporary exhibitions, which refocused the museum display of Māori culture: 'Te Kooti' in 1972 and 'Maori art' in 1978.

'The life of Te Kooti Rikirangi', originally a Waikato Art Museum exhibition, was curated by Frank Davis, who was a well-known Pakeha advocate of contemporary Māori art. It was a 'new look' display with an innovative mixture of carving, historical artefacts, photographs, contemporary paintings and poetry (*Dom*, 16 May 1972). The exhibition challenged Pakeha views of Te Kooti, presenting him as a prophet and leader rather than a 'rebel' and attracted considerable Māori interest from members of the Ringatū church that he founded ('Concerning Te Kooti Rikirangi Te Turuki' 1972). The institution had not grappled with controversial contemporary issues like this before. Recently appointed history curator Michael Fitzgerald (2001) recalled that the opening was a somewhat tense occasion with the presence of a Māori audience: a busload of Ringatū followers from Te Teko led by *kaumātua* Hemi Te Pōno (Figure 3.8), who were passionately interested in the representation of their founding leader. The Chairman of the Board, Ormond Wilson, at pains to reassure his visitors, reminded them in his speech of the Museum's honourable purpose. 'On an occasion

Figure 3.8 Hēmi Te Pōno of Te Teko with Ringatū flag at Te Kooti exhibition, National Museum, 1972 (Alexander Turnbull Library PAColl-7327-2 (EP/1972/2467/5-F)).

like this,' he said, the Museum can 'fulfill its place as a truly national institution – a sacred treasure house … of the history and culture of our nation' (TPA MU 2, 72).

In the process, the Museum discovered that adopting the role of 'a truly national institution' was at times fraught with difficulty. In 1974 it became caught up in an intertribal dispute over Raharuhi Rukupō, the carver of *Te Hau ki Tūranga*. One day a large group of Ngāti Porou from Te Araroa arrived in the Māori Hall, where they were welcomed by Charlie Tuarau and other staff in front of the meeting house. The self-proclaimed 'Lazarus Society' presented a series of genealogical plaques establishing their link to the carver of the house 'Raharuhi' (Lazarus) Rukupō, which were duly displayed inside (Bosch 1974). No sooner had this claim been lodged than the museum was criticized by the Halbert family from Gisborne who swore that Ngāti Porou were mistaken as Rukupō was *their* ancestor. Assistant director John Yaldwyn stated that the museum was not a land court adjudicating claims but a 'house of learning and a house for storing knowledge' (*Dom*, 15 February 1974). Former ethnologist Terry Barrow observed that the museum was 'merely a depository for artifacts…' (*Dom*, 15 February 1974). Whereas in the 1960s the Museum had avoided involvement in festivals and other Māori cultural initiatives, now it tried to engage a Māori audience, and therefore found it more difficult in situations like this to retreat to its former position of aloof disinterest.

Whatever the rights and wrongs of this incident, the *whare* at the centre of the debate was clearly attracting more Māori attention – the wrestle over the house reflected its rising *mana* and importance among tribal groups. The Maori Council magazine *Te Maori*, which covered the *pōwhiri*, referred to *Te Hau ki Tūranga* as a 'taonga whakairo' (Bosch 1974: 34). Museum ethnologist Roger Neich remembers hearing this term for the first time in 1974 during a conference of the Maori Artists and Writers Society at Wairoa (interview 29 May 2002).[3] The society (later called Nga Puna Waihanga) was founded at Te Kaha in 1973 in a spirit of cultural renewal. The objective of the organizer, poet Hone Tūwhare, was 'to renew ourselves, to draw sustenance from the deep roots of the *tangata whenua*, and the land' (Hocken Misc Ms 210). In a speech at this *hui*, Te Whānau-ā-Apanui *kaumātua* Eruera Stirling was reported as saying *Māoritanga* meant 'holding fast to the treasures of your ancestors' (Salmond 1980: 247).

During this decade a more widespread use of *taonga* in English is evident. Māori began to express, not simply a link to what was on display, but ownership of it. Older people still had positive feelings towards museums (Dansey 1971) but, to young people, carving and weaving were beginning to signify their own patrimony, whether or not the museum was officially the owner. Their response to *taonga* in museums was sharpened by urbanization and cultural dislocation. In 1975 anthropologist Anne Salmond observed that the *marae*, a matter-of-fact place for rural Māori, had become, for young Māori in the city, 'a sort of shrine, a holy place of *Maoritanga*' (Salmond 1975: 130). Like many indigenous heritage movements, this should not be misinterpreted as simply nostalgia for the past but a claim for the future based on a reappropriation of traditional culture (Sissons 2005: 11). For Māori, history was clearly a means of negotiating modernity.

The 'Te Kooti' exhibition and the Lazarus Society controversy shows that museum staff were aware of the heightened Māori interest in and political pressure on exhibited Māori culture. There had been no major changes to the Māori Hall after the mid 1960s. Internal files reveal considerable anxiety about the 'growing criticism' (TPA MU 16, 4/6). In the late 1970s and early 1980s, discussions were held about a complete redesign of the Dominion Museum, including the Māori Hall (AR 1981). A number of ideas from outside designers were then canvassed and these contained the seeds of a radical departure from convention. Māori architect John Scott wanted to create the atmosphere of another world and came up with the novel idea of entering the Hall from an underground tunnel (TPA MU 218, 25). Prompted by the views of Māori he consulted, who saw museums as 'dead', Wellington designer Murray Pilcher wanted to 'present objects in the context that their creators and cultures intended.' These ambitious plans were driven by John Yaldwyn, supported by key Māori figures on the Board. Graham Latimer of Ngā Puhi (Harrison 2002), a plain-spoken leader of the New Zealand Maori Council, had joined the Board in 1974. After 1978 Māui Pōmare (a descendant of the famous Dr Pōmare) asserted considerable influence as chairman (Hobbs 1999). For the time, there was a surprising amount of Māori consultation. Prominent individuals John Scott, Robert Māhuta, Kohe

Webster, Tipene O'Regan and Hirini Mead were involved at various stages of the project in an advisory capacity.

These innovative ideas for redesigning the Māori Hall did not see the light of day, but two key exhibitions in 1978 did explore some of the boundaries of display conventions. In the New Zealand Academy of Fine Arts, situated on the first floor of the museum building alongside the National Art Gallery, an exhibition called 'Maori Art' was staged with items from the Museum and Gallery collections. An initiative of artist and designer Guy Ngan, the director of the Academy, this groundbreaking exhibition displayed 'traditional' Māori objects as art in an art gallery setting alongside contemporary Māori art. There were a total of seventy pieces from the Dominion Museum, plus a selection of works by noted artist Ralph Hōtere from the National Art Gallery and other collections (AR 1979). Hōtere's *Song Cycle* banners and other abstract paintings formed a backdrop against the north wall, with carvings on plinths and smaller objects in cases down the centre and around the other walls (Figure 3.14). 'This exhibition invites you to set aside ethnographic considerations', wrote Roger Neich in the catalogue, 'and to enjoy the art for its own sake' (Neich 1978). The exhibition was the 'first of its kind – it is the first time Maori artefacts have been shown as art and also the first time ancient carvings have been linked with modern art' (*EP*, 2 January 1979).

The exhibition contained Māori art in the form of 'primitive art' (non-Western objects seen as art) alongside Māori art in the form of 'Māori modernism' (produced as art for art galleries). The white surfaces, minimal labels and complete absence of cultural information signalled that all the objects in the room were to be seen for their formal qualities rather than function or symbolic meaning. According to Neich's invaluable visitor survey, the exhibition was largely a success with the public, most of whom were receptive to the display of Māori objects as art (Neich 1980). Some visitors commented that the museum display needed to catch up with art galleries. 'It would be nice if you could bring the museum (downstairs) in line with your approach', said a non-Māori male aged twenty-eight. 'Now they are two completely different worlds.' Neich concluded that the 'New Zealand public are not yet prepared to accept and appreciate traditional Maori art simply as art…' (Neich 1980: 6–9). Māori made up quite a high proportion of the visitors attending 'Maori Art', comprising 11 per cent of the sample (Neich 1980: 7). Though the survey suggests these people came largely to see that particular exhibition rather than being regular visitors, Māori were nevertheless overrepresented at this exhibition, in contrast to the museum where, it appeared, Māori visitors were still a minority. Neich remembers that, while the National Museum had visiting Māori groups in the 1970s, regular Māori visitors were still the exception rather than the norm (2002). Tom Ward, who joined Ngāti Pōneke in the late 1950s, recalls that the club and its members had little contact with the National Museum despite its former links through Ngata in the 1930s and 1940s (personal communication, 27 May 2002). *Te Hau ki Tūranga*, described by Mataira in 1961 as 'mokemoke' (lonely), was still empty and 'cold' a decade later, peopled only by McDonald's model Māori warrior.

By the end of the 1970s Māori art, displayed in the style of temporary art gallery exhibitions, gained a foothold in the national institution. However, as refurbishment plans stalled, the permanent displays remained largely untouched and inertia continued to reign. Even when the National Museum produced a significant touring exhibition to China, the largest ever to leave the country, the effect on the museum's own permanent Māori exhibits was negligible (AR 1979). A trend away from expensive permanent galleries towards temporary exhibitions, a greater appreciation of Māori art, a stronger interest in New Zealand art and culture, and a new generation of museum staff – all played a part in these developments. As part of the proposed redesign of the Māori Hall, Bob Māhuta suggested a dialogue between the National Museum and Māori consisting of a series of *hui* culminating in a national gathering on the Museum's marae ('Development possibilities' 12 June 1980, TPA MU 16). The National Museum was not ready for such radical steps and its failure to respond to such challenges left them in a vulnerable position. Soon, Māori intervened, and took matters into their own hands.

'A NEW NET GOES FISHING': CONTEMPORARY MĀORI ART

Exhibiting modern painting and sculpture in art museums set 'art apart' from the broader field of visual culture (Pointon 1994). The display of Whiting's *Te wehenga o Rangi raua ko Papa* in a mainstream art gallery (Figure 3.1) shows that by the end of the period covered in this chapter, contemporary Māori art had become accepted as fine art. However, Māori art demanded to be seen not only as art, but as Māori. A few days after Cliff Whiting's art work was displayed in the National Art Gallery in February 1978, Māori critic Georgina Kirby argued that contemporary Māori art should not be displayed in the Pakeha art world but reintegrated with Māori traditions in a Māori-run cultural centre (Kirby 1978). If European fine art was enshrined in an autonomous realm set apart from the social, then Māori art had an arguably more integral relationship with its social setting, and a correspondingly ambiguous position within the history of exhibitions surveyed in this section.

From the 1940s to the 1960s, the National Art Gallery was distinguished from the Dominion Museum by its singular devotion to the display of art as an autonomous category. Rooms contained a single line of works hung at eye level on a neutral wall unencumbered by extraneous objects or labels (Figure 3.9). The 'wide open spaces' of the reconditioned galleries received a favourable response from critics and the public when they reopened in 1949 (*Listener*, 20 February 1949: 6–7). Rooms were arranged, as before, to show sculpture in the entrance gallery, a large range of British academic painting, and some New Zealand prints and paintings. The conservative content of the National Art Gallery reflected the recolonial society's focus on British culture. This attracted criticism from younger artists and critics for being 'unrepresentative' of New Zealand art (Garland 1951; Brasch 1954). The galleries with their ornately framed oils began to look old fashioned in relation to the new dealer galleries catering for the growing market in modern art (Brown and Keith 1988: 179). Ken Gorbey, formerly director of the Waikato Art Museum, remembered his

Figure 3.9   National Art Gallery, December 1950 (Alexander Turnbull
Library 34506 ½).

'depressing visit' in 1960. 'The works that hung in long standardised lines and clusters', he
wrote later, 'had a stillness to them that only comes with eons of undisturbed rest' (Gorbey
1984: 8). Understaffed and underfunded, the national institution could not keep up with
new trends embraced at the Auckland City Art Gallery, which, under Eric Westbrook and
Peter Tomory, had begun to modernize its exhibition spaces from the early 1950s (Brown
2000). The National Gallery lacked appeal to a broad audience because it catered mainly
for the Academy of Fine Arts, to the extent that people could not tell them apart. There
were complaints that the National Art Gallery was 'overruled' by the Academy (Simpson
1964: 38). Exhibitions at the Academy naturally reflected the tastes and values of the ageing
membership of wealthy patrons at the expense of the general public. For the Academy too
the 1950s were 'years of stagnation' (Eden and Kay 1983: 152). Cedric Savage described
prevailing tastes as 'the rule of the dilettante' (Savage cited in Brown 1981: 21).

Māori subjects were popular among New Zealand artists in the late 1940s and early 1950s,
although Gordon Brown has pointed out that this 'encounter' was 'minor and on the whole
superficial' (Brown 1981: 73). Aside from pictures *of* Māori, objects made *by* Māori were
rarely displayed as art. In 1950 a picture titled *Old Woman with Taiaha* (c.1939) by Linley
Richardson hung in a gallery of New Zealand painting, very similar to the works by the artist
included in the inaugural exhibition in 1936 (Figure 3.9). Richardson's portraits were now,
however, criticized as 'anthropological data', which did not belong in an art gallery (Garland

1951: 135). By the 1960s, temporary installations punctuated the semi-permanent hangs of the British and foreign collection at the National Art Gallery. Work by Inuit, Chinese and Aboriginal artists was displayed (AR 1960–70) but according to observers at the time neither Māori art, nor it seems many Māori visitors made much of an appearance on the first floor of the institution, despite their increasing visibility on the ground floor (Neich 2002). Māori people were only regarded as 'a fascinating subject for portraiture' as shown by one exhibition (*Maori Portraits* 1961). There may have been criticism that the National Art Gallery did not represent New Zealand art, but few at the time even considered its lack of Māori representation. In 1966 the Director Stewart Maclennan could still conclude that Māori art had no place within New Zealand art because integration had made Māori culture 'one with that of his European neighbours', whereas the arts of the past 'lingered on in practice only as traditional crafts' (Maclennan in McLintock 1966: 87). Māori arts and crafts, taken seriously by at least some Pakeha in the art world of the 1920s, were now regarded as tourist souvenirs and firmly divorced from modern art practice. Maclennan concluded that 'no Maori artist of stature has yet arrived' (Maclennan in McLintock 1966: 87).

Ironically several young Māori artists had already arrived on the scene. As Chapter 2 showed, European fine art in art galleries had been isolated from Māori arts and crafts in museums – an 'institutional separation of Maori and Pakeha art' (Renwick 1987: 18). This situation prevailed for much of the postwar period but in the 1960s gaps suddenly opened up. The decade saw pioneering breakthroughs: the first novel, play and book of poetry in English by Māori writers as well as forays into popular music, television, architecture and other fields (Beatson and Beatson 1994: 60–3). Dynamic new art forms, pioneered by a generation of Māori artists living in the cities, represented an enthusiastic embrace of modernity and modern art and a break with what was now referred to as 'museum art' (*Te Ao Hou* March 1964, 46: 25–7). Damian Skinner (2005) has shown how these artists abandoned traditional forms and subjects to enagage with the mainstream art world, creating 'another modernism' that experimented with Western styles and media. The appearance of 'brown art in white spaces' (Mané-Wheoki 1996) should be understood as a Māori entry into the most prestigious strata of Pakeha cultural capital. More broadly, contemporary art was the arena for a spirited Māori engagement with modern urban life which demanded not just a spot in the art gallery but a place for Māori within decolonized New Zealand society.

At first the new category of modern Māori art was more likely to be displayed at a *marae* or community hall, where works of art were often juxtaposed with arts and crafts of a more customary type, and the continuity of medium and the relevance of message was apparent to a Māori audience. This usually occurred at the Māori arts festivals that were held during the 1960s in Hamilton, Wellington and other centres. In 1963, for example, the first festival of Māori Arts was held at Tūrangawaewae *marae* in Ngāruawāhia near Hamilton, to mark the centennial of the King movement. Wood sculptures by Para Matchitt and Arnold Wilson, and paintings by Selwyn Muru, were placed against the 'striking background' of the *wharenui Mahinārangi,* with its heterogenous display of 'momentoes', as well as portraits by Goldie and Lindauer and decorated gourds by Theo Schoon (*Te Ao Hou* March 1964, 46: 28–9). A wide range of objects were haphazardly arranged on tables and standing panels like a school fair. According to a report in *Te Ao Hou,* the festival 'presented to an appreciative audience an impressive selection of Maori talent, providing a vantage point from which to view the achievements both of the past and the present' (*Te Ao Hou,* March 1964, 46: 28–9). In the extraordinary photographs of Ans Westra showing young Māori coming face to face with modern Māori art, we see how object and subject constitute one another through the culture of display (Figure 3.10).

Figure 3.10 Works by Para Matchitt at the Māori Festival of the Arts, Tūrangawaewae marae, Ngāruawahia, December 1963 (with the permission of Ans Westra/Alexander Turnbull Library Westra proofsheets M643).

The first large exhibition, staged in a Hamilton church hall for the Festival of Māori Arts in August 1966, displayed a range of contemporary work without the 'traditional' crafts that often accompanied them (Figure 3.11). These works were included alongside carving in an exhibition curated by Buck Nin at the Canterbury Museum later that year (*Te Ao Hou* May 1967, 58: 38–9). In 1967 this show travelled to another Māori arts festival in Wellington, and eventually toured Australia, Samoa, Singapore, Malaysia, Hong Kong and Japan ('New Zealand Maori culture and the contemporary scene,' TPA MU 2, 72/1).

The headline 'Row provoked by Maori art display' appeared on the front page of Wellington's *Dominion* in 1969 (*Dom*, 30 August 1969). It was a glaring sign of the gap between the National Art Gallery and the new visual culture of young urban Māori. Selwyn Muru coordinated 'The work of Maori artists' as part of the New Zealand Maori Council's

Figure 3.11   Artists Cliff Whiting (left) and Para Matchitt (right) at the exhibition of contemporary Māori art, St Paul's Methodist Centre, Hamilton, 1966 (Archives New Zealand AAQT 6539, A81942).

'Rangatahi weekend' which planned to 'highlight the contribution that our younger people are making to New Zealand as a whole' (*Te Ao Hou* 1970, 68: 38–9). The catalogue declared that Māori people were going through 'their own industrial revolution' (ATL Larry Pruden papers Ms 6664-15). A reviewer commented that the work indicated 'adjustment to a new age of science and culture' (*Dom*, 2 September 1969). The *pepeha* prominently positioned on the frontispiece – '*Ka pū te ruha, ka hao te rangatahi*' [The old net is cast aside, the new net goes fishing] – was a widely known statement of generational change (Mead and Grove 2001: 181). The cover featured a bold design by Muru in the style of synthetic Cubist works by Picasso and Braque (Figure 3.12). The words 'Maori' and 'art' emerge from a collage of

Figure 3.12   Cover of catalogue for 'The Work of Maori Artists', National Art Gallery, 1969 (with the permission of Selwyn Muru/Alexander Turnbull Library Pruden papers Ms 6664-15-01).

broken facets, suggesting the construction of a modern Māori identity through the medium of art.

Hopes were high for this first exhibition of contemporary Māori art at a public art gallery. Most of the artists in the Wellington exhibition (Matchitt, Wilson, Nin, Whiting, Adsett, Graham and Walters) had been exhibiting in dealer galleries for several years, and Nin's work had been shown in the Academy of Fine Arts. Hōtere was already represented in the National Art Gallery collection, as was Muru, whose *Kohatu* (1965) was on display in 1969 among a group of modern New Zealand and Australian paintings (*A Guidebook to the National Art Gallery* 1969: 12). This work (Figure 3.13), purchased in 1965, was the first by a Māori artist acquired by the National Art Gallery. Titled 'Rock' in Māori, the painting references the stylized figures of Māori rock art found in caves in the South Island.

The Maori Council exhibition, unfortunately, was far from a success. The steps that were taken by the Gallery management to vet the works, control the display and police the opening was an embarrassing illustration of the gap between Pakeha high culture and Māori people in the late 1960s ('Maori exhibition,' TPA MU 5, 10/69). After being approached by John Booth, the Pakeha director of the New Zealand Māori Council's Wellington office, the

Figure 3.13   Selwyn Muru *Kohatu* (1965) oil on hardboard (with the permission of Selwyn Muru/Museum of New Zealand Te Papa Tongarewa B.41030).

gallery responded diffidently. The new director was Melvin Day, a painter who had studied art history at the Courtauld Institute. He stipulated there should be a preview of works ten days before 'as the standard of work exhibited in the gallery must be vouched for' ('Report on developments and progress of Maori exhibition', 1969, TPA MU 5, 10/69). Muru was bitterly disappointed when Day selected the works without him, and 'damn well gave us a little space in the corners of the corridors...' (Muru personal communication, 16 February 2006). Of the seventy works originally submitted, only twenty were shown in one bay (gallery 6/L) at the National Art Gallery, while the remainder had to be accommodated at short notice at the Display Centre in Cuba Street (TPA MU 5, 10/69).

The Māori Council exhibition's opening was a rather tame social gathering with sherry, speeches and a poetry reading (Invitation 20 September 1969, TPA MU 5). The gallery staff badly mishandled the situation, giving the impression they were gatekeepers and that Māori people were not welcome. When they learned about the function, gallery staff panicked. 'Apparently it was thought a lot of Maoris would attend the function, misbehave and get drunk', a woman from the Māori Council office told reporters later (*Dom*, 30 August 1969). An anxious Day rang Booth asking: 'What will you do if there is any trouble?' (TPA MU 5, 10/69). An emergency meeting of the building and finance committee was held and a 'rude and abrupt' letter was sent to the Māori Council dictating the rules to be observed. The artists present, far from being accepted by the art establishment, received the distinct impression that Māori art and Māori people were not welcome. 'I can remember a letter too, a most offensive letter', John Bevan Ford said later, 'about how we ought to conduct ourselves in this gallery' (cited in *Taikaka* 1991). According to Cliff Whiting (2000), the argument was about 'whether Māori should be displaying art in a place like this ... they suggested that if they displayed our art, Maori art, up there, then you would have all these people eating kai, having parties ... *in the galleries!*'

This incident, with the accusation of prejudice and the public censure from the editor of the *Dominion*, the Māori Council, and Māori MPs, raised serious questions about democratic access at public art galleries (Editorial, *Dom*, 2 September 1969). Whether it was the result of institutional racism or simply a series of innocent blunders is perhaps less important than the consequences. The gallery itself came under increasing pressure to include Māori art and artists in the national collection, to represent not just New Zealand artists but Māori artists. Eventually the National Art Gallery changed its style of installation design, moving away from the Academy and closer to progressive institutions which promoted contemporary art. The galleries took on the same austere look: skylights were covered up, overhead track lighting installed, battens removed and the walls painted a neutral white. Rather than collection hangs in which pictures were left permanently on view, by the 1970s most public art galleries had a roster of exhibitions with regular changeovers which were organized internally or from travelling exhibitions (McCredie 1999). This change in display was matched by new art practices and a shift in focus to modern New Zealand art, through acquisitions and exhibitions which sometimes included work by Māori artists like

Ralph Hōtere, who worked in a Western medium (Day 1972). Visiting exhibitions from Australia, Asia and North America exposed the gallery audience to modern indigenous art, and articles by liberal Pakeha critics and writers stimulated a climate of support for modern Māori art (Davis 1976; Wilson 1976; Orbell 1978).

Meanwhile, many Māori artists continued their efforts to gain access to the mainstream art institutions. Some like Matchitt and Whiting preferred community marae projects to art galleries. Whiting explained the link between his artistic practice and the setting of the *marae* in terms of social relationships: 'There on the marae the significance of Maori art is made apparent. There a whole network is sewn together by social relationships, and art can make the ties manifest' (McLaughlin 1975: 25). Other Māori artists wanted to show their work in art galleries and have it recognized as art in its own right. Ralph Hōtere, for example, simply wanted to be seen as an artist not a Māori artist (Hōtere in Davis 1976: 9). For others, however, art had a political agenda. Just as Māori people at the time were trying to win some autonomy within the wider society, Māori artists wanted room within the white cube which framed the display of modern art. 'Everything we were doing', Arnold Wilson said later, 'was based around the hope of having a space of our own, a Maori space' (Wilson cited in Pound 1994: 115). At the Dowse Art Museum in Lower Hutt in 1979, when Selwyn Muru displayed a series of highly political paintings about the prophet Te Whiti, the exhibition space was transformed into a *marae* for the opening with guests sleeping on the floor (Thomson 1981: 40, 41). Muru declared that: 'Our galleries must reek with human odour. They have become too sterile, with the paintings like icons, and not to be touched' (Skinner 2005: 204).

In the late 1970s it was the regional institutions in Rotorua, Hamilton and Gisborne, rather than the large metropolitan ones, which mounted significant exhibitions of contemporary Māori art. *Contemporary Maori Art* at the Waikato Art Museum in Hamilton in 1976 was initiated by Buck Nin and other local artists. Nin's acrylic paintings mixed *kōwhaiwhai* pattern with elements of modern art (Figure 3.14), typical of the kind of work included in this show. Commentators at the time saw these exhibitions not only as artistic milestones, but as expressions of what Māori writer Witi Ihimaera called a 'brown revolution' (Ihimaera in *Contemporary Maori Art* 1977: 4). Frank Davis hailed a 'vigorous reassertion of Maori identity', which showed that Māori people were 'distinctly and proudly different from other New Zealanders' (*Contemporary Maori Art* 1976: 7). Critic Peter Cape (1979: 89) sounded a note of caution, suggesting that the art establishment was still resisting the inclusion of Māori art which was 'more likely to be seen on the marae than in the local gallery.' Within the discourse of Pakeha cultural nationalism Māori artists gradually carved out a separate space within which 'contemporary Maori art' would mark itself off as a distinct field within New Zealand art. Like indigenous groups in other postsettler countries, these courageous artists defied their 'otherness' and entered the forbidden space of modernity, not just to make a historical claim on it, but to challenge the discourses which defined and protected its boundaries (Araeen in King 1998: 16).

Figure 3.14   Buck Nin *Ko Wai te Waka e Kau Mai Nei?* [*What is this Canoe that Swims My Way?*] (1976) acrylic on board (with the permission of Carol Nin/Museum of New Zealand Te Papa Tongarewa MA 1.006127).

Against this background of change, a large touring exhibition of contemporary Māori art was being developed at the National Art Gallery in 1977 in partnership with the Maori Artists and Writers Society and the Queen Elizabeth II Arts Council of New Zealand. This project was promoted by younger staff such as Exhibitions Officer Nicholas Spill and Ian Hunter as acting director (in the absence of Melvin Day). The ambitious exhibition comprised forty to fifty works by twelve to eighteen artists which would travel around the country during 1978 ('Exhibition proposals 1977', TPA MU 6, 121B/6). Tentatively titled 'Te Ao Marama', it was to have an opening that included Māori ceremonial followed by a *pōwhiri* at Takapuwāhia *marae* in Porirua. As the title suggested, contemporary Māori art was seen to be emerging from the darkness of obscurity into a 'world of light'.

In planning 'Te Ao Marama', the National Art Gallery made concessions to its conventional fine arts aesthetic. The process of working with Māori artists and Georgina Kirby, secretary of the Maori Artists and Writers Society, encouraged staff to step outside the parameters that usually determined the display of art. The initial proposal stated categorically that the exhibition was to include painting, sculpture and works on paper but not 'Maori crafts' ('The proposal', early 1977, TPA MU 6, 121B/6). But a later version says that because arts and crafts are 'not differentiated in Maori culture' the exhibition would include 'more traditional Maori crafts'. 'It is hoped such an amalgamation of different media will form a visually coherent whole', Nicholas Spill reassured the Gallery Council, 'and will help to break down barriers between pakeha compartmentalised concepts separating art from craft' (Memorandum 22 August 1977, TPA MU 6, 121B/6). Pakeha staff struggled to reconcile a liberal desire to be inclusive with their own values and tastes. This tension could not be resolved and after some debate the exhibition was abandoned in November 1977, only two months out from the opening, due to concerns over the quality of work submitted. Instead, a truncated exhibition of work by three artists – Ralph Hōtere, Matt Pine, and Cliff Whiting – was hastily assembled for two weeks in March 1978. There were *karakia,* but no *pōwhiri* or other *tikanga* to interrupt what was otherwise a conventional gallery opening attended by an audience made up of the art lovers from the Friends of the Gallery.

Although the exhibition was generally well received, critics did not quite know what to make of Whiting's work and its combination of Māori and European elements (Figure 3.1). To critic Neil Rowe this 'group marae project' may be art, but not very good art (*EP,* 18 March 1978). Hōtere's restrained abstract work, which incorporated the poetry of Bill Manhire, had been produced for an avant garde multimedia performance (Figure 3.15). In contrast to Hōtere's 'powerful and original' works, already in the national collection, Whiting's 'mural' was not acquired by the National Art Gallery (*EP,* 18 March 1978). Although it showed such work in a temporary exhibition, the gallery restricted its purchases to the kind of formalist painting and sculpture that was more easily absorbed into a modern art context. Those, like Hōtere or Pine, working in a style or medium most easily assimilated into the mainstream art market, were regarded as contemporary New Zealand artists, whereas others like Whiting were identified by their political content or craft style as 'Maori artists'. While some Māori had success as artists rather than as Māori, others were not prepared to set their art apart. Contemporary Māori art had been accepted as art in the art museum, but only by divesting itself of links to traditional art and, by implication, leaving its own audience at the door.[4]

In a number of 'Māori exhibitions' in this period people wrestled with problems of the classification of objects, collections and exhibitions – what is Māori art, where do we put it, and how do we exhibit it? Yet something was missing from these experimental exhibitions despite attempts to bring museum display up to date. That crucial absence was audience. In the 1980s cultural institutions became the focus of an indigenous nationalist discourse as their once quiet halls were filled with people. With the dramatic arrival of a Māori audience came the demand that art was not set apart from the people, but reunited with them.

Figure 3.15   Ralph Hōtere *Song Cycle II* (1975) oil on unstretched canvas (with the permission of Ralph Hōtere/ Museum of New Zealand Te Papa Tongarewa B.8861).

NOTES

1. In the US, anthropology had long moved away from museums, whose displays were no longer considered up to date (Conn 1998: 26) but in postwar New Zealand museums retained a closer association with anthropology (Henare 2003).
2. This is a line from the popular song 'My old man's an All Black' (1963). The word 'hori', now considered offensive, was New Zealand English slang for a stereotypical Māori male (Orsman 1997: 359).
3. Dr Roger Neich was one of a new generation of ethnologists whose work was influenced by new developments in academic anthropology, in particular the work of Nelson Graburn (1976) on tourist arts. He was closely involved in the Pacific Arts Association, an organization which was exploring new approaches to the study of indigenous cultures.
4. In contrast to the Māori audience who attended the Māori art exhibition at the Academy, this exhibition reportedly attracted few Māori visitors (Neich 2002).

4 'EMBLEMS OF IDENTITY', 1980–90

> Objects, like words and bodies, are not 'themselves,' but symbols of themselves, and
> through them we are continuously at the game of resymbolising ourselves.
>
> (Pearce 1997)

In the 'Te Maori' exhibition at the National Museum in August 1986 (Figure 4.1), worn
wooden remnants of an eighteenth-century *pātaka* are suspended against a white wall and
displayed with the spot lighting and minimal labelling formerly reserved for works of art.
The object, far from being seen as a functional structure, is made visible in terms of formal
qualities of shape and surface decoration. The same institution that formerly regarded its
Māori collections as artefacts or, at most, as primitive art, now displayed them as 'Art', on
a par with fine art.

The venue is crowded with Māori people. An indigenous category of display – *taonga*
– is at work. Gathered around the *pātaka* listening to speaker Māui Pōmare, these people
are part of a Māori ceremony which acknowledges their own cultural values. They look at
the same carving, not just as art, but as *taonga tuku iho*, a treasure 'handed down' from the
ancestors. Because museum display was now powerfully linked with the Māori past, carvings
became symbols of the Māori present. Museum exhibitions, once a representation of the
colonization of the indigenous people, now evinced decolonization. Through this process,
two distinct categories in the culture of display – art and *taonga*– became intertwined in the
late twentieth century. As several critics at the time recognized, 'Te Maori' was an event that
shook up the conventions of display and ushered in a period of change. Ian Wedde, the art
critic for Wellington's *Evening Post*, wrote:

> The day Te Maori ... opened at the National Museum, all the pictures in our place were
> shaken askew on their walls by a small earthquake ... What is being shaken by Te hokinga
> mai are the cultural assumptions on which the collection economies of museums and
> galleries rest. These curatorial framing devices ... which we are used to seeing present art,
> are being made to look crooked... (*EP*, 27 August 1986)

This chapter examines the culture of display in the 1980s before, during and after the
groundbreaking 'Te Maori' exhibition. It emphasizes the reconstruction of *taonga* as a Māori
way of displaying and interpreting Māori objects in a museum setting and the consolidation
of 'contemporary Māori art' in art galleries. These modes of display circulated, clashed
and coalesced throughout the 1980s, but generally moved up the cultural hierarchy as

Figure 4.1   Māui Pōmare at the opening ceremony of 'Te Maori: Te hokinga mai', National Museum, Wellington, August 1986 (Museum of New Zealand Te Papa Tongarewa F.465/7).

government policy on 'race relations' shifted from integration to biculturalism. When the poetics and the politics of exhibiting converged, Māori objects became what Bill Renwick called 'emblems of identity' (Renwick 1987).

DECOLONIZATION'S CULTURE: THE TREATY, BICULTURALISM AND MĀORI EXHIBITIONS

'Te Maori' marked a turning point in New Zealand history (Brooking 1999: 196–7). In the 1980s, years of great social and cultural change, the exhibition represented a highpoint of Māori assertiveness on the national stage. The decade began as the previous one had ended, with vigorous protest. Opposition to the South African rugby tour of New Zealand by the Springboks in 1981 turned the spotlight on racism in New Zealand. There were annual protests at Waitangi, as the Treaty became a focus for Māori grievances and Pakeha attempts to settle them. From 1975 to 1984, however, the National government resisted giving much power to the Waitangi Tribunal, which had been set up to hear land claims under the previous Labour government (Belich 2001: 474). The situation for most Māori in the early 1980s was starkly different from that of the postwar generation who at least had found work in the cities – many Māori were unemployed and social statistics in poverty, health, education and incarceration were chilling. Māori were now 80 per cent urban, and 50 per cent were aged under 25 (Sciascia in Mead 1984a: 158).

The pace of change accelerated when the fourth Labour government headed by Prime Minister David Lange swept Robert Muldoon out of power in 1984. Finance Minister Roger Douglas' reforms were launched at the same time as a series of popular nationalist platforms (for example, an independent foreign policy, and nuclear free legislation). Although Māori suffered economically from free market reforms, they made considerable political advances in this period and sparked yet another cultural revival through strategic collaboration with Pakehadom. As Belich argues, Māori history converged with mainstream New Zealand history, and resurgent Māori and their issues moved in from the wings to centre stage:

> On the one hand, a partial Maori 'decolonisation' took place, with a huge increase in Maori activism, radicalism, and political and cultural-self assertion. Pakeha were somewhat readier to listen to it, partly because they themselves were decolonising and liberalising to some extent, and partly because a large and urbanised Maori population was less easily ignored than a small and rural one. (2001: 475)

This time, however, the courts were the most effective means of redress due to the increasing legal status of the Treaty of Waitangi. When in 1985 the government gave the Waitangi Tribunal the power to examine claims back to the colonial period, it took a major step in addressing longstanding disputes (Walker 1992: 514–19). The Taranaki tribes, Tainui in the Waikato, and Kai Tahu in the South Island lost no time in filing major land claims and expectations were raised that *iwi* would regain an economic base for separate development. Optimism was heightened when Ngāti Whātua settled their long standing claim over Ōrākei-Bastion Point in 1987 (Belich 2001: 478-80). The Tribunal report on Muriwhenua established the principles of 'partnership' between Māori and the Crown which underlay the Treaty, one of the ideological planks for the policy of biculturalism which had supplanted integration in government parlance (Poata-Smith 1996: 108).

'TE MAORI', 1981–6

'Te Maori' was an international exhibition made up of collections from New Zealand museums. It opened at the Metropolitan Museum in New York in 1984 and toured several US cities from 1984 to 1986 before returning to New Zealand and opening in the four main centres over 1986/7. Its historical significance lies in the ways in which the project overlapped with indigenous discourses. In the early 1980s, at the same time that 'Te Maori' was being developed, a new generation of Māori leaders set out to use Māori customary culture for social and political ends. Kara Puketapu of Te Āti Awa, Secretary of the Department of Māori Affairs, had just embarked on a series of programmes designed to enhance Māori self-reliance and independence. Puketapu was looking for a way to imbue the younger generation of urban Māori with a sense of identity based on traditional values. 'Te Maori' was the answer. 'We hope this exhibition will stimulate young Maoris', said Puketapu, 'and raise their awareness of their rich culture and heritage' (cited in Barber 1984: 13). Hirini Mead of Ngāti Awa, Professor of Māori Studies at Victoria University of Wellington, was another of these leaders. At first Mead framed the museum display of Māori culture as an anthropological problem, in which meeting houses were analogues to Western models of cultural maintenance (Mead 1983). Now more politicized, he believed the answer to contemporary problems was to reinforce Māori identity by returning to a strong cultural base. At a conference in New York just before 'Te Maori' opened, Mead described the objects in the exhibition as 'symbols of identity' (Mead 1990).

When the exhibition that became 'Te Maori' was first mooted in the early 1970s it was little different from a number of projects that highlighted the artistic qualities of Pacific art. In contrast to those early proposals, when it was revived in the early 1980s unprecedented levels of Māori participation were called for. Puketapu recalled:

> One of the things that had to be made clear from the beginning … was that there was not going to be *any* Maori art exhibition unless Maori people are involved and agree. Now that is pretty critical. No government is going to allow any artefacts to go overseas if there is any sort of political row going on in the country and I'm pretty sure that would have occurred if Maori people weren't consulted. (Puketapu in Murphy 1983)

This process of consultation with *iwi* was a crucial initiative, which required gaining approval from tribes before items in museum collections from their region could travel to the US. Though suggested by Pakeha, it was picked up with enthusiasm by a Māori sub-committee backed by the Department of Māori Affairs. The negotiations had the effect of raising Māori consciousness about their cultural heritage and ensuring their enthusiastic involvement in the ceremonies accompanying the exhibition. According to one *kaumātua*, it was a 'wonderful opportunity' for a small people 'to be seen by the whole world' (Sciascia in Murphy 1983). Māori were fully aware of the political impact of an international exhibition on the domestic scene. The Kai Tahu discussions hinged on the 'opportunity to increase the mana of the Maori heritage in the eyes of the wider community…' As its report recognized, 'the surest way to raise Pakeha awareness of the value of anything is for distinguished overseas institutions to pay laudatory attention to it' (O'Regan report, 5 January 1981, TPA MU 28, 1/1).

Correspondence between Māori Affairs and *iwi* show that most individuals and groups referred to the contested objects as *taonga*. It is at this point that the word, until now used within Māori communities in *te reo* Māori, seeped into English usage among exhibition developers and the museum professionals they came into contact with. At meetings the term *taonga*, new to many Pakeha, was frequently heard and recorded in documents. The link between *taonga* and expressions of ownership in the political climate of the time was a key element in the diffusion and popularizing of the word in Māori circles. For Pakeha it was a useful Māori term for a museum object that acknowledged Māori spiritual values. Linguist Harry Orsman noted its usage in English in the 1980s as a 'treasured artefact' (1997: 813), a phenomenon directly related to 'Te Maori'.

By the middle of 1981, an interdepartmental organizing committee was set up that included the Arts Council, Foreign Affairs, Māori Affairs, Internal Affairs, Tourist and Publicity, and Trade and Industry. These government officials were joined by representatives from major museums who liased with curator Douglas Newton at the Metropolitan Museum and the American Federation of Arts. Though the group was large and unwieldy, the balance of power lay with a core group of educated articulate Māori working in universities, government departments and arts organizations. Puketapu was chair, Piri Sciascia was executive officer, and others like Dr Tāmati Reedy and Hamu Mitchell were closely involved (*Te Maori: A Report* 1988). Puketapu later said this was a key step 'because it recognised that Maori people must take the major role in planning' (*Dom*, 14 November 1983).

The presence of these assertive Māori, together with the many *kaumātua* and *kuia* who became swept along with the exciting project, ensured that Pakeha museum directors and curators were exposed to Māori values and responses to their visual culture. Despite the scepticism of professionals used to dealing with exhibits simply as objects, museum practices were challenged and stretched by Māori demands. Committee minutes show how Māori adopted different approaches to museological issues. An example was the use of the word *taonga* in place of artefacts and their novel classification in terms of their tribal groupings ('Minutes of meeting, Nov. 10, 1981', Dr Yaldwyn's files TPA MU 28, 1/1). Māori insisted that the exhibition be accompanied by 'the complete package' comprising elders, opening ceremonies, oratory, prayers and so forth. This was not simply to acknowledge the *tapu* of the objects as *taonga* but also because they wanted to present their art as part of their culture, not leaving the visual arts 'to stand alone' but integrating them with the performing arts and oral arts (Sciascia in Murphy 1983). Before the exhibition even left the country, elder Sonny Waru of Parihaka told a reporter that the Māori people who were to accompany it were 'part and parcel of the exhibition, caretakers of their sacred heirlooms' which were 'the living embodiments of our ancestors' (cited in *Dom*, 14 November 1983).

Mead, nominated by Newton as co-curator, was primarily responsible for articulating the notion of *taonga* as a Māori category of display within a discourse of political independence. These Māori views of their visual culture were disseminated widely to the New Zealand public through the best-selling exhibition catalogue. Mead (1984a: 32–3) wrote that 'the rise of mana Maori' was the theme of the exhibition, adding that Māori were no longer content to be 'silent partners' but wanted to 'speak for themselves.' He argued that the group of bilingual scholars who worked on the book, unlike their predecessors, took note of 'Maori understandings of their art'. According to Mead (1984a: 21), *taonga tuku iho* was a 'highly prized object that has been handed down from the ancestors'. While this definition appears to refer mainly to family heirlooms and old tribal treasures with genealogical connections, Mead (1984a: 22) does acknowledge the modern popular understanding of a *taonga* as 'a highly prized possession to which is attached *korero* (text or story).' This *kōrero* clothes and embellishes the *taonga*, so that when it is viewed the layers of *kōrero* are dispersed among the people present through discussion, the performance of *waiata* and so on. Mead's (1984a: 21) articulation of *taonga* overlapped with more conventional concepts of fine art without being equivalent to them. Rather than the disinterested aesthetic appreciation of European tradition, which values a distant viewer who prizes the formal qualities of an isolated object, Māori people respond in a direct, often physical, way to *taonga*.

Time magazine described the opening of 'Te Maori' in September 1984 (Figure 4.2) as the 'most unusual opening in the 114-year history of the Metropolitan Museum of Art' (Blake 1984). The extensive media coverage suggested the single most newsworthy feature of the event was the large Māori delegation with their solemn ceremonies (*New York Times*, 24 September 1984). Mead later described the 'breakthrough' as the moment when their *taonga* became art:

> By the time … we had finished our karakia, the frenzied clicking of the cameras of the international press present at the ceremony assured us all that this was a historical

Figure 4.2　Opening ceremony 'Te Maori', Metropolitan Museum, New York, September 1984 (Mobil).

moment, a break through of some significance, a grand entrance into the world of art. We had suddenly become visible. (Mead 1984b: 24–5)

For many Māori present, seeing their *taonga* in the Metropolitan for the first time was a deeply moving, spiritual experience. East Coast *kaumātua* Monita Delamere told his *whānau* on his return to New Zealand that 'he felt that all his tūpuna were alive there' (Con Te Rata Jones, personal communication, 19 August 2002). As Kirshenblatt-Gimblett has observed of exhibitions at the National Museum of the American Indian, for indigenous viewers objects are proxies for persons and so the liveness of the thing becomes an index for the connection between the living and the dead (1998: 159). The opening ceremonies at the four US venues, which involved almost 100 *kaumātua* and another 100 performers and artists, provided context for what was otherwise a conventional art museum design. Some Māori felt that categories of art and *taonga* operated simultaneously. Mina McKenzie, the director of the Manawatu Museum and a member of the 'Te Maori' management committee, was present at the opening. 'While the Americans and Douglas (Newton) were looking at Te Maori for the excellence of its sculptural form', she reflected later, 'Maori people were being re-united with their ancestors. Energy was flowing between the two concepts' (McKenzie in Butler 1996: 77).

The museum's intention was clearly to display these objects primarily as art – with some attention to their cultural context – in other words, a judicious combination of the art/artefact categories that had dominated American museum display for several decades (Kahn 1995: 325–6; Welsch in Herle, Stanley, Stevenson and Welsch 2002: 5). Although Newton was aware of different Māori responses, he thought about the objects in terms of primitive fine art (Newton in Murphy 1983). Many objects were displayed as primitive sculpture, placed against clear glass vitrines or white walls in such a way as to emphasize their formal qualities (Figure 4.2). Reviews and comments revealed a range of responses. Mead praised the 'uncluttered' installation, saying that each item was treated as 'an artwork in its own right rather than being part of a larger context' (Mead 1985a: 2–3). He felt that the art style presentation was a little closer to the Māori concept of *taonga*, in that individual objects were singled out and highlighted rather than being grouped together with other examples of that type (Mead 2006). Some New Zealand viewers thought the installation was cold and lacked life. Māui Pōmare criticized the unrepresentative selection and lack of Māori presence (Report, 7 June 1985, TPA MU 255). But some Americans thought that the show was actually part of a trend towards *more* context in art exhibitions, pointing out that this installation was evocative of locale with the simulation of a 'cliffside village' within a palisaded fence (Preston 1985).

The exhibition attracted a great deal of interest among scholars because of contemporary academic debates about the politics of representing other cultures. At the same time that 'Te Maori' was at the Metropolitan on Fifth Avenue, it was business as usual on the other side of Central Park in the Margaret Mead Hall of Pacific Peoples at the American Museum of Natural History, while downtown at the Museum of Modern Art the controversial

'Primitivism' exhibition was making waves (McEvilley 1992). In a series of experimental exhibitions at the Center for African Art in New York, curator Susan Vogel responded to the 'Primitivism' controversy by reviewing a century of different approaches to the display of African objects, showing how the presentation became simpler and more aestheticized as they became accepted as 'art' (Muller, Roberts and Vogel 1994). Whether they displayed things as beautiful art or as interesting artefacts, anthropologist James Clifford (1985: 171–2) accused both art museums and anthropology museums of ignoring the contemporary lives of tribal cultures 'in the name either of constituting authentic, "traditional" worlds or of appreciating their products in the timeless category of "art".' Critics were divided too about the recategorization of carving as art in the 'Te Maori' exhibition. While many New Zealanders, Māori and Pakeha, basked in art world acclaim, others were critical. Canadian museum anthropologist Michael Ames called the exhibition 'romantic primitivism' because the 'continuing existence of Maori people' was ignored (Ames in *Taonga Maori Conference* 1990: 34). However, Clifford thought Māori allowed their *taonga* to be appropriated as art in order to enhance their national claims: 'Everybody [was] using everybody', said Clifford, 'and the objects move into new places and old contexts' (Clifford in Foster 1987: 150). Most *kaumātua* in New York interviewed by Tipene O'Regan said that the important thing about 'Te Maori' was the effect of international attention on Pakeha (O'Regan 1984: 15). If art, with a nod to artefact, was the mode of visual display at the world's greatest art museum, and if that raised their *mana* as a people back home, then that was good enough for them.

The experience in the US had a profound affect on the subsequent response of Māori to museum display in New Zealand. From September 1984 to June 1986 'Te Maori' was seen in museums in New York, St Louis, San Francisco and Chicago. Māori perceptions of the display turned on the contrast between the lavish attention shown their *taonga* in the US and what they saw as their neglected state in New Zealand museums. 'We see them (*taonga*) displayed here in a way that they've never been displayed before,' said James Henare, of Ngā Puhi ('Kaleidoscope reviewed' 1984). For Tūhoe's John Rangihau the Metropolitan's display gave the *taonga mana*. 'You see them displayed with the attention they need, and they are asking for', he said. For him the change was not from a museum to a gallery, nor from artefact to art, but from neglect to respect:

> They represent living things for us as Maori, they have to be seen and not left in a corner, or down in the basements of the museums of New Zealand... Here they are being displayed in a most artistic way, in a way that says something about the culture of the people who made them. It says: 'We are here, we stand tall.' ('Kaleidoscope reviewed: Te Maori', 1984)

The experience of visiting 'Te Maori' was particularly moving for young people, and became intimately bound up with a heightened sense of Māori identity. 'It drew me closer to my Maori side', said eighteen year-old university student Atawhai Tibble of Ngāti Porou who attended the opening at the Field Museum in Chicago. 'When I saw the way the

Americans had arranged it', he said, 'it was almost as though the *taonga* (treasures) were talking to me, breathing, reaching out to me' (*Sunday Star Times*, 17 August 1986). In numerous reports like this of visitors encountering their exhibited culture, the individual is said to be called by ancestral voices, like the visitors who are welcomed onto the *marae* by the *karanga*. The carvings, weaving, weapons and other things, seen in Western terms as inanimate objects, become in Maori eyes active living agents – *taonga tuku iho* – which make connections to tribal identity and *whakapapa* (McCarthy 2006). When Māori people say that pieces of wood are alive and they communicate with them, 'living' indexes the relation of the objects to living persons so that to show the *taonga* under the right conditions is to make those to whom they matter visible too.

New Zealand museums were initially reluctant to get involved in 'Te Maori'. As the momentum of the planning process accelerated over the years 1981 to 1983, major museums were inexorably dragged into the project despite fears over the governance of collections and inexperience in working with Māori communities. The National Museum itself had for several years been trying to update its displays in the face of public criticism and was slowly working its way towards incorporating Māori views. Much of this work was the initiative of Dr J.C. Yaldwyn, who became the new director in February 1980 after several years as a very active deputy to Dick Dell. A scientist who had a genuine interest in Māori and Pacific Island culture, Yaldwyn took an active part in the public face of the institution (Hobbs 1990). When plans for redevelopment were delayed, Māori resentment was expressed in the following outburst by Graham Latimer recorded in the minutes of the Museum Council:

> The Maori people had waited a long time for the adequate housing of their heritage and now it appeared that the National Museum could not provide this. He would have to go back and tell his people about this and possibly the collection should now be housed in other museums in other parts of New Zealand, perhaps in Parihaka, Rotorua or Waitangi. (29 September 1983, TPA MU 247)

Things were changing, although perhaps not fast enough for Māori. In the 1983 Annual Report, the word *taonga* (in italics) appeared for the first time, in connection with 'Te Maori' (AR 1983: 17). Acquisitions were listed with their Māori names italicized: *mere, poupou, pātaka, patu onewa, tewhatewha* etc (AR 1983: 21). After several years of delay, during which attempts were made to find a carver to replace Tuarau, Bill Cooper was finally appointed 'Advisory Officer (Maoritanga)' in May 1984 (AR 1985). The presence of Cooper, followed in the next few years by more Māori staff, reinforced the reforms and made cultural norms and values concrete. 'Clearly the National Museum is going through a period of great change, uncertainty and frustration', wrote the director, 'but could move into a period of great opportunity if strong action is taken now' (AR 1984: 25).

A revealing example of the Museum's attempt to move with the times was its bid to enliven the presentation of *Te Hau ki Tūranga*, the interior of which had remained unchanged since the 1940s, apart from the addition of carpet and spotlights (Figure 4.3). The idea was to give

Figure 4.3   Interior of *Te Hau ki Tūranga* c.1936
(Alexander Turnbull Library Hall-Raine PAColl-0346-02).

the house a sense of atmosphere through an audio narrated by well-known broadcaster Bill Kerekere of Ngāti Porou. The script, initially a rather academic monologue, went through several drafts as phrases such as 'ritual magic', considered inappropriate, were edited out by John Yaldwyn. After the audio had been recorded, Yaldwyn admitted in a letter to Kerekere that by doing an English only version 'we have inadvertently committed the common error of ignoring the true Maori side of things' (Yaldwyn in O'Rourke 1994). The director then asked him to write and record their first Māori language commentary for the house. 'I would most sincerely like to have something that was truly and deeply Maori in its own right, spoken with feeling from the heart,' wrote Yaldwyn, 'possibly saying things that might be difficult to translate or at least were obviously Maori thoughts and not translated European thoughts' (Yaldwyn in O'Rourke 1994).

The temporary exhibitions at the National Museum in the early 1980s were the most influenced by debate surrounding 'Te Maori' and least hampered by internal constraints. They continued the display experiments of the late 1970s. Roger Neich contributed to this increased activity with a rejuvenated display team under Gavin Kee. In December 1983, the thirty-eight pieces from the museum collection destined for 'Te Maori' in America were displayed for a month in the Academy of Fine Arts on the first floor. In 'Maori art for America' the newly cleaned objects made quite an impression 'spread around an otherwise empty gallery against a uniform background' (EP, 13 January 1984). Another innovative show was held in the reopened temporary exhibitions gallery two months later. This exhibition was originally titled 'New national treasures' but the name was changed to 'Nga taonga hou o Aotearoa' before it opened in March 1984 (TPA MU 504, 3/2–3). This was the first instance of the word *taonga* appearing in an exhibition title and suggests that the staff were now quite familiar with the word. The name was not the only change. A draft of the press release described it as a selection of artefacts with the words 'and art' written in by hand (TPA MU 504, 3/2–3). In an article in the magazine *Pacific Way*, Neich (1984) referred to 'ancient Maori *taonga* (treasures of the ancestors)'. It employed a spare, aesthetic design, avoiding too much information or signage by providing only short object labels. It was good to see individual pieces 'displayed for their quality as works of art', Neich said, but added that there was a need for balance as 'people liked to know the background and importance of Maori art works' (EP, 30 March 1984). Māori art was therefore already established as a category of museum display in the early 1980s. But the missing element, in contrast to 'Te Maori', was a substantial Māori audience.

Though there were precedents for its display of *taonga* and art, as an international exhibition 'Te Maori' had a profound impact on New Zealand museums. 'The Te Maori Exhibition has changed forever the perceived reason for New Zealand museums to hold, study, and display Maori objects', declared the National Museum Annual Report in 1985. 'No longer can the uninformed public hold the stereotypic idea that Maori culture is 'collected' by natural history museums', it continued, 'as part of an academic and majority culture fascination with things primitive, quaint, tribal, exotic' (AR 1985). The moves toward bicultural reform in museum practices which had been slowly building up since the early 1980s were accelerated with debate surrounding 'Te Maori' disseminated through the national museums organization AGMANZ (Art Gallery and Museums Association of New Zealand). The pages of the *AGMANZ Journal* were full of debate about how New Zealand institutions should display *taonga*. Rodney Wilson, director of the Auckland City Art Gallery, argued that these 'transcendental' objects were art and should be rehoused in art galleries (1984: 18). The Manawatū Museum director, Richard Cassells, disagreed, pointing out that 'a display technique based on the philosophy that "the art speaks for itself" simply does not work for a different culture'. To deal adequately with *taonga*, he said, the curator must become an anthropologist and the gallery become a museum (Cassells 1985: 25–7). Meanwhile, the region's museums were simply getting on with forging new relationships with local communities. In describing plans for redeveloping the Ngāti Kahungunu exhibit at the Hawkes Bay Art Gallery and Museum, curator David Butts looked beyond Western categories to address the issue of *mana Māori*. 'A successful exhibition should communicate something more than an analytical series of cases exposing aspects of a lifestyle', he wrote. 'Somehow the mana of the people must come through' (Butts 1984: 23–4).

While Pakeha quibbled about categories of display, Māori concentrated on the exhibition's political significance for their people generally and Māori collections in museums specifically. Hirini Mead believed the experience was a 'turning point' for the relationship of Māori to museums. He acknowledged that 'leisurely' change had started to occur before 'Te Maori' but claimed that Māori people did not make a practice of visiting their local museums which were run by Pakeha ethnologists (Mead 1985b: 4). His newly politicized perspective is obvious in the following demand for self determination:

> The Maori people want to control their own heritage; they want to be the people who handle their *taonga*; they want to have the knowledge to explain them to other cultures; they want to explain them to their own people; they want to define their past and present existence, they want to control their own knowledge (*matauranga Maori*) and they want to present themselves their way to the world and to themselves. (Mead 1985a: 4)

The National Museum started to feel the heat almost as soon as the Māori delegation returned from New York. Māori politicians visited and demanded answers to questions about the state of the collections and displays. There was also internal pressure. By the end of 1985, the Museum Council, chaired by Māui Pōmare, included forthright Māori like Tipene O'Regan and Graham Latimer, who were supported by Pakeha liberals like museologist Keith Thomson and art critic Hamish Keith. John Yaldwyn continued his campaign to modernize the institution, appointing more Māori staff and revising the old cases in the Māori Hall. He told the Museum Council that he found the old labels 'condescending and offensive' and took steps to have them updated, reworded and reset in a uniform style as part of Kee's ongoing display overhaul (TPA MU 255–8). Temporary exhibitions continued the trend towards aestheticized display. 'The Art of War', staged in

Figure 4.4   'The Art of War', Academy of Fine Arts, January 1986
(Museum of New Zealand Te Papa Tongarewa F.414/9).

the Academy of Fine Arts in December 1985 (Figure 4.4), contained weapons in a starkly minimal setting. In February 1986, 'Whakaahua tinana: The human form in Maori art', was installed in the refurbished special exhibitions gallery in the north wing of the National Museum. Displayed as 'Maori art in an art gallery setting' the small selection of carvings, jewellery and weapons demonstrated how the Māori artist explored the 'formal possibilities' of the figure (TPA MU 504, 2/8). A novel step was the inclusion of bilingual labels and bicultural protocol, provided by staff and students from the Māori Department at the Polytechnic next door.

With the exhibition 'Tarawera' the museum stepped outside its comfort zone and into the community. This series of photographs, marking the centenary of the eruption of Mt

Tarawera, travelled around *marae* in the Rotorua area in June and July 1986 attracting a great deal of Māori interest. Curated by Peter Waaka, it was a simple display consisting of historic images on movable panels ('Tarawera: A Memorial Exhibition' 1986). At the Wahiao *marae* at Whakarewarewa (Figure 4.5), the exhibition was inside the meeting house – according to local informant Pita Tapsell the first time this had ever been done (*Dom*, August 1986: 9). In contrast to the National Museum's Māori art exhibitions for their traditional Pakeha audiences, this was an interesting example of the Māori agency of display. *Whāriki* were laid on the floor, plants were added, and the photographs supplemented with cloaks, carvings and heirlooms from local families in display cases. The constant presence of people kept the *taonga* 'warm', a custom that reflected the Māori concept of *taonga* as living things (Mead 1986a: 15). Here on the *marae* the display became integrated into the everyday life of the community – it even had to share the *wharenui* with a *tangihanga* (funeral). Waaka later complained that the museum's design elements, the white panels, advertising and abundant signage, did not fit with the décor of the *wharenui*. Māori ideas of display were clearly

Figure 4.5 'Tarawera' exhibition at Wahiao marae, Whakarewarewa, 1986 (Museum of New Zealand Te Papa Tongarewa B.016813).

governed less by aesthetics than by *mana*. For example portraits were hung according to the rank of the individuals represented. 'While the importance of customs such as these may go unrecognized in some of our institutions', Waaka later pointed out, 'we cannot afford to ignore them when displaying local material in our meeting houses' (Waaka report 1986 TPA MU 5, 16). On the eve of 'Te Maori's' return to New Zealand the aestheticized display of Māori culture as art, whether in a museum or gallery setting, still occurred in isolation from significant Māori visitation. That, however, was about to change.

'TE MAORI: TE HOKINGA MAI', 1986–7

For the National Museum, hosting 'Te Maori: Te hokinga mai [The return]' was a major challenge. Staff decided not to install it in the Māori Hall because the lofty space would 'overwhelm' the exhibition, opting instead for the bird and mammal gallery, a 'cleaner and more intimate display space' (TPA MU 255). Carpeted floors, closed in windows, the lowered ceiling with modern light tracks, and false walls provided an environment similar to the American art museums. Ross Ritchie, an artist and exhibition designer at the Auckland City Art Gallery, was responsible for overall display throughout the New Zealand tour with some input from staff at each venue. He opted for an art gallery style of display: 'too much information could draw attention away from the actual pieces', which 'spoke for themselves' (*EP*, 14 August 1986).

The spot lighting, bare white walls and minimal labelling made the space look more like the National Art Gallery upstairs than the other museum galleries (Figure 4.6). *Poutokomanawa* and *pou* were placed against walls to emphasize their form. *Toki*, previously grouped by type, were placed by themselves in cases. The gateway mask (Mead 1984: 2) was placed flat on the wall, its lighting throwing mysterious shadows onto the eye sockets and mouth. *Uenuku*, the famous Tainui *atua* from the Te Awamutu Museum, was treated like a monumental sculpture and positioned free-standing in the middle of the room (Figure 4.7). *Pūkaki*, which was mounted on a wall suggesting the height of a gateway, and the *waka tūpāpaku*, which were put in a dark corner suggestive of a cave tomb, were the only concessions to context. The *maihi* from the Te Kaha storehouse, *Te Potaka*, were placed on a large rectangular wall, with the other side of the same wall containing the bargeboards from Rotoiti, in a way that did not at all suggest their architectural setting (Figure 4.1). This design met negative internal reaction. John Yaldwyn told the Museum council he was dissatisfied with the two-dimensional treatment of large objects like the *maihi* which were handled like works in an art gallery. In a letter to the 'Te Maori' management committee, Yaldwyn passed on critical comments including the mounting of weapons and other objects upside down or out of context. He recommended, unsuccessfully, that an ethnologist should be present when the exhibition was set up at each venue (TPA MU 260).

'Te Maori: Te hokinga mai' opened with a dawn ceremony on 16 August 1986. The visitor response to the exhibition exceeded all expectations: 12,000 the first week, and a record 185,000 by the time it closed only two months later (AR 1987). Extraordinary scenes

Figure 4.6 'Te Maori', National Museum, August 1986 (Museum of New Zealand Te Papa Tongarewa F.469/7).

transformed the Māori Hall into a national *marae*. Elders occupied the *paepae* in front of the old meeting house, where visitors were greeted in twice-daily *pōwhiri*. Tribes competed fiercely with one another at dramatic handover ceremonies each week. The museum rang to the sound of speeches, song and *haka*. In the exhibition space there was rapt attention, communal discussion and performance, laughter and tears (Figure 4.7). The young Māori guides led visitors through the crowded throng to look at the *taonga*, which were addressed, stroked, and festooned with *kawakawa* leaves as a sign of their living presence. The impact on the institution was equally unprecedented. The Museum had adopted a 'truly bicultural approach to display' and must never be allowed to 'return to its monocultural ways again' (AR 1987).

Figure 4.7 Tainui visitors with *Uenuku*, 'Te Maori'
exhibition, National Museum, Wellington, 1986
(with the permission of Tainui/Brian Brake estate/Mobil).

There was a mixed public reaction to the exhibition's design at its four New Zealand venues in Wellington, Dunedin, Christchurch and Auckland. Māori critics generally thought 'Te Maori' at home was not on a par with the US. Tipene O'Regan on the other hand preferred the display in Wellington. He thought the weaving exhibition and 'Maori art today', the contemporary art show at the Craft Council, added a living dimension that was missing in America where Māori were seen as people 'looking to the past' (O'Regan 1986).

Jonathan Smart observed that 'Te Maori' was almost out of place in the Robert McDougall Art Gallery in Christchurch: 'Friendly and passionate, hot and noisy, it is the opposite of the McDougall's normally hallowed calm' (Smart 1986). For Priscilla Pitts the installation looked 'marvellous' at the Auckland City Art Gallery. 'It's a work of art in itself', she said, 'classical, simple, the works isolated in clear white spaces' (*Herald*, 27 June 1987). Amidst the praise, there were unfavourable notes (Lynch 2000: 35–8). Bernie Kernot criticized the narrow selection of objects: the cutoff date of 1860, the absence of women's art, and the scarcity of transitional objects showing Pakeha influence. Though there were advantages in regarding objects as art rather than artefact, Kernot reminded people that none of these things had been made just to look at like Western artworks, a point overlooked by those praising the discovery of carving-as-art (Kernot 1987: 5).

When the exhibition arrived in Auckland, the Auckland City Art Gallery controversially won the right to host 'Te Maori' ahead of the claims of the Auckland Museum. This tussle reflected Māori preferences for the art gallery because of its higher status. Mead (1985a) had argued that art gallery settings 'freed' Māori art from the natural history context of museums. American art museums had 'elevated' Māori art, Mead maintained, transforming it from 'an ethnographic art' known only by an elite few to 'an internationally recognised world-class art' (*Listener*, 25 October 1986: 8). This aestheticized appreciation of *taonga* as art was captured in the photographs of Brian Brake that featured in books, calendars and posters (Figure 4.8). As Western critics have observed, bestowing on tribal objects the status of art makes them fetishes of quite another kind (Conn 1998: 257). But this view overlooks the agency at work in this recategorization. Displaying objects with the aestheticized aura of art works served to heighten their reception as *taonga* by Māori visitors. This revivified notion of *taonga* was not the intention of the exhibition design, but a result of the way Māori visitors interacted with the objects shown in a new light. In the 'Te Maori' exhibition, *taonga* were performed not installed. Objects on display activated social relations with the people who viewed them. As indices of the relations between ancestors and living descendants, *taonga* worked against art because the web of social interactions and customary practices nullified a design intended to isolate objects for disinterested aesthetic interest. Many Māori visitors did not seem to care about the style of presentation, as it was the performances of *waiata* and *karakia*, the contact with *kaiārahi* (guides) and *kaumātua*, which made objects *taonga* and not the particular way they were presented. Some of the *kaumātua* who went to 'Te Maori', like Waho Tibble from Ngāti Porou, did not even go into the exhibition – for them the gathering of the tribes on the *marae* was the real attraction (personal communication, 19 August 2002).

As observers at the time noted, the overwhelming presence of Māori people – the elders conducting rituals, the tribal groups being welcomed, the *kaiārahi* meeting and talking to visitors – took the museological commentary away from the institution and returned it to *iwi*. The presence of *kaiārahi* in the exhibition space and their popular guided tours were a key initiative in the New Zealand experience. Although sometimes criticized by

Figure 4.8 *Hei tiki*, 'Te Maori' exhibition, 1986–7
(with the permission of the Brian Brake estate/Museum of
New Zealand Te Papa Tongarewa B.069050).

museum staff about the content of their narratives, this popular newly traditional knowledge functioned to contest the institution's academic interpretation of Māori culture. Young people told a variety of colourful stories in response to visitors' questions about mythological meanings: the three-fingered hands on carved figures, the red, black and white colours on cloaks, and the seemingly magical powers of ancient *taonga* (O'Regan in Lowenthal and Gathercole 1994: 104). Mead later pointed out in defence of the programme that for Māori people language was a means of recapturing an alienated culture from the hands of what he called the 'professional few' (*Listener*, 25 October 1986). For example, *kaiārahi* were able to categorize *taonga* using Mead's chronological model based on plant growth (e.g. *te puāwaitanga* [the flowering]) rather than art historical models for date, provenance and so on. The word *taonga* itself was a 'tool of explanation' that allowed Māori to repossess their art. 'Maori art', said Mead, 'has become a means of enculturation' (Mead in *Taonga Maori Conference* 1991: 168).

Ironically, the temple of Western modern art was the setting for the remaking of indigenous traditions. For the Māori who flocked to the exhibition, public museums and galleries became 'shrines' (Kernot 1987: 6). The fusion of art with *taonga* combined elements of both categories but left others in tension. From the customary concept of *taonga* came the ceremonies and links to people, but the religious overtones, popular taste and modernist art practice of contemporary Māori society were edited out. Similarly the aesthetic style and high culture status of art was employed, without the disinterested appreciation that usually accompanied it. There is a danger that, if their fictiveness is not recognized, unifying anticolonial narratives can lead to a form of ethnic 'fundamentalism'. The modern Māori vision of 'traditional' culture, while performed in a context of decolonisation, was arguably an 'oppressive authenticity' that confirmed old stereotypes of Māori as spiritual and natural, making modern urban indigeneity somewhat anomalous (Thomas 1999: 188–92; Sissons 2005: 39).

MĀORI PATRONAGE

'*He aha te mea nui i te ao? Māku e kī atu: he tangata, he tangata, he tangata*' [What is the most important thing in the world? It is people, people, people.] There is an echo of this well-known proverb in Mead's comment about the 'Te Maori' exhibition. 'If there are messages in TE MAORI', he wrote, 'one of them would surely be that art is for people, is about people and is people' (Mead 1986a: 74).

Māori embraced this exhibition despite a history of low visitation at the National Museum. Rather than refer to Māori people like other museum 'audiences' in the museological terminology adopted in the 1980s, they are, instead, 'patrons'. This word better conveys the distinctive relations between this particular ethnic group and their exhibited culture because it allows for the active role of indigenous subjectivities in their encounter with the objects on display. Māori patrons have an extra-ordinary connection with the museum, not simply as visitors who happen to look at exhibitions (although the term encompasses this) but as communities who have a distinctive social and political investment in them, as stakeholders. If display constitutes subjects, then exhibiting Māori in the 1980s created indigenous patrons who were to have a decisive influence on the future direction of the National Museum.

International research suggests that museum going is socially stratified (Bourdieu and Darbel 1991; Merriman 1991; Bennett, Emmison and Frow 1999). The existing visitor statistics in New Zealand suggest that museum audiences are dominated by wealthy, tertiary-educated Pakeha (Thomson 1981; Harker 1986; Cockburn 1989, 1990).[1] Greg McManus (1988) argued that Māori were underrepresented among visitors to New Zealand museums even though their culture was prominently displayed there. Suddenly, with the 'Te Maori' exhibition, this changed. Hirini Mead claimed that of the first 100,000 visitors to 'Te Maori' at the National Museum, 'over half were Maori.' Mead implied that museums before had been elite Pakeha enclaves but now 'there is no doubt about the predominance of brown faces in the crowds' (*Listener*, 25 October 1986).

Despite the paucity of hard evidence to confirm reports of high Māori attendance, the political traction generated by this sudden upsurge in Māori patronage is beyond question. In a series of speeches and articles, Hirini Mead spearheaded a campaign for '*mana motuhake*' (self-determination) in the realm of museum display. 'There is a felt need among the people', Mead (1985c) declared, 'to be reunited with their heritage and to regain control of it.' This was reflected in 1985 in a far-reaching proposal *Nga taonga o te motu: Treasures of the nation*. Promoted by several museum professionals backed by Māori MP Pita Tapsell, who was an active Minister of Internal Affairs, it advocated a new national museum incorporating a Polynesian cultural centre titled 'Te marae taonga o Aotearoa' (*Nga taonga* 1985). The very use of the word *taonga* indicated that a 'new' understanding of Māori cultural treasures was a prominent part of the concept. The Māori department, titled 'Te whare taonga tangata whenua' was to be separate from the art and natural environment sections. This bold repackaging of the constituent parts of the existing collections, with its clear demarcation of Māori responsibility for Māori culture, was revolutionary.

The Māori submissions to the report, from *iwi* as well as community organizations, were enthusiastic about a Māori-focused cultural facility and insisted on strong Māori representation. One referred to *taonga* in their 'dungeons' (TPA MU 496 box 2/2). The major submission was a report from a large *hui* held at the National Museum during the 'Te Maori' exhibition, which supported the proposal but reflected the widespread interest in Māori-run cultural centres as an alternative to Pakeha-run museums (21 October 1986, TPA MU 487/1 box 2). The 'Te Maori' exhibition report went further in recommending that 'every effort be made to put Māori people in charge of their art heritage in New Zealand museums, art galleries and cultural institutions' (*Te Maori: He tukunga korero* 1988: 12).

In the context of the late 1980s, it was expected that the appearance of Māori visitors in the museum would be accompanied by claims for a greater say in those museums. The engine of political progress was not protest, as in the 1970s, but the courts, which upheld the legal status of the Treaty of Waitangi through a series of landmark decisions (Belich 2001: 479–80). Citing the principles of the Treaty, Māori organizations in a number of sectors sought greater self-determination. Progress with Treaty claims prompted Māori commentators to link the Treaty and its implications of partnership to the governance of museums. In a paper on the new museum concept, lawyer Moana Jackson interpreted article two of the Treaty, which guaranteed Māori 'complete Maori authority over all their taonga', in terms of Māori exhibits in museums. The Treaty placed an 'obligation on museum authorities and Māori to be equally involved in the planning, design, staffing, and management of the institution' (Jackson 1988: 2).

By 1990, with the government-sponsored sesquicentennial celebrating 150 years since the signing of the Treaty, public attention to biculturalism reached its height. In November of that year, the 'Taonga Maori' conference at the National Museum witnessed continued calls for Māori control of their heritage. In the following decade, as we shall see in the next chapter, museums in New Zealand continued to receive close attention from an 'articulate Maori lobby', which was 'making new demands on collections, care and interpretation' (Legget 1995). Seen in the international context, this degree of indigenous influence was extraordinary. The museum, once the colonial artefact par excellence, had in turn become the object of 'postcolonial revenge' (Ghandi cited in Chakrabarty 2000: 16).

'TAONGA MAORI' AND 'TREASURES', 1987–90

From the close of the New Zealand tour of 'Te Maori' in 1987 until the opening of 'Taonga Maori' in late 1990, there were rapid internal changes at what was now referred to as the 'National Museum of New Zealand': an increase in Māori staff, the adoption of customary practices and the official policy of biculturalism. Bill Cooper was the first Māori staff member in 1984, followed by curators Gerard O'Regan in 1985, Arapata Hakiwai in 1987, and Awhina Tamarapa in 1989. By 1990, when a number of students were hired as guides, the Museum employed by far the largest proportion of Māori staff in any New Zealand museum. In 1988 a new mission statement declared that the museum was a 'guardian of Maori *taonga* or traditional treasures' and in 1989 it recognized the Treaty and Māori 'rangatiratanga' (chieftainship/sovereignty) over 'taonga tuku iho' (AR 1988, 1989). In addition to a Māori title, 'Te Whare Taonga o Aotearoa' the Museum created Māori names for its galleries, and in the Māori Hall the country's first bilingual labels appeared in a long-term exhibition (TPA MU 269). Some time during 1989, a sign was set up outside *Te Hau ki Tūranga* requesting visitors take their shoes off before entering, according to Māori custom. Perhaps most significant of all, the word *taonga* came to be used throughout the institution by staff and in 1989 it appeared for the first time in the Annual Report without italics (AR 1989).

In terms of display, change was more fitful. Notwithstanding the refurbishment of cases in the Māori Hall, the National Museum's permanent exhibits received even more adverse attention than before as a result of 'Te Maori' (TPA MU 264). In the meantime the best the Museum could do was mount temporary exhibitions. Two major exhibitions show how *taonga* became consolidated as a category of museum display, overlapping with both artefact and art and another Pakeha sibling – 'treasure.' Originally conceived as a sequel to 'Te Maori', the 'Taonga Maori' exhibition opened in October 1989 at the Australian Museum in Sydney and then toured to Brisbane and Melbourne. It was a more inclusive project than its predecessor as it contained woven textiles as well as objects in wood, stone and bone, transitional work from the late nineteenth century and 'contemporary *taonga*' in 'traditionally derived styles' (Davidson 1989: 15). Exhibition developers chose not to include a wide range of contemporary Māori art in 'Taonga Maori' despite debating the issue at some length. Tipene O'Regan argued unsuccessfully for the inclusion of contemporary Māori work, which he referred to as 'the *taonga* of the future' (Council minutes, 28 July 1988, TPA MU 270). Another point of difference was that, unlike 'Te Maori', a number of Māori people had direct input into 'Taonga Maori' working alongside museum professionals. These included Board members O'Regan and Pōmare, as well as museum staff Bill Cooper and later Arapata Hakiwai and Walter Waipara. The ethnologists assigned to the exhibition, Betty McFadgen and archaeologist Janet Davidson (who replaced Roger Neich) went to great lengths to involve young Māori trainees in their work (Davidson 2000).

The 'Taonga Maori' installation was more artefact than art in style of presentation. Comprising well over 200 items, the exhibition was large and comprehensive, including full sized structures such as the façades of the Tainui meeting house *Tokopikowhakahau*, and the Te Arawa storehouse *Pukehina* (*Te Awhi*). The Australian designer, Bodo Matzick, moved away from the 'art gallery effect' of 'Te Maori' where things were 'looked at' for their visual qualities. He set out to contextualize objects within a narrative which not only talked about Māori origins and history but reminded visitors that 'Maori culture was alive today' (cited in 'Taonga Maori' *Muse* 1989: 4, 9). Visitors entered the exhibition through Neke Kapua's *waharoa* as if they were arriving at a marae. Next, a *pare* and *tauihu*, positioned as props to illustrate the story of the Māori creation and migration to Aotearoa, were intended to situate visitors within a Māori world view. Throughout the exhibition labels and graphics placed objects within the context of Māori culture. The colour scheme, made up of various shades of green, created a forest-like setting for the objects and reinforced the image of a people closely connected with the natural world.

Hakiwai, Cooper, and other Māori staff were largely happy with the design, which, aiming to 'explain' Māori culture to Australians, also provided the sort of didactic information Māori living in Australia were seeking. Janet Davidson felt that the exhibition text and the catalogue was a successful balance of academic and Māori perspectives (2000). There was some criticism in Australia of what was seen as the idealized presentation of traditional Māori culture (Thomas 1999: 187–95). Ironically, this misinterpreted Māori intentions to show a culture that was not 'fixed in time' but 'that is dynamic and fluid' (Hakiwai in *Taonga Maori Conference* 1990). The *kaupapa* (issue) for Māori developers was the social and educational role the exhibition would play, particularly for young Māori in Australia. Maamari Stephens's recollections of being a *kaiārahi* at the Queensland Museum suggest that to be involved with 'Taonga Maori' represented a 'political statement' for Māori in Australia. Among Australian-born Māori, she was aware of a certain 'ambivalence' about cultural identity, a 'dislocation' that sprang from growing up away from cultural roots in Aotearoa. 'Somehow we'd gone back to this exhibition', she said, 'to try and find a sense of belonging' (Stephens 2002). Judging by the comments of Māori visitors to the exhibition in Sydney and Brisbane, these people saw 'Taonga Maori' in terms of their current cultural identity (TPA MU 63, 1/1-3).

Meanwhile back in Wellington, another major show marked the sesquicentennial year of 1990. 'Treasures and Landmarks' was the first joint exhibition hosted by the National Art Gallery and Museum. The driving force behind the revamp of the Māori Hall which accompanied 'Treasures' was new Assistant Director James Mack, who was well known for his design flair and penchant for craft art and social issues. Mack saw the meeting house as 'a treasure/*taonga*' and its presentation as 'a proclamation of its special qualities and an invitation for museum goers to encounter it' (*EP*, 24 February 1990). An English word often used in translation for *taonga*, 'treasure', operated as a loose Pakeha equivalent to it, although it was also associated with high culture values of rarity and traditional heritage.

When the 'Treasures' exhibition opened at the National Museum in February 1990 (Figure 4.9), it contained the same objects that had been in the Māori Hall for half a century. But the presentation of the *whare*, *waka* and *pātaka*, was very different. *Te Hau ki Tūranga* remained in its customary central position, but it was framed by spiky *harakeke* plants. A huge greenstone boulder, representing *mauri* or spiritual essence, sat in the centre of the floor. Approaching the hall through the doors, the visitor saw *Te Hau ki Tūranga* in front of them, its façade spotlit against the backdrop of the wall newly painted in pale green and cream with the art deco detailing picked out in ochre. The *marae* was showered with dappled light like a glade. *Te Tākinga* loomed out of the darkness, the *paua* shell eyes of the

Figure 4.9 'Treasures' exhibition, Māori Hall, National Museum, June 1990
(Museum of New Zealand Te Papa Tongarewa F.000981/05).

carved figures flickering in the dim light. Fresh green *kawakawa* leaves were placed on the cases, acknowledging the *taonga* as living symbols of ancestral *mana*.

The new design transformed the atmosphere of the Māori Hall. The layout created an impressionistic glimpse of a mysterious Māori world rather than the scientific dissection of a primitive culture. The lighting, with the dramatic contrast of light and dark, created a sense of awe compared with the clear dispassionate light in which objects were previously bathed. This heightened emotion was meant to express the spiritual power of Māori *taonga* as 'living treasures'. According to Mack, with proper cultural awareness, Māori exhibitions could display the culture 'from the inside out'. Arguing that Māori beliefs had not been handled well in museums, Mack wanted to let in the light, to allow the spirituality of objects to 'radiate' and touch the viewer (*Taonga Maori Conference* 1990: 113–14). In the absence of recorded Māori responses, it is difficult to judge whether the exhibition achieved this insider view, or whether it was seen as a Pakeha expression of those aspects of Māori culture that appealed to a national sense of identity. As the product of a Pakeha designer with some Māori input, the exhibition reflects the bicultural compromise typical of the late 1980s. At the same time, by neglecting to represent modern Māori society it was open to the accusation that it betrayed the same 'primitivist' vision of a Māori past that was displayed in the Māori Hall in the 1950s and 1960s.

The themes and tensions evident in the design reflect converging discourses in New Zealand society after the separatist agitation early in the decade. An accommodation had been reached between the resurgent Māori fringe and the liberal Pakeha centre through a policy of biculturalism centred on the Treaty (Fleras and Spoonley 1999: 121). However, the enthusiastic Pakeha adoption of a new Māori culture of display should not conceal the fact that Māori often had quite a different agenda. In contrast to Pakeha cultural nationalism, Māori nationalism centred on gaining independent control of their own resources – including their cultural heritage – for the purpose of social development. Just as Māori had wrested concessions from Pakeha discourses in the past, at the end of the twentieth century biculturalism was a convergence of their cultural needs and Māori *realpolitik*.

After 'Treasures' closed, 'Taonga Maori' opened at the National Museum in November 1990 following its Australian tour. The installation of this exhibition afforded the opportunity of giving the Māori Hall a complete facelift. The old showcases were hidden behind screens and *Te Hau ki Tūranga*, *Te Tākinga* and *Teremoe* were left in place. The items from the new exhibition were laid out around them in a way that replicated the narrative sequence of the exhibition's original concept, with three metre walls creating enclosed settings for each section and maintaining a flow through the open space. But James Mack made several changes to the exhibition, downplaying the Australian contextual approach, which in New Zealand perhaps appeared too 'ethnographic' (particularly for Māori sensibilities), instead opting for a celebration of *taonga*. Text panels were reworked, objects shifted around and a dramatic audio-visual narrated by actor Rangimoana Taylor was set up in the entrance. The exhibition presented a greater diversity of material culture, with examples of contemporary

Figure 4.10 'Taonga Maori' exhibition, Māori Hall, National Museum, November 1990 (Museum of New Zealand Te Papa Tongarewa F.000959/13).

weaving and hybrid carvings such as Tene Waitere's naturalistic panels (Figure 4.10). Mack injected a heightened sense of drama through music, lighting and layout that, curator Arapata Hakiwai argued, appealed to the emotions of Māori viewers (*Taonga Maori Conference* 1990: 118–19).

If 'Taonga Maori' in Australia was more artefact than art, in New Zealand the opposite was true. There was much more aesthetic isolation of individual objects: the *waka* cenotaph rising up behind *Teremoe*, for example, or the sequence of *taurapa* arranged against the blank wall behind. An evaluation study suggested that the show was seen by some visitors as an art gallery-style display, which they found confusing because there was a lack of context in which to understand the objects (Wizevich 1993: 48–50). Yet compared with the disembodied allure of 'Treasures', there was more sense of cultural origin in 'Taonga Maori', albeit a stripped-back version of the original didactic structure. This was the outcome of the strong Māori involvement in its development balanced with Mack's aesthetic impulses. Overall, Arapata Hakiwai felt that the display found a middle ground between art and context (*Taonga Maori Conference* 1990: 119). Pakeha reviewers noticed the tone of aestheticized reverence. *The Evening Post* reviewer said the exhibition captured the 'the spirituality of

Maori life...' (*EP*, 31 October 1990). Rob Taylor thought the museum was treated as 'a sanctified space full of holy relics' (*Dom*, 14 November 1990). The guided tours and events for 'Taonga Maori' proved popular but the exhibition was something of an anti-climax that could not match the numbers or excited clamour of 'Te Maori'. Rather than wanting another museum exhibition of Māori culture, many Māori people had moved on and were now more concerned with what they saw as the next step – the repatriation of *taonga* and tribal museums (Hakiwai 1990).

'GATHER ONLY THE HEARTWOOD': CONTEMPORARY MĀORI ART AT THE NATIONAL ART GALLERY

Upstairs in the National Art Gallery in 1986, the scene was very different. Critic Ian Wedde contrasted the 'flow of people about the taonga' at 'Te Maori' with an exhibition of prints displayed 'demurely within these Modernist gallery walls'. He argued that 'The crowds that attended Te Maori implicitly removed it from the museum context – in every sense that matters, they took it away with them.'

> Downstairs (if you could get in) the building was filled with people – with ceremony, emotion, song, and with what might still be called an educative process which ran completely counter to the formalities of museum display... Upstairs, though, you could have the whole place to yourself. There was no noise, no emotion, and nothing that remotely questioned the authority of the display conventions. (*EP*, 29 October 1986)

But contemporary Māori art had in fact already permeated the art world. Para Matchitt's *Huakina*, a dramatic wood and steel sculpture depicting Te Kooti's battle flag, was installed in the entrance to the National Art Gallery during 'Te Maori'. This powerful work bristled with injustice, barely contained within the frame of fine art. If the Museum was guilty of displaying *taonga* as art without the *kōrero* (talk) which clothed them, then the Gallery tried to display Māori art purely as art, stripping it of the history that gave it value and meaning (Panoho 1987–8).

In the late 1980s, after the triumph of 'Te Maori' in museums, the growth of 'Māori exhibitions' in art galleries showed that contemporary Māori art, after several false starts, had arrived. Art galleries had already incorporated a model of 'Māori art', although it was not the one that many Māori artists themselves advocated. Theirs was more closely tied to a community context, to a popular audience and to cultural identity rather than modernist aesthetics. After a decade spent evading and then flirting with Māori modernism, the form of Māori art closest to their tastes, gallery staff took the unheralded step of handing over their spaces for Māori to display their work themselves. 'Taikaka', a Treaty-based partnership with Māori artists, organizations and *iwi*, was an experiment in display that embraced a loose category of visual culture ranging from fine art to craft to *taonga* and back again.

Like the National Museum, the National Art Gallery underwent enormous change in the 1980s, although it was comparatively sheltered from the currents of Māori nationalism

enveloping the Māori exhibitions. Weaned from the Academy, it became a distinct professional organization with its own small, elite audience.[2] In late 1979, Luit Bieringa became
director, replacing Melvin Day's ambivalence towards New Zealand contemporary art with
strong support for local artists. With the new director and the presence on the Gallery's
Council of Hamish Keith and Hirini Mead, who played key roles in 'Te Maori', there was
promise of more interaction with Māori artists after the disappointments of the late 1970s.
According to the 1980 Annual Report, the gallery was developing new policies in a number
of areas 'notably Maori and Polynesian art' (AR 1980). The gallery staff in the mid- and late
1980s were certainly aware of Māori political issues and their implications for the display
of art and watched closely as events unfolded downstairs. Para Matchitt's *Huakina* was
purchased in 1987 but Bieringa admitted that 'the gallery has yet to address the question of
significant Maori representation' (AR 1987). After 'Te Maori' the New Zealand art world
paid more attention to the Māoriness of Māori art in reviews, catalogues and books, and the
trickle of Māori art exhibitions became a flood (Hanham 2000).

A new curator, Tim Walker, made more acquisitions and curated a steady stream of small
exhibitions at Buckle Street and in the Gallery's renovated space on the waterfront known
as Shed 11: The temporary/contemporary. Staff installed these exhibitions in the same way
as work by other contemporary New Zealand artists: as autonomous works of art in a fine
art setting with minimal labelling or interpretation (Figure 4.11). Only one-off events like
the opening of 'Taki Toru', where *kapa haka* and a reggae band attracted a large number of
young Māori, interrupted the prevailing atmosphere. Although the National Art Gallery
was never fully a 'white cube' along the lines of contemporary art museums overseas, it
employed the same kind of spartan space which simultaneously sanctioned the taste of the
cultural elite (Bennett 1995: 171).

However, in late 1990, by which time Jenny Harper had become director, the National
Art Gallery embarked on an ambitious project that had similar ramifications for the art
world that 'Te Maori' had for museums. This venture was described as a 'milestone in the
cultural decolonisation of Aotearoa-New Zealand' (Brunt 2004: 222). 'Kohia ko taikaka
anake [Gather only the heartwood]' was developed in 'a spirit of equal partnership' based
on the Treaty, with the gallery working once again with Ngā Puna Waihanga and Te Waka
Toi (the Māori branch of the Arts Council). The National Art Gallery handed over space,
resources and curatorial control. Walker acted as coodinator alongside artist-curators Para
Matchitt and Sandy Adsett (*Kohia ko Taikaka* 1993: 10–11). A partnership approach was
taken, Walker explained, 'so that the artists could have some involvement in defining
what was seen, the way it was shown, and the whole kaupapa of the exhibition' (Walker in
'Taikaka' video 1991). In doing so, the Gallery hoped to debate the 'limiting parameters
within which art institutions have cast "contemporary Maori art' (Walker in *Kohia ko
Taikaka* 1993: 7).

Not surprisingly, it was a major challenge for a professional organization used to maintaining 'standards'. Rather than being 'gatekeepers', staff became 'ushers' who had to stand

Figure 4.11 National Art Gallery, 1980s (Museum of New Zealand
Te Papa Tongarewa B.033174).

back and let artists, groups and *iwi* do things their way. Open over the same time as 'Taonga
Maori' in the museum, 'Taikaka' attracted a good deal of attention and a high proportion
of first-time Māori visitors. Alongside the typical upper class income/professional visitation,
there was a significant Māori patronage. Whereas nationally Māori made up only 7.4 per
cent of the art gallery audience, they made up 14.9 per cent at the National Art Gallery,
probably as a result of 'Taikaka' over the summer and autumn of 1990–1 (Stafford 1991:
20).

'Taikaka' was the country's largest ever exhibition of contemporary Māori art. The work
of 160 artists from throughout the country was seen over four months (AR 1991). It filled
the entire fourteen galleries on the first floor, which had been reopened once the collection
was moved out to a new storage facility at the rear of the building. Eight 'founding'
artists each produced a series of works or assemblages in 'installation galleries', while the
works of 'second-generation' artists were combined in 'exhibition galleries'. The layout
was indistinguishable from most public art galleries at this time: the works were placed

in bare rooms or against white walls with minimal labelling, which had more to do with the rushed process of setting up the exhibition than curatorial intention (Walker, personal communication, 31 August 2002). The *iwi* and regional galleries took a different approach, with a surprising variety of work shown side by side in the same space: pottery, jewellery, weaving, carving, painting and mixed media (Figure 4.12). Tim Walker commented later that the 'abundance and diversity' of work in 'Taikaka' changed the 'physical appearance' of the Gallery (*Kohia ko Taikaka* 1993: 8). While it proved a challenge to the gallery's old audience, who were used to 'a more formal and ordered aesthetic', it encouraged the new Māori audience (*Kohia ko Taikaka* 1993: 8). Perhaps the most remarkable feature of 'Taikaka' was the way that the national institution, which until recently had operated as the arbiter of taste and cultural capital, effectively allowed itself to be taken over. The Gallery suddenly renounced its 'jurisdiction over an aesthetic ideology of "high art," the basis of colonial exclusion in the past' (Brunt 2004: 227).

Figure 4.12 Tākitimu gallery, 'Kohia ko Taikaka anake' exhibition, National Art Gallery, 1991 (Museum of New Zealand Te Papa Tongarewa F.001422/05).

Art critics welcomed the exhibition's timeliness rather than its content. Rob Taylor wrote that the huge display was 'a good start' but much of the work was disappointing (*Dom*, 19 December 1990). Samoan writer Albert Wendt praised the show for setting out a 'different art history' (1991: 16). Māori critics were also more positive. Bob Jahnke responded to questions of lowered standards in these terms:

> One may be justified in criticising the uneven quality of the show. However, one must consider the exhibition philosophy which Nga Puna Waihanga has maintained since its inception in 1973 ... a philosophy that defines art from a cultural perspective. The western division of 'craft' and 'fine art' becomes superfluous rhetoric in this context. (Jahnke 1991: 32)

Despite its success in breaking down barriers and bringing in new audiences, questions remained. At the time, debate centred on the exclusions from an exhibition that set out to be inclusive. The question of identity so central to many of the artists was, it seems, the very reason why Ralph Hōtere declined to participate, as always avoiding the label 'Māori artist'. Yet other postmodern Māori artists like Michael Parekōwhai, whose work questioned an essentialized Māori identity, also took part in the show. Questions of gender joined those of ethnicity. The exhibition was boycotted by Haeata, the Māori women artists collective, on the grounds that it excluded Māori women artists. If the so-called first generation male artists involved in the show wrote themselves into the history of Māori art, then female artists were written out (Harper 1991: 58–9). The fact that gender had been overlooked threw doubt on the efficacy of Māoriness or tribal affiliation as a prerequisite for 'Māori art'.

As an exercise in partnership, 'Taikaka' was the culmination of a period of breathless change in New Zealand society. Whatever its failings in terms of conventional art standards, the exhibition did attract a new Māori patronage. Contemporary art gained relevance with a wider Māori audience by addressing Māori issues at a national level. The 1980s was therefore a crucial decade in New Zealand cultural history because it marked the highpoint of decolonization. It encouraged the exploration of a new independent sense of identity in many different fields. A burgeoning Pakeha nationalism created space for Māori culture to emerge on its own terms as the government policy of biculturalism attempted to ameliorate Māori demands for greater independence (Durie 1994: 102–4). Māori made major strides in advancing their political causes, and latched on to the 'Te Maori' exhibition as an expression of resurgent cultural nationalism.

When Māori people occupied museum spaces *en masse* their tribal heirlooms were re-articulated as '*taonga*' – touchstones of decolonized cultural identity – which simultaneously functioned as a new badge of bicultural nationhood for Pakeha. Because of the nature and intensity of their relationship with Māori exhibitions, Māori patrons became an important presence both on the exhibition floor and in the offices and boardrooms of museums around the country. Clearly more than simply an 'audience' for Māori exhibitions, Māori patrons supported, encouraged, criticized, and cajoled, inserting themselves into the exhibitionary apparatus. So long a tool of colonization and recolonization, museum display now became the means of decolonization.

NOTES

1. Māori were underrepresented at six per cent, whereas they made up thirteen per cent of the national population in the 1991 Census (Cockburn 1990: 12).
2. According to Cockburn, the audience was predominantly tertiary educated, professional and Pakeha (1990: 1). The impression I got from my visits to the gallery from 1984, and my time working there from 1988, was of an institution that was regularly visited by a small number of enthusiastic art lovers.

5 MANA TAONGA, 1991–2001

That a national institution can simultaneously so thoroughly marginalise empire and embrace 'race' when the two are intrinsically bound together in New Zealand's history since the late eighteenth century signifies the complex, often contradictory, unravelling of interwoven threads of colonialism in a former settler colony at the end of the twentieth century.

(Macdonald 1999: 2)

The presentation of *Te Hau ki Tūranga* in the 1990s owed much to previous cultures of display (Figure 5.1). Still flanked by a *pātaka*, it sat at the centre of a *kāinga* in an echo of the Māori village arrangement of the postwar period, when carvings were seen as artefacts of a distant past. The way in which texture and form were singled out for their aesthetic beauty

Figure 5.1   'Mana Whenua' exhibition, Te Papa, 1998 (Museum of New Zealand Te Papa Tongarewa Mana Whenua2).

echoed the art exhibitions of the 1970s and 1980s. But the agency of display, the question of who the exhibit was *by* and *for*, alerts us to subtle differences in the way the objects were now seen. The *whare* and the *pātaka* were positioned so that they no longer crossed over each other's 'view', but were spaced out to respect their individual authority and power (*mana*). The display enhanced this *mana*: *Te Tākinga* was adorned with feathers and bathed in spot lighting, and *Te Hau ki Tūranga* was raised up on a platform as if it sat on a hill. The label text, which addressed the visitor from the point of view of the tribe, made explicit the connection between *iwi* and their ancestral treasures.

If *taonga* can be defined as inalienable possessions (Weiner 1992), then what was on display here was the ownership of the social group. It was a Māori category of visual display at work within a Māori cultural framework, that is to say, *taonga* within a Māori discourse of survival and strength: *mana taonga*. The phrase *mana taonga* (power, authority of *taonga*) is usually understood to refer to Te Papa's policy of giving people who have *taonga* in the museum the *mana* to stand on the *marae* and claim the museum as 'their place' (*tūrangawaewae* or place to stand) (Mahuika 1991; AR 1995: 16). Because this pan-tribal inclusion within a national body overrules the monopoly of the local tribe, Tapsell (in McIntyre and Wehner 2001) has criticized the policy as an appropriation of Māori values that turns 'tribal space' into 'our place'. In this chapter I use 'mana taonga' in a genealogical sense to describe the period when the *mana* of *taonga* returned to Māori hands (Mead cited in *Taonga Maori* 1991: 186).

Mana taonga was the sign that the control of representation in museums had returned to Māori people. The modern *pepeha – Mana taonga, mana tangata –* suggests that the authority and prestige of *taonga* is bound up with social power and vice versa. The exhibitors, and who they exhibit for, are more important than what is exhibited and how. Like postcolonial exhibitions of indigenous culture in other settler colonies, this self-representation reflected a broader museological shift to a contestatory culture of display in which the academic and legal authority of the museum was sidelined (MacClancy 1997; Simpson 1996). Intimate, emotional and even romantic, this style of presentation was the product of the *tangata whenua* looking at themselves, rather than being observed by Pakeha. The Other, once the object of the colonizer's gaze, had become self and the object subject. After 140 years of Māori exclusion, collusion and consultation, they were the displayers in 'Mana whenua', the exhibition in which *Te Hau ki Tūranga* sat and which is analysed in this final chapter.

MUSEUMS IN THE 1990s: POSTCOLONIAL OR POSTMODERN?

A remarkable moment in New Zealand history occurred in 1995, when a British queen apologized to a Māori one. In addition to a royal apology, the Crown paid $170 million in compensation to the Tainui tribe for breaches of the Treaty of Waitangi committed during the war in the Waikato in the 1860s. The symbolic gesture that sealed the event was the handover by Prime Minister Jim Bolger of 'Korotangi' to the Māori queen Te Atairangikahu on the *marae* at Tūrangawaewae (Legget 1995). This small sculpture of a bird, which, according to tradition, came to *Aotearoa* with the Tainui *waka* many generations ago, had been in the collection of the National Museum for many years. The return of this *taonga* was a sign of the times. It was what James Clifford called a 'taxonomic moment' (1988: 228) when an object shifts categories – in this case a museum artefact became a tribal heirloom once more, a pre-eminent symbol of *mana taonga*. But above all, this remarkable event demonstrated that Māori had resumed responsibility for their own affairs. New Zealand's long period of colonization and recolonization were over, and decolonization was here to stay.

According to demographic statistics, Māori were in a much stronger position than they had been a century before, and they could no longer be ignored on the national or local stage.[1] Despite its antipathy to many Māori demands, the National government oversaw the settlement of the Tainui claim in 1995 and the Kai Tahu claim in 1998. Greater political representation boosted Māori assertiveness. After the 1994 election, organized under the new mixed-member proportional representation system (MMP), the new parliament contained fifteen Māori MPs spread across the political spectrum. Protest became symbolic rather than social – focusing on trees or statues of colonial politicians rather than spilling out on to the streets (Belich 2001: 479–80). The new coalition government's support for repatriation efforts, which culminated in Tau Henare's 1996 Taonga Māori Bill, demonstrated that there was broad consensus for protecting and preserving what were seen as cultural treasures – a mood not dissimilar to that at the turn of the century, as noted in Chapter 1.

Though the Bill and Henare's political career were short lived, there was a real sense of Māori confidence at this time, which seemed to be leading to a form of separate Māori nationhood. But the Māori struggle for *tino rangatiratanga*, a measure of sovereignty based on article two of the Treaty, was countered by the state's insistence on democracy for all. The state policy of biculturalism, an attempt to ameliorate Māori calls for a measure of self-government, had a profound impact on education, the environment, and the arts. By promoting the idea of two peoples living in one country, this official discourse allowed a measure of Māori autonomy but tried to maintain control over Māori independence. Whereas, in the nineteenth century, museums reflected the colonial conflict between settler and native, at the end of the twentieth century they were the scenes of attempts to reconcile different forms of decolonization – Pakeha cultural democracy and Māori cultural sovereignty.

In 1992, the former National Art Gallery and National Museum were integrated to form the Museum of New Zealand Te Papa Tongarewa. The Museum of New Zealand, which became known as Te Papa in 1997, opened in a new building on the Wellington waterfront in 1998. The process that led to Te Papa began in the aftermath of 'Te Maori' in the late 1980s and was contemporaneous with the appearance of the 'new museology'. This chapter does not focus on the Museum of New Zealand project itself, which has been the subject of much discussion, but analyses the development of Māori exhibitions up to the opening of Te Papa in 1998 and its first few years of operation. The analysis of Te Papa and its exhibitions is framed within a genealogy of display and it brings in the perspective of those developing the exhibition and those who visited it. With the availability of visitor research, I am able to demonstrate the links between audience and the culture of display with far greater quality and quantity of information than is available for earlier periods. Through visitor surveys I am able to articulate in detail the relational nature of the museum, its links to new indigenous subjectivities, postmodernity and future imaginings.

Decolonization and biculturalism were inscribed into the architecture of the new national museum. The building's exterior had a European and a Polynesian side: the rectilinear European façade faced the city and the curvilinear side of the building with the *marae* like a hilltop *pā* looked out over the sea. The whole structure was split in two by the huge granite wall representing the earthquake faultline that runs right through the capital city (Figure 5.2). On entering the building, a grand staircase to the foyer led to exhibitions about the natural environment on level two. Here visitors were met by Neke Kapua's *waharoa* (Figure I.2). From the foyer visitors made their way up to level four where the history and art exhibitions were located (Figure 5.3). The people and their culture were seen to grow out of the land, in a updated version of settler identity (expressed in the museum's by-line 'our place'). Levels three and five contained smaller function and temporary exhibition spaces.

A huge glass facsimile of the Treaty of Waitangi hung in the centre of level four and is the focal point of the entire space. This feature display of the Treaty operated conceptually and architecturally as the hinge of the nation, cleaving the museum into Māori and Pakeha

Figure 5.2   View of Te Papa from the waterfront, Wellington, October 1997 (Museum of New Zealand Te Papa Tongarewa F.004449/7).

Figure 5.3　View across level 4, Te Papa, 1998 (Museum of New Zealand
Te Papa Tongarewa F.004899/44).

sections in their separate spaces. In the layout of level four the Māori exhibition zone, which contained 'Mana whenua' and the changing *iwi* exhibitions, was positioned on the side of the building next to the sea where according to tradition the explorer Kupe arrived from the ancestral homeland *Hawaiki*. The contemporary *marae, Rongomaraeroa,* faced the rising sun in the East, while the Pakeha portion of the museum with its grid-like plan looked out on Wellington where Europeans settled. The building therefore rendered into concrete and glass the tripartite concept developed in 1989: *Papatūānuku, Tangata Whenua* and *Tangata Tiriti* (the land, people of the land, people of the Treaty). Māori-Pakeha relations were reformulated through the Treaty as a founding document. 'Icons' of Pakeha New Zealand identity – Jeff Thompson's corrugated iron Holden and John Britten's superbike – were displayed on one side of the central core opposite an old *waka taua: Tangata Whenua* and *Tangata Tiriti* were separated out into distinct areas, modernity in one and, it seemed, a timeless present in the other. Although 'our nation's story' had been made over, and Māori were given equal status to their Treaty partner, the same two protagonists were inextricably meshed together in an ambiguous relationship (Phillips 1996; Macdonald 1999; Neill 2004).

The last quarter of the twentieth century has been called the postmodern age, character-ized by global communication and multicultural diversity with an attendant loss of faith in traditional certainties and master narratives (Bhabha in Nelson and Shiff 1996). The 'new museology' (Vergo 1989) translated elements of postmodern theory into the field of museum practice in the 1980s and 1990s as museums interrogated their own exhibitionary strategies by exposing audiences to the constructedness of representation and the partiality of knowledge. Attention focused on the visitor experience rather than collections, shifting emphasis from the object to the audience. It is possible to see the postmodern museum's dissonance, synaesthesia and blurring of collection boundaries as a 'heterotopia', a space in which the syntax that holds together words and things has collapsed (Rajchman 1985; Foucault cited in Rajchman 1988: 49). Te Papa's design and layout shows many of the elements of the new museology and of the postcolonial inclusiveness which sought to redeem postsettler nations (Simpson 1996; Muckle and Veracini 2002; Dibley 2005).

The display of the war canoe on level four suggests, however, a tension between a distinct indigenous domain within a postmodern space. With *Teremoe,* dramatic new techniques overlap with customary Māori values. Positioned outside the 'Mana Whenua' exhibition, the *waka* is mounted on an angle as if mounting the crest of a wave (Figure 5.4). Rippling lights play on the underside and spots pick out the details of carving along the *rauawa*. The sound of the sea can be heard on an audio. At the end of the *waka* stands a plaque, containing a graphic of the Whanganui River and a photograph of Mr and Mrs Hipango who donated the canoe to the museum in 1930. By stipulating that their photograph had to accompany the exhibit, these Māori patrons articulated the link between display and tribal patrimony. The label describes the *waka* as their *taonga,* a treasured heirloom of Te Āti Haunui-ā-Pāpārangi, which they donated to the museum to be preserved and admired. It is

Figure 5.4   Entrance to 'Mana Whenua', showing *Teremoe* on left, Te
Papa, 1998 (Museum of New Zealand Te Papa Tongarewa F.004919/07).

displayed with a sense of respect, like a church relic, its *mana* derived from rich associations
with revered ancestors and the tumultuous events of the battle of Moutoa in the 1860s.
There are traces of the new museology here – the multimedia animation and narrative style
– but they are subsumed into a Māori-centric style of display – essentialized, reverential,
and utopian – which is definitely not postmodern. How did elements of postmodernism
and postcolonialism shape the museum display of Māori objects at the end of the twentieth
century? How did this compromise between the discourses of Māori nationalism and Pakeha
biculturalism, between *iwi* and the new museology, come about?

CULTURAL DEMOCRACY AND CULTURAL SOVEREIGNTY

In the last two decades of the twentieth century, museums around the world ushered in a
period of experimentation and change in the exhibitionary apparatus. In addition to new
media and interactive technologies, exhibition developers and designers looked back to

the long history of leisure, spectacle and immersion that paralleled the birth of the public museum. Boundaries between high and low culture were broken down and replaced by an apparently haphazard order which harked back to the wonder cabinets of the premodern era (Bann 2003). These new generation museums were often the subject of academic criticism for their various ideological sins: racism, nationalism, commercialism and populism. As Prior points out, however, many museums in the 'hypermodern' era were 'more plural, open and contingent than the mass culture or elite image suggest'. Diverse, self-reflexive and composite structures, museums inhabited a 'more democratic "third space" beyond elitism and consumerism' (Prior in McClellan 2003: 68). Andrea Witcomb (2003: 169) also takes issue with critiques of the museum from left and right, arguing that museums have always been mediators between high and popular culture.

Ethnicity was reconfigured as process, as African objects in American museums were exhibited as the mixed products of messy histories (Lidchi in Hall 1997: 201). Museums in former settler colonies, under attack for their links to colonization, found new ways to display national histories and indigenous objects: using self-reflexivity or dialogue, including transitional and syncretic objects and consulting those represented to have a say in how their culture was shown (Casey 2001; Davison 2002). In New Zealand, Australia, Canada and the Pacific, museums received negative reviews for the way that they negotiated questions of indigenous, settler and national identity (Gillespie 2001; McIntyre and Wehner 2001; Williams 2005). Critical museum theory dismissed indigenous exhibitions as cultural inventions or 'theoretically incorrect' essentialism (Dibley 1997; Brown 2002). Some scholars have since reconsidered this criticism, recognizing how Māori exhibitions effectively advanced Māori claims for the museum (Thomas 1995b). As Clifford notes, dismissing syncretic traditions as inauthentic is tantamount to 'another kind of intellectual imperialism' (Clifford 1997: 180). When 'critical barbarity' results in a campaign of antifetishism against anything smacking of identity formation, then social critique has run out of steam (Latour 2004). In this chapter I question the perceived wisdom of much postmodern theory by suggesting that a strategic use of older museum practices better served the interests of Māori patronage.

In the 1990s the culture of display was transformed, at the same time as the museum display of Māori culture in New Zealand settled into a new orthodoxy. At the old National Museum building at Buckle Street 'Taonga Maori' lingered on in the Māori Hall, while at Auckland and other metropolitan museums permanent displays were updated in line with this restrained fusion of art and taonga which was the legacy of the overwhelming success of 'Te Maori.' The most important Polynesian exhibition of the decade outside New Zealand was 'Maori' at the British Museum in 1998, which, although containing modern work in a customary style, retained elements of the ethnographic and artistic presentation of the 1980s and earlier (Starzecka 1998; Gathercole 1999).

The call for social inclusion drove many of the new audience-focused exhibition practices adopted by the Museum of New Zealand project in the early 1990s (Sandell and Dodd

2001; Sandell 2002). Museums in Australia and New Zealand embarked on visitor research in an attempt to broaden their visitation and reach new publics. Public accountability became one of the requirements of the Museum of New Zealand when the taxpayer-funded facility set out to become a 'museum for all New Zealanders' (AR 1995: 19). Art historian Jenny Harper (1990: 41), then working on the museum project, declared that the biggest challenge facing museums was to change 'our overall orientation from that of self-serving collection-based organisations to being audience-orientated.' From 1995 to 1996, the Museum of New Zealand initiated its own audience research with a particular focus on Māori who were still underrepresented in New Zealand museums (O'Regan 1997: 65). Exhibition interpreter Neil Anderson (2000) established an audience-focused process that ensured exhibitions would appeal to a broad range of people. Narratives and personal stories in a conversational tone replaced the terminology of academic disciplines on label text. Marketing strategies, which responded directly to negative perceptions of the Museum at Buckle Street, deliberately repositioned the institution as an attractive leisure destination for visitors in direct contrast to the 'quiet contemplation of objects in a cathedral of culture...' (Kirshenblatt-Gimblett 1998: 139).

At this juncture, just as at critical periods in the past, Māori and Pakeha aspirations became entwined. The new museology's emphasis on democratizing the audience coincided with a Māori concern to address the historical alienation of their people from museums. The politics of Māori 'cultural sovereignty' (Tamarapa 1996b: 171) resulted in a new approach to museum display, which set out to include *iwi* in the process of developing Māori exhibitions as part of the new museology's focus on audience. The National Museum did have a small but supportive group of Māori patrons, in spite of the fact that wealthy middle-class Pakeha were generally overrepresented amongst its visitors (Cockburn 1989, 1990; *Admission Charges* 1994). There was now a concerted effort to attract more Māori visitors to the new museum. From the beginning, the Māori staff working on the Museum of New Zealand project were adamant that Māori exhibitions had a primary 'target audience' of Māori. Exhibition planning documents made frequent reference to the importance of using text, design and other features to create an environment where Māori people felt comfortable ('Mana whenua 100% concept design' 1996: 46, TPA MU 361).

There were growing expectations that the new museum would carry on from where 'Te Maori' had left off. Ken Gorbey, who headed the project's planning team, described biculturalism as 'an historical imperative' that arose out of the Treaty' (1991: 7). The Museum saw itself as a *kaitiaki* (guardian) rather than owner of *taonga*, and began a long process of *iwi* liaison with major tribes in preparation for the exhibitions in the waterfront building. Over the next few years, it became the laboratory for the initiatives that were a feature of New Zealand museums (Murphy 1999). This Māori 'seizure' of museum space (Jahnke 1999: 197) was enacted through the reframing of collections and exhibitions within *tikanga Māori* – customary Māori protocol and practices. The protocols, handling, classification, storage and conservation of Māori collections were modified (Tamarapa 1996a). In line with the laws of *tapu* and *noa*, water bowls were placed near collection stores, everyday objects were kept apart from those for ceremonial use, and *kōiwi tangata* and *mokamokai* (human remains) were placed in a special enclosure or *wāhi tapu*. With *taonga*, staff observed restrictions on food, and laid out fresh green leaves signifying their status as living things.[2] Rather than being organized by type or provenance, *taonga* were now classified by tribal affiliation. These changes had the effect of making Māori visitors more comfortable with the display and management of their *taonga* which they felt were being 'kept warm' by the Māori who looked after them (Tamarapa 2000; Rewi 2001).

The Museum of New Zealand now carried the bilingual title Te Papa Tongarewa and claimed to be a 'bicultural' museum (AR 1989, 1993). Alongside Cheryll Sotheran, who was appointed CEO in 1993, Māori artist Cliff Whiting became Kaihautū, or the navigator of the canoe, in 1995 (AR 1994/1996). Internal classifications were made over in line with a new conceptual framework, revealing that this new museum, despite its attempts to suggest a break with the past, was just as much a product of social forces as its predecessors (*A Concept for the Museum of New Zealand* 1991). Within the new tripartite concept, anomalies quickly surfaced. The department of Maori Art and History oversaw the Māori collections, which consisted of the material from the former Ethnology department, although contemporary Māori 'art' was handled by Māori curators in the 'Art and History' department within the concept of 'Tangata Tiriti'. Museum discourse – the language of staff communication, exhibition text, internal documents and publications – reveal that terminology was being reshaped in line with the times. *Taonga* became firmly consolidated and widely used internally, while the term 'artefact' became rare. Māori names for objects were uniformly used without italics, and from 1996 *iwi* affiliation was added where known. Other words and phrases overlapping with *taonga* revealed ambiguities within Māori categories, particularly when applied to Museum activities. The Annual Report stated that 'traditional taonga' were acquired by Māori curators, whereas works by Ralph Hōtere and Robyn Kahukiwa were bought by art curators (1996). Anxious to lay claim to their patrimony, Māori policymakers defined the culture in ways which failed to incorporate the diversity of contemporary expression. The Museum's Pacific team, in contrast, operated with more fluid categories, avoiding the word 'traditional' and collecting and displaying an eclectic range of contemporary visual and material culture (Mallon, personal communication, 16 February 2004).

Despite attempts to pin down the meanings of this ambiguous concept, there is evidence that the meaning of the term *taonga* in English continued to change (Hedley 2004: 64–8). Researcher Hineihaea Murphy (1999: 2) found that defining *taonga* was 'a difficult and somewhat contentious task. Linguist Harry Orsman (1997: 813), for example, recorded a shift from 'goods' to 'a treasured artifact or person'. Visitor research suggested many Māori people saw *taonga Māori* as old items found in museums, *marae* or family collections (McCauley 1996). The meaning of *taonga* came to be applied to 'traditional' cultural treasures: land, people, the language, and what Mead has called 'art heritage' (Mead 1993: 225; 2003: 261). As used in the Māori titles of organizations or programmes, *taonga* referred to something precious and historic that needed to be saved, not unlike the connotations in English of the word 'heritage'.[3]

According to Paul Tapsell, *taonga* were 'any tangible or intangible item, object or thing that represents a kin group's genealogical identity in relation to its estates and resources and is passed down through generations' (2000: 169). Tapsell's neotraditional definition is itself a product of a period when *iwi* sought the repossession of alienated resources in Treaty claims, made demands for repatriation and fostered debates about intellectual property rights (Henare 2005: 94–5; Hedley 2004: 57). Ethnolegalistic definitions of *taonga* as ancestral property rights rested on a formulation advanced by Hugh Kawharu in 1987 (1989: 321). The 'retrospective' history associated with the Waitangi Tribunal and its legalistic constructions of Māori tradition have been debated by several scholars (Oliver 2001; Byrnes 2003; Belgrave 2005; Sissons 2005). Critics warn that chauvinistic nativism is no answer to Eurocentrism and may merely reproduce its binary oppositions (Chakrabarty 2000: 16, 106). One of the drawbacks of 'resurgent culturalisms' is that they police the boundaries of tradition to 'suppress the diversity within' (Dirlik in Dirlik, Bahl and Gran 2000: 248). While it has been has been claimed that the triumph of artefact-as-*taonga* has achieved a postcolonial denouement for New Zealand museums (Tapsell 2000), I believe there is a need for theoretical and historical analysis that lays bare the process by which certain objects, once curios and then artefacts, *became taonga*. 'The task,' as Sharon Macdonald put it, 'is also to explore the consequences of particular forms of representation in terms of the distribution of power: who is empowered or disempowered by certain modes of display?' (1998: 4).

'MĀORI TALKING ABOUT MĀORI': THE DEVELOPMENT OF 'MANA WHENUA'

The politics of cultural sovereignty meshed with the Museum of New Zealand project in the internal development of the 'Mana Whenua' exhibition. From the outset Māori staff saw themselves as overturning outmoded practices. Awhina Tamarapa, Māori curator and concept leader on the Museum of New Zealand project, argued that the problem with conventional museum displays was that Māori *taonga* were grouped according to criteria such as form and function, rather than by the tribal affiliation and genealogical histories that animated them. 'All cultural treasures in museums', Tamarapa argued, 'should be displayed in partnership between the people who created them, the people who held them, and the people who will see them on display' (1996a: 167).

Visitor research assisted the developers by providing feedback about the 'Māori audience', their responses to museums and their display preferences. In one study most of the people surveyed were critical of 'static' displays and favoured more dynamic methods such as reconstructions, oral histories, hands-on displays, and audiovisuals (Fitzgerald and MacLennan 1994: 54). Above all, these studies pointed to the difficulty of the interpretative task for 'Mana whenua' given the complexity of its primary target audience – Māori people were plainly not all the same, but had different backgrounds, experience, expectations and tastes. Given that the Māori exhibition team was encouraged to address a broad audience, like other exhibition developers on the Te Papa project, it was not surprising that the original concept for 'Mana Whenua' was expansive. The overall conceptual shape had initially been provided by a Cliff Whiting sketch, which envisaged Māori culture as a continuous stream (Gorbey 2000). It encompassed *taonga* in the broadest sense including carving, weaving, and contemporary paintings through to language, land, *waiata*, and people. In addition to 'traditional' *taonga*, there were plans for ancillary exhibitions covering modern social history and contemporary Māori art. The breadth of the concept was expressed most clearly in 'Te Huka a Tai', the childrens' discovery centre next to 'Mana Whenua', which contained children's selections of their own '*taonga*' including everything from commercially produced bone carvings to books about Egypt and plastic toys.

By the end of 1994, the exhibition concept comprised three main sections: 'Mana waka' would tell the story of the Māori arrival in Aotearoa, 'Mana Whenua' the Māori settlement of the land, and 'Mana tangata' the contemporary perspective ('Mana Whenua concept development report', TPA MU 361, 3).[4] According to the objectives:

> The 'Mana whenua' exhibition tries to capture and convey the richness, complexity and dynamism of the culture of the tangata whenua... The relationship to the land, the struggles of survival, the adaptations and changes, and the strong connections to the whenua today are explored. ('Mana Whenua 90% developed design' September 1996)

A series of peer reviews with Māori leaders and experts endorsed this plan. They liked the combination of old and new, and urged the team to emphasize the innovative aspects of what were often seen as traditional objects, warning against the 'glorification of the past' ('Minutes of Te Komiti Tikanga Maori hui', 2 March 1995). In debates with the members of the exhibition team a broad notion of *taonga* emerged which encompassed the competing categories of art and artefact. There were conflicts. Sandy Adsett argued that more art should be included, criticizing the exhibition for being boring because of the 'historical perspective'. Tipene O'Regan disagreed, criticizing the recent bias toward art, which he argued was the fault of the 'Te Maori' exhibition, which 'had proclaimed taonga in an art arena' ('Minutes of Te Komiti Tikanga Maori hui' 1995).

Faced with a range of opinion, staff working on the exhibition had to come up with their own working compromises. Designer Marcus Smiler explained his approach, showing how a traditional genealogical category could be extended to embrace modern objects:

> My understanding of the concept of taonga was that each item had a history ... behind them. They all link into a holistic story through their own whakapapa links, and therefore are more than just artefacts or objects ... I viewed each object in the exhibition as a taonga, whether old or relatively young. (Smiler, personal communication, 10 December 2001)

Māori staff had to overturn what they felt was a discredited style of museum display, although they were less certain about what to replace it with. Exhibition documents declared that Māori were 'a living people … not a lifeless, dead culture that museums continue to perpetuate' ('Mana Whenua concept development', 1994: 11). The new Māori exhibition will 'deliver interpretations from "within the culture' ('Mana Whenua concept development' 1994: 24). 'The vital relationship between Māori people and their taonga is critical in the development of this exhibition', declared another document ('Mana whenua 90% developed design report' September 1996: 199). Concept developer Arapata Hakiwai said they had set out to animate objects, to 'make them live' by acknowledging the *mauri* (living life force) of *taonga* (1999: 11). Designer Henare Walmsley felt that it was a 'distinctly Māori' process – the group operated like a '*whānau*' where decisions were made by consensus (personal communication, 14 December 2001). Tamarapa thought that the design and interpretation of 'Mana Whenua' reflected a Māori perspective because being Maori meant the developers took certain things, such as the concept of *taonga*, for granted (2000). Smiler felt that they produced 'unmistakeably Māori' elements: the *ngutu kaka* pattern on the floor tiles, the curvilinear layout and organic forms, the sounds of native birds, the '*mānuka* branch' handrails and the earthy green colours. When it came to displaying things as *taonga*, the designers tried to give them 'presence and *mana*' by presenting them 'in the best conditions and environment that suited them' rather than 'just objects in a room' (Smiler, personal communication, 14 December 2001).

From early 1995 as the exhibition concept was refined and edited through the development process, the team struggled to maintain the focus on their original objectives as they had to economize. The 'Mana Whenua' section was retained, while other elements were incorporated into it. When segments dealing with modern society were deleted, and contemporary art commissions failed to materialize due to a lack of funding, staff fell back on the same collection items that were on display in the Māori Hall at the old National Museum in Buckle Street. Despite the best intentions of the team, and a storyline emphasizing adaptation to a new land, the completed exhibition had a much more 'traditional' look. Due partly to the failure of plans for guides and interactives, there was a predominance of old carvings in the space. Yet, this is only part of the story. In another sense, the 'traditional' look of the exhibition was intentional. By the early 1990s, the style of display for *taonga*, established in the late 1980s with key exhibitions, was considered appropriate amongst Māori people as a way of treating their cultural heritage objects (Thomas 2001: 306–7). To treat revered cultural treasures with experimental display techniques or postmodern irony would therefore have been regarded as almost disrespectful.

It was difficult to distinguish in design terms how *taonga* in 'Mana Whenua' were treated differently to other exhibitions throughout Te Papa. Subdued versions of standard design approaches were favoured, perhaps as a way of avoiding being coopted by the kind of deconstruction and bricolage applied to art exhibits (Goldsmith 2001). *Taonga* were given respect, honoured, elevated and heightened by scale, layout, words, graphics – they were not deconstructed and certainly not classified, dated or analysed in an academic or scientific way. Atmosphere and mood were created with lighting, music and space, so as to give objects a sense of *mana* as *taonga*. Multi-media technology such as videos, audios and soundscapes were employed to simulate the life force of object-beings in the act of communicating with the Māori descendants. *Taonga* were perhaps best thought of as responses, rather than as objects, constituted not in inherent qualities but through the *mana* bestowed by the patrons who were the owner-spectators. Artefacts and art were thus transformed into ancestral treasures by representing, alongside the object, the owning group's relationship to the object. As Hakiwai explained:

> Our mission was to literally break down the walls of the museum, reconnecting the umbilical cord between *taonga* and people, building two-way highways so that life could be given back to *taonga* that had been sleeping for years. (1999: 12)

Apart from difficulties with the communication of Māori values and ideas within the museum setting, the 'Mana Whenua' team had to grapple with the challenging process of *iwi* liaison, which was a new departure in exhibit development in New Zealand. In this process the display of each major *taonga* in 'Mana Whenua' was negotiated with *iwi* as Treaty partners. As Awhina Tamarapa (2000) described it, their intention was to 'reconnect' tribes with their *taonga* by asking them how they would like to see it displayed. In 'taking the exhibition to the people', they hoped to 'speak through the people' (2000). By focusing on how people today valued their *taonga*, the team hoped to get away from 'a static, museum-oriented exhibition' that 'lacked the real and living people dimension' ('Mana Whenua concept development', 1994: 20). Instead of a museum voice speaking for Māori, the display was intended to speak on behalf of *iwi*, and in many cases in their own voice. With the *pounamu* segment, for example, the exhibition team liaised with Maika Mason and a group of Kai Tahu from the West Coast of the South Island. The controversial Moriori segment was similarly developed jointly by staff in consultation with Māui Solomon and Te Iwi Moriori. All major decisions concerning the display of these *taonga* – the concepts, conservation, interpretation, design and signage – were discussed and approved by *iwi* in addition to the museum approvals process.

Similarly, the conservation and display of *Te Tākinga* was led by museum staff Awhina Tamarapa and Rose Evans who employed people from Ngāti Pikiao to work on the project and liaised with a committee who met every month (Evans 1999: 14–15). The tribe approved the proposal to interpret the exhibit through a computer interactive, despite initial reservations about the use of technology. They were enthusiastic about the idea of visitors having access to the interior of the storehouse where an audio explained the preservation of food. But they were not happy with the plan to place a large label 'dominating the frontal appearance of their taonga.' This proposal, which came from the way finding committee (the group responsible for visitor orientation inside the building) was roundly rejected ('Mana Whenua team responses … 90% presentation', January 1996). Height was another consideration. As Tamarapa recalled, tribal representatives were keen to see their *taonga* elevated to give it more *mana* (Personal communication, 17 October 2001). The major issue for them was, in fact, the placement of *Te Tākinga* rather than the details of design because the question of where their prized *taonga* sat in relation to the *wharenui* alongside it was a question of tribal *mana*.

The label outside *Te Tākinga* introduced the 'magnificent' *pātaka* not only as part of the 'proud heritage' of Ngāti Pikiao, but as 'evidence of our mana'. The Māori text elaborated by describing it as a 'great taonga', one of the 'beating hearts of Te Arawa', the display of which embodies the 'mana of the tribe'. This text also made it clear that the research, planning and reconstruction of the display was the work of 'our elders' who worked in 'a cooperative relationship' with Te Papa. Ngāti Pikiao have 'made this house our own again' under the patronage of 'Tāne-whakapiripiri (Tāne-who-unites), the guardian of these and all other taonga in the museum'.[5] In the case of *Mākōtukutuku*, museum archaeologists Janet Davidson and Foss Leach worked alongside Hāmi Te Whaiti and a group of Māori people in the Wairarapa, to build a reconstruction of an ancient *wharepuni*, the remains of which had been discovered in Palliser Bay. Together they made the tools, collected local resources, built the house and constructed props such as nets and traps – all in the style of their ancestors 500 years before. The collaborative process led the team to discard the 'archaeological/ethnographic approach' because it 'infuriates Maori people and does not convey any sense of our history and meanings we attach to taonga' ('Concept development', 1994: 24). The comments from local people in the accompanying video suggest that this process was more about *iwi* development than archaeology, and this has indeed been borne out in a range of joint projects.

The best example of the museum-*iwi* partnership at work was *Te Hau ki Tūranga*. The complex two-year process of moving the *wharenui* from Buckle Street to the new building in Cable Street was part of an 'ongoing relationship' with the Rongowhakaata people of Gisborne. Project manager Walter Waipara, of Rongowhakaata descent, was guided by *iwi* committees. A team of tribal technicians and other Māori staff were responsible for conservation, relocation, and reinstallation of *Te Hau ki Tūranga*. Its placement in 'Mana Whenua' was also determined to a large extent by *iwi*. They wanted the *whare* to be presented as a free-standing structure, facing north, in a prominent position. In the finished exhibition, *Te Hau ki Tūranga* was placed centrally against a back drop of stockade posts, its raised position accentuated by the steps and the sweeping lines of the ramp. The image of a 'dramatic, elevated position', as if the house stood within a *pā* on the crest of a hill, was intended to express tribal wishes to see the house 'uplifted' in order to 'give it mana'. As Walmsley recalled, the platform had a 'status effect' that not only gave the house prominence within the overall exhibition but also moved it forward of the *pātaka* beside it – a subtle example of inter-tribal *mana taonga* (Personal communication, 14 December 2001). There were some criticisms on 'aesthetic' or 'historical' grounds about aspects of the design, such as the interior with its lowered floor, but Hakiwai regarded these views as unimportant in relation to the views of *iwi* themselves. As concept developer of the exhibition, Hakiwai tried to empower the tribe so that the final form it took reflected its views:

> If the iwi didn't like it, we wouldn't have gone with it. I think our role ... drastically changed from curators as authoritative voice to facilitators of a process. So it [the exhibit] *does* speak with authority, it speaks with the authority of the people, and the people are engaged as participators, are fully involved in the process... (Hakiwai 2000)

Tribal approval was not given lightly, and, as Hakiwai discovered, the museum/*iwi* relationship was often a slow and difficult process. When Hakiwai arrived in Gisborne with a film crew to produce the video, he discovered that the production company's script had not been approved. They were told in no uncertain terms that they could all go back to Wellington. Once Rongowhakaata approved the concept, and participated in selecting the stories, locations, and elders that were to be to be filmed, then the project proceeded smoothly (Hakiwai 2000). In the completed video *Te Hau ki Tūranga* is described as 'a treasure for the nation', a formulation that recalls the way in which Māori leaders at the turn of the century talked about gifts to museums. The label says that the house 'symbolises the proud identity of Rongowhakaata, our contribution to the nation, and our commitment to a bicultural partnership...' The Māori text explicitly states that the house is displayed here to strengthen the *mana* of the *iwi*, and is a gift not just to the nation but to the world.

By 1996, 'Mana Whenua' had entered its final stage of development and budget cuts created conflict between the exhibition team and the project management. The most inflammatory issue was the standardized design of the display cases and the unilateral decision to encase all small collection items. Hakiwai complained bitterly about what he saw as an obstruction of their plans to make *taonga* physically accessible to visitors. 'If this is the case,' he wrote with a sardonic pun, 'then we should put a plinth around *Te Hau ki Tūranga*, *Teremoe* and *Te Tākinga*!' (email Hakiwai to Walmsley, 30 August 1996, Hakiwai files, TPA MU 361). Hakiwai's comments in an internal email made it plain that issues of display for Māori (staff and patrons) were a question of *mana*:

> We (includes iwi) have selected the taonga and this includes what we say, how they should be displayed etc ... surely an extension of the interpretation of the taonga is the way that it is presented... After all whose exhibition is this? (Hakiwai to Walmsley, 30 August 1996)

The 'Mana Whenua' exhibition was finally signed off and installed in 1997, ready for the opening of Te Papa in February 1998. The public's first glimpse of the finished exhibition was the large carved entrance way or *tomokanga* beside *Teremoe* (Figure 5.4), which featured Ross Hemera's contemporary art work 'He Whakamārama'. Once inside the exhibition, visitors received the impression they had entered a gloomy forest, suggested by shafts of light and the sounds of birdsong. Two *poutokomanawa* figures stood guard at the entrance, displayed against a deep blue curving wall, the aged patina of the polished *tōtara* and the absence of barriers inviting people to touch. These figures, placed as free-standing posts in the viewer's space had a more human scale and animated presence than artefacts under glass. Behind the figures on a curving wall hung a luminous panel announcing the title of the exhibition, 'Mana Whenua' and underneath the words 'Mai i a Rangi ki a Papa: The people, the spirit that binds.' There were images of the natural world and the people who claim *mana* over it – their authority arising from ancestral connections to land.

A little further along the pathway was the centre point of the exhibition where visitors saw a vista of the feature objects and major segments of 'Mana Whenua' (Figure 5.1). The space was dominated by the *wharenui Te Hau ki Tūranga* in the centre with the *pātaka Te Tākinga* to its right (Figure 5.5). On the opposite wall was the voyaging canoe *Te Aurere* (Figure 5.6). In a large rippling island case in the middle of the exhibition was the segment devoted to the Moriori of the Chatham Islands (Figure 5.7) and opposite that the small *raupō whare Mākōtukutuku* (Figure 5.8).

It was their genealogical connections, the *whakapapa,* which wrapped them in social relations, which showed that *taonga* were not simply functional structures, artworks or artefacts. A *taonga* acts as a repository of connections – a living tradition – which brings the past down into the present. Moreover, the *taonga* is seen by the descendants not as a relic but as something living in a present which encompasses the future. When 'dead' artefacts become living *taonga* the culture of the people who made them gained *mana*, along with the visitors who saw them. Exhibiting Māori became an act of empowerment because the museum display of objects made visible the people and their culture. *Mana Māori* implies the power, respect, and authority of the indigenous people. This 'new' approach to the old objects was made possible by the Māori exhibitors' partnerships with *iwi*, which unseated the conventional position of the museum curator. If the exhibitionary apparatus was used by Māori for Māori, then exhibiting Māori acknowledged the *mana* of *taonga*.

The completed installation design of 'Mana Whenua' was a compromise between the developers' political aspirations and the Museum's overall goal of communicating to a mass audience. Māori staff felt that they had been strong advocates for the Māori target audience, resulting in an exhibition that presented *taonga* from an *iwi* perspective. Walmsley said later that the exhibition was different to earlier ones because it had *mana* that came from 'Iwi engaging in their taonga'. He felt that this gave 'Mana Whenua' a *wairua*, an atmosphere and spiritual ethos, that visitors felt as soon as they entered the space (Walmsley, personal communication, 14 December 2001). The developers employed Māori understandings of *taonga* as social agents to connect with Māori people. In the wider context, the exhibition is comparable to displays of native peoples in North America and Australia, particularly in the ways in which it made visible the presence of those who are absent in ethnographic exhibitions, the living descendants of exhibited objects. As Kirshenblatt-Gimblett observed of the National Museum of the American Indian in New York:

> What is on display above all is the presence, the vitality, the survival of Native Americans themselves… What visitors discover in these galleries is what the objects on display mean to Native Americans today. (1998: 159)

Figure 5.5   *Te Tākinga*, 'Mana Whenua', Te Papa, 1998 (with the permission of Ngāti Pikiao/Museum of New Zealand Te Papa Tongarewa B.042448).

Figure 5.6   *Te Aurere iti*, 'Mana Whenua', Te Papa, 1998 (with the
permission of Hec Busby/Museum of New Zealand Te Papa Tongarewa
F.005489).

Figure 5.7   Te Iwi Moriori, 'Mana Whenua', Te Papa, 1998 (with the
permission of Te Iwi Moriori/Museum of New Zealand
Te Papa Tongarewa F.004920/09).

The exhibition developers, determined to present *taonga* in a postcolonial light, shied away from some elements of postmodernism. Radical elements were toned down: there was little undercutting of the narrative, problematizing of tradition or questioning of identity. The exhibition's design was not fundamentally different to the models of the late 1980s, which presented *taonga* as essential foundations of 'traditional' Māori culture. But despite the criticism of some within the Museum that it was museologically 'old fashioned' in comparison to some other exhibitions, the celebratory tone dignified what were seen as the great works of the ancestors and was the result of a genuine empowering of *iwi* to tell their own story as they saw it. Māori patronage was more important to Māori developers than Pakeha ones, and Māori staff were correspondingly less willing to push the boundaries in ways that would alienate the people they had to answer to in meetings, *iwi* liaison and ceremonies where people forcefully expressed their interests and preferences.

Figure 5.8 *Mākōtukutuku*, 'Mana Whenua', Te Papa, 1998 (with the permission of Ngāti Hinewaka/Museum of New Zealand Te Papa Tongarewa F.004920/03).

An ambitious programme of changing *iwi* exhibitions every two years aimed to supplement 'Mana Whenua' with a focus on individual tribes. These exhibitions – thus far Te Āti Awa, Te Aupōuri, Tūhoe, Whanganui and Kai Tahu – illuminate some of the issues underlying the design of 'Mana Whenua'. One scholar has commented that the *iwi* exhibitions 'add notes of vibrant *contemporaneity* to otherwise sombre Maori displays' (Henare 2005: 251). 'Te Aupōuri iwi', featuring the people of the far North of New Zealand (Figure 5.9), opened in 1999 (AR 2000). It was in some ways a reaction against the traditional content and ethereal style of 'Mana Whenua'. There were contemporary art works, a nineteenth-century Māori Bible and even a bottle of *Waha wera*, a local chilli sauce ('Te Aupōuri iwi exhibition', April 1999, TPA MU 361). In one notable example, a modern manufactured object assumed the status of *taonga* through its association with people and events in the history of the tribe. This was Hone Tahitahi's prayer book, dating from the First World War, which the soldier wore in his breast pocket at this mother's bidding. At Gallipoli in 1916, it saved his life when it stopped a Turkish bullet. Complete with the bullet still embedded in it, the little book was placed in a small reliquary on the *marae* at Te Kao ('Te Aupōuri iwi' 1999). The Tūhoe and Whanganui exhibitions were presented in

Figure 5.9   Segment of 'Te Aupōuri iwi' exhibition, Te Papa, 1999
(with the permission of Te Aupōuri/Museum of New Zealand Te Papa
Tongarewa CT.012266/22).

the now-orthodox style associated with the traditional material culture that dominated the colonial archive and museum collections. The Kai Tahu exhibition, opened in mid 2006, focused on current developments with this South Island *iwi* whose postindigenous identity and economic successes after the settlement of their Treaty claims were quite different from the experiences of North Island tribes (Sissons 2005: 52–3).

As we saw in earlier chapters, the issue of 'contemporary Māori art' and where to put it was closely related to this genealogy of display. The self-reflexive quality of postmodern Māori art raises questions about the approach to display favoured in 'Mana Whenua'. What does the newly traditional concept of *taonga* exclude? Is there a tension between its conservative vision of rural Māori life and the reality of young urban Māori? Some works by young Māori artists successfully wrestled with the politics of identity and representation. A key example was *Native portraits n.19897* (1998), an installation by artist Lisa Reihana on level four at Te Papa (Figure 5.10). This quirky video-*waharoa* echoed and responded to Neke Kapua's 1906 *waharoa* on level two and Ross Hemera's 1998 work at the entrance to 'Mana Whenua'. In a bold use of new media, Reihana looked back to the past, to the museum and its archive and reimagined the ways Māori people and their culture were and are represented. The monitors depicted a bewildering array of images of Māori that blurred past and present, tradition and modernity, Māori and Pakeha – an example is a disconcerting shot of a Māori woman in Victorian dress sporting a *tā moko* and staring

Figure 5.10 Lisa Reihana *Native Portraits n.19897* (1998) video discs,
audio discs, video monitors, museum cases, in the exhibition 'Facing It',
Te Papa, 1998 (with the permission of Lisa Reihana/Museum of New
Zealand Te Papa Tongarewa MA/1.028470).

back at the viewer. The *waharoa* framed Reihana's critical, postmodern 'portrait' of Māori identity today, and invited the visitor to enter future realms through a reassessment of the past and its legacy (Tamati-Quennell 1998).

'TAONGA ARE TREATED AS TAONGA': RESPONSES TO 'MANA WHENUA'

From the time that Te Papa opened in February 1998, it attracted unprecedented numbers of visitors. The new museum exceeded its annual target of 700,000 in three months. One million visitors went in five months, and over two million in the first year (AR 1999). Three and a half years after opening, the national museum boasted a total attendance in excess of 5.5 million people (*Sunday Star Times*, 21 October 2001). In terms of audience, it was immediately noticeable from statistics that a broad cross-section of New Zealanders visited Te Papa. Its popularity with Māori visitors was truly groundbreaking: they constituted thirteen per cent of New Zealand visitors – and in some quarters up to fifteen per cent – equivalent to their proportion of the general population (AR 1999). According to exit surveys, 'Mana Whenua' itself attracted a very high proportion of Māori visitors at seventeen per cent (McCarthy 2001: 18).[6] Exhibition evaluation revealed that over forty per cent of the New Zealand visitors to 'Mana Whenua' were Māori.[7] In comparison with earlier figures for Māori museum visitation, this study proves conclusively that previous trends have been reversed and Māori people have taken up museum going on an unprecedented scale.

Despite, or because of, this success there was continuing debate about aspects of display at Te Papa. There were negative reviews from critics who disliked the innovations and the unconventional display of art, calling the museum a 'giant amusement arcade', a 'glitzy expo' or the 'MTV of museums' (*New Statesman*, 1 February 1999; Chamberlain 2000: 50). As anthropologist Michael Goldsmith (2001) observed, criticizing Te Papa was almost a national sport. Reviews from art critics and cultural commentators were more likely to be negative, whereas lay people tended to be more positive. 'Everybody hates Te Papa', commented the *Evening Post*, 'except the public' (*EP*, 5 October 1998). In New Zealand, as elsewhere, conflict over museum display was now a part of the 'culture wars', a debate that was in the end about the ownership of culture (Heller 1997; Cossons 2000; Millard 2001).

Challenged by the postmodern collapse of art into culture, late modernist artists and writers complained that Pakeha culture was taken off its pedestal whereas Māori objects were reified and put back on one (Harper 1997; Williams 2003; Wedde 2004). Some critics compared 'Mana Whenua' favourably to the visual culture exhibition 'Parade' because they thought *taonga* were treated with the respect art objects were not (Brown 2002). Others noted a more solemn and reverential tone in the Māori exhibitions, in contrast to the postmodern irony of the art and history exhibitions, that marked them off as the spiritual centre of bicultural museumhood (Goldsmith 2003; Dyson 2005). The display of contemporary art and Māori life today, however, did not always meet with the approval of many Pakeha visitors who preferred to see Māori art and culture along more conventionally 'traditional' lines. The contemporary *marae* designed by Cliff Whiting (Figure 5.11), *Te Hono ki Hawaiki*, was a brightly coloured, custom-wood construction that functioned as a venue for welcome ceremonies and performances. Some visitors accepted this 'souped-up and modernised marae' (*The Taranaki Daily News*, 14 February 1998) but many felt it was tacky, gaudy or demeaning in contrast with the 'real' Māori art on display in 'Mana Whenua' (Watson 1997: fn. 176).

The presentation of objects as *taonga* in 'Mana Whenua' had a largely positive reception from mainstream critics (*EP*, 10 February 1998). At times, however, critics felt uncomfortable with old objects placed alongside contemporary art, popular culture or technology. One spoke of the 'beauty' of these 'extraordinary objects' but felt they needed 'more space in

Figure 5.11 *Te Hono Ki Hawaiki* on the contemporary marae with
Dalvanius Prime and the Pātea Māori Club, Te Papa, February 1998
(Museum of New Zealand Te Papa Tongarewa F.4836).

which to breathe' (Faggetter 1998). The *Sunday Star Times* noted the contrast between the
waharoa standing 'regally' on level 2 and the flashing neon sign for the commercial rides of
the 'Time Warp' and complained that it was difficult to tell 'whether an artefact was a modern
reproduction or an ancient taonga' (14 October 2001). An English critic complained of the
'insult' to Māori because the 'finest examples of their magnificent woodcarving art ... are
placed in the midst of the household detritus of modern New Zealand' (*New Statesman*, 1
February 1999). When these comments were repeated by Finlay MacDonald in a negative
Listener editorial (5 February 2000), a series of letters defended Māori initiatives at the new
museum. In one, Danny Butt pointed out that Te Papa's attempts at biculturalism, whatever
their faults, 'makes the *Listener* look pretty honkey [white] in comparison...' and was an
improvement on 'the good old days of dusty glass cases that so many Pakeha critics yearn

for'. Butt noted the irony of quoting an English critic on insults to Māori: 'Why not ask the owners of the cultural material in question?' (*Listener*, 26 February 2000). The following letter from Māori readers gave an indication of what these 'owners' thought:

> So the white folks at the *Listener* are getting antsy about Te Papa's success? What a surprise! We know it may be hard to bear, but New Zealanders are well travelled and well educated and we vote with our feet... But, of course, what really upsets the snobs and the cynics is seeing so many of us brown faces visiting the place. Such a change from the usual gallery experience, where a token Maori is employed as a curator or guard and the small coterie of visitors are a nice, safe pale colour. (*Listener*, 26 February 2000)

There were a range of responses by Māori critics and academics to the Māori exhibitions at Te Papa. Ranginui Walker (2001: 43) approved of the display of *Te Hau ki Tūranga* as a 'cultural icon'. Witi Ihimaera complained that it had been sidelined by the new *marae*, and that its 'forbidding tapu' was 'diminished' by the audio-visual gadgets of a 'Virtual village' (Ihimaera and Ellis 2002: 47). One particular debate about the Moriori exhibit (Figure 5.7) threw into relief different views about the authority of museum scholarship. The Moriori people of the Chatham Islands, some 800 km east of New Zealand, are closely related to Māori but have long been misrepresented either as their primitive forebears or as having 'died out'. This controversy erupted when Peter Munz, Emeritus Professor of History at Victoria University, criticized the labels which did not mention the 1835 massacre of Moriori by Taranaki Māori, calling it a 'historical distortion' and 'political propaganda' (Munz 2000: 13–16). Munz was in turn attacked by a Māori scholar, Professor Mason Durie of Massey University, who advocated the validation of *mātauranga Māori* (Māori knowledge) on a par with Western systems of knowledge (Solomon cited in Williams 2003: 20). Moriori leader Māui Solomon told museum staff that they chose not to dwell on this episode simply because they did not want to be depicted yet again as 'victims' (Hakiwai 2000). Māori staff were unrepentant, and did not see it as a deliberate 'omission'. If *iwi* were genuinely 'empowered to tell their story', explained Hakiwai (2000), 'and if they chose certain things that were important to them and not others ... so be it'.

These public debates highlighted the difference between popular responses and those of critics, whether Māori or Pakeha. There was a tendency for academic critics to simply 'read off' meanings from museum exhibits, resulting in interpretations that did not take into account the diverse responses of people who actually saw them (Thomas 1996: 297; Witcomb 2003: 14). Surveys suggested meanwhile that 'Mana Whenua' was being given a very enthusiastic response by visitors despite the troubled comments of a few individuals. There was undoubtedly genuine interest from *iwi* in 'Mana Whenua'. This was reflected on several occasions when tribal groups accompanied the transfer of their *taonga* from Buckle Street to the new museum. Video footage of the series of well-attended ceremonial openings in late 1997 (among them Rongowhakaata, Ngāti Pikiao, and Te Āti Haunui-ā-Pāpārangi) show *iwi* groups interacting with their *taonga* in a form of communal celebration (Jodie Wylie video tapes 1995–7, TPA MU 215). Tamarapa felt the partnership with *iwi* gave

'Mana Whenua' an 'endorsement' because they felt that it was 'their' exhibition. She believes that this prompted people to visit the exhibition after opening (2000). During my own experience of working in the exhibition from 1998 to 2000, I often saw tribal groups visit their *taonga*. On one occasion I took a Kura Kaupapa (Māori immersion primary school) with accompanying adults from the East Coast to *Te Hau ki Tūranga*. They did not seem to be much interested in specific aspects of display or the details of the house's history, but used it as an *aide memoire* to teach the children. They sang a famous *waiata tawhito*, 'Pine pine te kura', and listened to a speech by one of their *kaumātua* about *tīpuna* depicted in the *poupou*. Response to *taonga* took the form of affirming group identity and *mana*, often through the act of performing *whakapapa* connections.

In terms of the partnership with tribal groups, audience research suggests there was a favourable response to 'Te Aupōuri iwi'. In focus groups and interviews, respondents said that the exhibition was a successful statement of tribal identity, which had raised the profile of their people on the national and international stage, and that it spoke to current political developments such as the progress of their claim before the Waitangi Tribunal (McCarthy 2004: 323). In addition to confirming that Te Papa's Māori exhibitions attracted a broad cross-section of New Zealanders and a disproportionately large proportion of Māori, visitor research allows us to be much more precise about the overall response of Māori visitors to Te Papa. In contrast to the underrepresentation of ethnic minorities elsewhere (*Audience Research* 2000), Te Papa was seen as fun, accessible, and family-friendly for Māori visitors. The data from the Te Papa Visitor Profile showed that almost ninety per cent of Māori visitors rated their experience at Te Papa as 'good to excellent' and gave it an average rating of eight out of ten (Kay Haughey, personal communication, 25 October 2001). Many of these Māori were new museum visitors. Only twenty per cent of Māori visitors to the exhibition said they had been to the Museum in Buckle Street (McCarthy 2001: 54). This new-found enthusiasm for museums is reflected in comments from Māori respondents. A homesick young woman from the Tainui tribe in the Waikato told the interviewer that the museum was good, 'cos I'm away from home but home's right here' (McCarthy 2000: respondent no. 81).

My own research, a summative evaluation comprising interviews with over 150 visitors, showed that Māori visitors in particular responded very favourably to the exhibition (McCarthy 2001: 14). Through interviews with visitors, summative evaluation attempted to provide a more complete record of how visitors actually looked at and interpreted 'Mana Whenua'.[8] While confirming that the exhibition successfully engaged with Māori patrons, it did throw up issues which were dealt with in a redesign in late 2001; including changes to the lighting, labels, and the number of *taonga* on display. The rethink dealt with the problem of contemporaneity by expanding the segment on *Te Aurere* and the current revival of *waka* culture. The designers, Smiler and Walmsley, introduced more variety into the colour schemes and layout in order to 'spice' it up (Smiler, personal communication 14 December 2001).

The research revealed three main findings. First, the exhibition was clearly very popular with Māori visitors, who thought it was better than other Māori exhibitions they had seen before. Second, there was a strong perception from visitors overall, but particularly Māori, that there had been changes in the museum display of Māori culture, with the advent of a more open, accessible style that was more culturally appropriate. Third, one of the major reasons visitors liked the exhibition was the clear sense of *iwi* involvement, which they felt was communicated in the installation design. The comments of Māori visitors, while similar to those of visitors overall, at times reveal distinctive Māori responses to the presentational style of 'Mana Whenua' and a positive reaction to the way that, as one visitor put it, 'taonga are treated as taonga' (McCarthy 2001: 63). Again, the detail of these responses reinforce the idea that what is on display is less the objects than their relationship to the people who identify with them.

Overall, eighty-four per cent of visitors, and an even higher proportion of Māori, thought 'Mana Whenua' was better than exhibitions they had seen at Buckle Street or at other museums. Many commented postively on what they saw as the updated installation design of the exhibition, saying that it was more in keeping with Māori values and attitudes towards *taonga* than other museums or exhibitions in the past. One Māori visitor, for example, suggested that 'the way the stuff has been exhibited gives it the deference it deserves, the honour. Each piece has been exhibited like a jewel' (McCarthy 2001: 49). Another Māori visitor said 'Mana Whenua' was:

> Less cluttered, more dynamic, less static. Objects have a context, that's what the ethos of the museum and education do, whereas the traditional way was to collect large numbers of things for the narrow interest of specific people. (2001: 58)

Another Māori visitor contrasted the old-fashioned, scientific displays of the past with the approach in 'Mana Whenua', which provided more context for Māori visitors:

> What this has created here is space ... before it was categorised and closed in. This is open – you can sit and look as long as you like. You've got the Pacific here too – that helps us identify [ourselves, helps us to] trace our tūpunas back ... [there's a] relationship. (2001: 58)

Māori responses often mentioned the access to *taonga* that they observed in 'Mana Whenua.' 'You can get a lot closer,' responded a Māori visitor, things were 'not glassed off. You can feel a part of it, immersed in it' (2001: 63). One Māori commented that, compared to Auckland Museum, there was 'a different feeling ... a feeling that I wanted to go into it.' They enjoyed sitting inside *Mākōtukutuku* because 'it made us feel we were in that time' (McCarthy 2000: respondent no. 38). Another Māori visitor commented that *Te Hau ki Tūranga* 'draws you into it ... you feel part of it. Touching is allowed' (McCarthy 2001: 59). Compared to old museum displays where they 'plonk the poupou all in a row', it was felt 'Mana Whenua' treated carvings like 'my tīpuna ... I want people to know where they're from' (2001: 63). One Pakeha-Māori couple contrasted what they saw as the objective approach of the Canterbury Museum displays with the inclusive character of 'Mana Whenua', which was 'far superior':

> Canterbury Museum felt like Pakeha explaining something they didn't understand. There wasn't a valuing of those people. Canterbury Museum tries to stand back and look, and look from afar. Here you can enter right into it. Here it's in a context of things Māori ... this is a welcoming atmosphere. (2001: 59)

The single most popular exhibit was *Te Hau ki Tūranga*, which was seen by ninety per cent of Māori visitors. 'It's so imposing. It looked big, it has mana', commented one Māori visitor, when asked why she was drawn to it. When prompted as to why it has mana, she commented; 'Cos it's set up on the steps [it] has more mana' (2001: 36). The other houses and large carved *taonga*, *Mākōtukutuku*, *Te Tākinga*, *Te Aurere* and *Teremoe*, were also popular, as were the *pounamu* and *kākahu* segments, but many Māori mentioned a range of *taonga* as the highlights of the exhibition because of some personal connection. Often a particular *taonga* was chosen, not for aesthetic reasons but simply because it was from the respondent's own *iwi*. One Māori visitor, for example, liked the 'meeting house' most about the exhibition because 'it's from Gisborne where I'm from' (2001: 36). Māori visitors from the far north often mentioned exhibits in the Te Aupōuri exhibition as their favourites (2001: 49). One young Māori woman articulated the Māori sense of connection to place captured in a video which talked 'about Mt Hikurangi and the land being theirs forever.' 'I am Waikato', she said, 'the river is me' (McCarthy 2000: respondent no. 81).

Most visitors thought that the way Māori art and culture had been displayed in museums had changed (McCarthy 2001: 61). 'The people whose taonga it was are consulted, in a respectful way', one Māori explained, 'it appears that there is an effort to protect, preserve and present in ways which are appropriate' (2001: 64). Other visitors remarked on what they saw as a move from an objective mode of display to something more intimate. 'Taonga are more open to touch, not behind glass cases,' said another Māori visitor. Another thought there were 'more taonga around' in museums now, and that they were not behind glass but 'out to mirimiri'. 'There appears to be a greater sensitivity to the cultural needs of the taonga presented', agreed a Māori visitor, because 'Māori customs, art, etc. recognise Māori validity' (2001: 63–5). Even Pakeha visitors agreed that now Māori objects were represented 'much more from a Māori point of view' (McCarthy 2000: respondent no. 90). For instance:

> Things used to be in glass cases with little information, in English not Māori. 'European displays of foreign objects.' There was no appreciation of Māori tikanga... It was like exhibiting dead taonga. They were objects presented in isolation. There is now a strong effort to display in a true context. (2000: respondent no. 90)

Māori visitor comments on this point make it clear that changes in the museum display of Māori culture were a question of *mana*, and were closely connected with social changes in the wider society:

Māori are a lot more free with their taonga and their reo than they used to be – they used to keep their stuff back. Because of the change of the government, the freeing up of the museum issues that were on the backburner, the pressure groups have said: 'We are here. This is what we're about.' People are now more aware that it's a taonga, a treasure rather than an item there for a few. These taonga are treated as taonga here. (McCarthy 2001: 63)

The summative evaluation also shows conclusively that Māori visitors saw 'Mana Whenua' as a Māori exhibition, that is, as an exhibition *by* Māori rather than simply *about* Māori. It was, in the words of one Māori visitor, a case of 'Māori talking about Māori.' Another Māori visitor commented that the 'information seems to come from Māori people themselves not museum curators' (2001: 64). Another thought this was to be expected given the changes in Māori-Pakeha relations: '...if the iwi didn't participate you wouldn't have all these taonga. Today a lot of iwi are reluctant to give up taonga cos a lot of it has been lost. Now it's a partnership thing' (2001: 49). The following comment suggests that partnership is a matter of the museum adopting Māori ways of dealing with their *taonga*, thus ensuring a welcoming environment for Māori visitors: 'People are named. Tikanga is there. People have expressed a wish how their taonga are to be treated and the museum has done it ... It's a comfortable space (2001: 49).

The partnership approach was the strongest message but 'Mana Whenua' was not so successful at getting across the point about Māori culture being living and dynamic. Research shows that most visitors thought the exhibition was about Māori in the past not today. A Māori visitor said they thought 'Mana Whenua' was about 'Māori people and how they used to live' (McCarthy 2000: respondent no. 29), and another saw it as 'just historic stuff...' (2000: respondent no. 1). Other Māori read the exhibition differently, however. Some praised the combination of old and new, and thought the exhibition showed how Māori had survived in the modern world. Far from seeing old objects as problematic in representing an idealized past, Māori visitors seemed to see it as something that gave them and their culture strength in the current context. One 'felt a lot of pride going through the exhibition, and feel that it is still a living history, more so today' (McCarthy 2001: 46). Once again, material culture is a symbol of *mana* and ongoing cultural vitality for many Māori today. 'Our Māori taonga are being preserved', said one Māori visitor. 'They are an example of what the past was like in order for us to treasure it' (2001: 47). At the close of the twentieth century, the distinctive Māori appropriation of 'traditional' heritage was directed toward the same aim as at the beginning of the century, the imagining of new futures through a negotiation with the modern and postmodern world.

Museum display in the contemporary period, as in the past, was a complex and multi-faceted phenomenon. Māori museum staff saw themselves as being in the front lines of a struggle for cultural sovereignty, making the most of openings in museum practice created by the new museology. After 'taonga' appeared in the previous decade, the 1990s was a period of continuing decolonization and the consolidation of this rearticulated indigenous category, partly unshackled from 'art.' There were tensions with new forms of postmodern Māori art, the notion of 'artefact' was now seen as old-fashioned, and *taonga* reigned supreme. In many ways, however, this latest stage of exhibitionary culture was little different as elements of art and artefact remained. In the 1990s Māori patronage was unquestionably integral to the discursive formation of *mana taonga* as can be seen in the parallel construction of Māori categories and discourses along with the appearance of Māori museum patrons.

'Mana Whenua' proved popular with visitors, and in particular the Māori visitors who began to attend the museum in large numbers. Some Pakeha found its 'conservative' cultural nationalism not to their taste but, understood in a wider social context, 'Mana Whenua' was the expression of a genuine Māori museum poetic which was governed as always by its politics. The exhibition adopted a classical modernist style that flirted with essentialist models of identity to bolster the case for separate Māori development. While in contemporary art, Māori engaged with postmodernism, this exhibition and its embrace by Māori represented a significant critique of postmodernism, and a demonstration of the limits of postmodern critique.

NOTES

1. In 1900 Māori comprised a tiny rural minority but by 2000 the *tangata whenua* were numerous (600,000 or fifteen per cent of the total), urbanized (eighty-three per cent in cities), industrialized and politicized (Belich 2001: 471–4).
2. For an explanation of these Māori customary concepts, see: Mead 2003; Barlow 1991; Salmond 1975.
3. In a recent interview, Hirini Mead (2006) referred to *taonga* as 'heritage items' (2006).
4. All exhibition documents are from TPA MU 361.
5. All video and label text is taken from: 'Mana Whenua' exhibition, Museum of New Zealand Te Papa Tongarewa, Wellington 1998.
6. That is to say those visitors randomly sampled as they were coming out of the exhibition (McCarthy 2001: 26).
7. For my audience research Māori ethnicity was treated as a matter of self-definition. Ethnic identity cannot be demarcated by a single boundary, being constituted by a number of variables including ethnicity, ancestry, and tribal affiliation (Levine 1999).
8. This form of audience research evaluates the outcomes of the exhibition by identifying the kinds of visitors who actually go and assesses how effective the exhibition has been with the intended audience in terms of its stated objectives (Screven 1976).

CONCLUSION: THE SUBALTERN SPEAKS

This book has considered the question of how and why the display of Māori culture changed so dramatically from the nineteenth century up to the beginning of the twenty-first century. The meeting house *Te Hau ki Tūranga*, for example, has been seen at various times as a symbol of chiefly *mana* (authority), a trophy, a curio, a specimen, an artefact, a model of arts and crafts, a national treasure, a masterpiece of primitive art, and then as a *taonga* (cultural treasure). By analysing exhibitions within their cultures of display, I have traced these transformations through different kinds of installation that shaped, and were shaped by, a wider network of social relations. In 1998, the house was reconstructed once more at Te Papa, this time with the participation of Rongowhakaata themselves. In its most recent incarnation, the *mana taonga* of the *wharenui* was to the fore – a Māori way of exhibiting Māori in which the poetics of museum display were governed by its politics. As the twenty-first century begins, what will the future hold for this meeting house? Since the report of the Waitangi Tribunal into the Tūranga (Gisborne) claim, the house has been the subject of delicate negotiations between the Rongowhakaata people and Te Papa. Will it remain at the museum, and undergo yet another transformation as the mode of installation design changes again? Or will it return to the people of Manutūke, and play a different role – the model perhaps for a future revival of the Gisborne school of carving or a symbol of tribal independence within Aotearoa/New Zealand?

Exhibiting Māori presents a different picture of indigenous people and museums to that rehearsed in postcolonial theory and repeated in local accounts of New Zealand museums. Contrary to the notion that Māori contact with museums began with 'Te Maori', I have shown that this exhibition had a long prehistory stretching back many years. Many instances of Māori interaction and involvement with exhibitions demonstrate again and again the presence rather than the absence of the *tangata whenua*. I have characterized the museum's expanding group of Māori visitors as patrons rather than simply audience. Like Friends organizations, business stakeholders and other interest groups, Māori patrons were not simply consumers of services but were closely bound up with the institution and its display of their culture. A key finding of this study is the relational nature of museums, how through their display material things can and do embody a living relation to living peoples.

The history of Māori participation in the colonial cultures of display shows a series of indigenous accommodations with Western museology, and Pakeha accommodations with an indigenous heritage movement. The story reveals surprising twists and turns. The commercial representation of Māori in the early colonial period, against expectations, was more benign than later ethnographic views. The early 1900s, the 1920s and early 1930s, and then the mid-1980s were high points of Māori participation. Under Hector (1865–1903) and Falla (1947–66) there was little contact with Māori, whereas under Hamilton (1903–13) and Yaldwyn (1980–9) the museum underwent significant change. Unfashionably, this account has given some weight to individual agency as well as social structure, so that influential actions of staff and patrons preclude over-determining the analysis.

Another feature of this genealogy is the continuity as well as the discontinuity. Although many years apart, the 'Te Maori' exhibition in 1986 and the Christchurch exhibition in 1906 were comparable social phenomenon with similar political messages for Māori people. Similarly, the spectacle of the 'new museum' can be seen in both the Māori Hall at the Dominion Museum in 1936, and the 'Mana Whenua' exhibition at Te Papa in 1998. The process of exhibiting Māori did not progress in a smooth line from ignorance to enlightenment but moved in fits and starts. Some may claim *taonga* had always been *taonga* but this study has shown that indigenous forms of display also have a history. Each visual category – from curio to *taonga* – appeared to be the definitive statement of the exhibitionary apparatus, only to be succeeded by another formulation as the interaction of objects, audience, practices and discourse was shuffled and reshuffled in each particular period. It is clear that Māori exhibitions today are not better or more progressive than their predecessors, and that current categories are merely the latest episode in an ongoing story. Whatever the latest trend in design, aesthetics or epistemology, the next phase might take place in museums run by Māori themselves on their own *marae*, the subject perhaps of the next stage of this genealogy.

In New Zealand today the clamour for repatriation may outstrip the ability or willingness of mainstream museums to meet the demands for Māori independence, or indeed Māori capacity to care for their own treasures. In the twenty-first century, indigenous people may well free themselves from Western obsessions with primitivism and identity only to fall foul of their own obsession with ownership (Brown 2003; Sissons 2005: 140–1; Appiah 2006). It is too early to say whether the new generation of Māori exhibitions represent a post-colonial accommodation of nation and native, or merely a crude inversion of the self/other equation that retains the same old Manichaean allegory of colonizer/colonized (Nederveen Pieterse 1997; Brunt in Erikson, Neumann and Thomas 1999). Simon During (1992) contends that it is the silence of the archive that leads to the production of homogenous and a-historical notions of indigenous tradition. But if the archive is *not* silent, as I show in this study, then traces of Māori responses to colonization recovered through a genealogy of display leave open the possibility not only of new Māori views of their own past but a different relationship between Pakeha and Māori. Indeed, as Sissons (2005: 154–5) points out, decolonization is a process that affects everybody, providing the opportunity for all parties to rearticulate their relations with one another.

Māori exhibitions in the year 2001 represented an updating of the political project that has occupied Māori since early in the previous century. Before they claimed a place within modernity by staging their past as heritage; now they are wrestling with postmodernity and globalization on their own terms. Not surprisingly, indigenous peoples are selective in this regard, preferring postcolonialism's critique of Western dominance to postmodernism's critique of representation. Though many first peoples have freed themselves of oppressive notions of authenticity that were themselves products of colonization, they are often unwilling to abandon cultural practices that are deemed untenable by mainstream Western critics. As Sahlins (1993: 18) reminds us, syncretism does not contradict indigenous claims of authenticity or autonomy but helps them to maintain a critical distance from global modernity. Neither completely assimilated by, or shut out of, colonial processes, contemporary indigenous society is 'beyond the space and time of colonial modernity and postmodernity' (Thomas 1999: 17).

To many indigenous peoples, the 'tyranny of post colonial theory' (Araeen, Cubitt and Sardar 2002: 336–43) and the postmodern obsession with hybridity were not unlike the old European stereotypes of ethnic authenticity – both maintained colonial distinctions and denied natives a postindigenous identity (Sissons 2005: 57). Though Western scholars caution against the re-enchantment of art and culture (Gell 1992; Thomas and Pinney 2001), why should indigenous people take any notice if fine art continues to avoid demystification? It is unlikely that the emerging Māori culture of display will defer to academic theory, design fashions or museological practice and it will almost certainly develop outside museums in the more open field of tourism and tribal cultural centres.

Postcolonial writing about museums often reproduces North Atlantic ideas formed in other contexts without modification. It overlooks submerged histories of indigenous resistance. Scholarship in this area requires a balance between such big factors as discourse and the sweep of history, as well as the small elements – material culture, cultural practices and individual agency. The methodology employed here contrasts with some cultural studies approaches to museums in combining social theory with archival research and interviews, thereby equipping researchers to create more nuanced scholarship. Comprehensive exhibition evaluation along with a detailed internal account of exhibition development provides an interpretation of display which avoids the pitfalls of much academic analysis that divorces theory from practice (McCarthy and Labrum 2005).

The particular way that issues of culture and display were inflected by colonization, race and nationhood in museums in the South Pacific are important not just for scholars and museum professionals in those countries. The case study I have presented is intended to reopen debate about postcoloniality and settler societies. It demands the re-examination of well-worn concepts of critical theory: strategic essentialism, the imbrication of Self and Other, the disingenuous invention of tradition, anthropology and its native interlocuters, and speaking subalterns. The work of Foucault, Bourdieu, Said and other scholars *can* be successfully applied to specific situations but must be tested out in the light of the evidence and not simply reiterated using the local as exemplars of the global. For example, this study has been informed by Bourdieu's theories of social distinction, yet its conclusions are rather less bleak and pessimistic about the possibility of change. Challenging their social exclusion, Māori mounted a response to Pakeha cultural capital that was as effective as their military and political resistance. Not content with being depicted as a 'dying race' at international exhibitions, Māori recast ethnographic exhibits as symbols of survival. Contemporary Māori art took its place in the art gallery, *taonga* were hailed as the art works of a 'great civilization' at the Metropolitan, and Te Papa was, in many ways, the 'National Maori Museum' that Carroll and Hamilton dreamed of.

This New Zealand case study therefore contains lessons for museum history and theory internationally. While the museum was itself a colonial artefact, it was never an unchallenged tool of settler rule and Māori always attempted to steer it towards their own ends. Māori responses to museums may not always have been enthusiastic but museum going has recently become a popular activity. Māori now go to museums because museums are more Māori. This may very well be an exception but it is a reminder that postsettler states should listen out for indigenous voices even when they are drowned out. It is a reminder, too, that social institutions are not impermeable, that power is fluid and contestable, and the process of colonization far from inevitable. If the museum, and indeed modernity itself, can be indigenized, then it should not be so difficult to envision an indigenous future.

APPENDIX

INSTITUTIONAL TITLES

The Colonial Museum (1865–1907)
The Dominion Museum (1907–72)
The National Art Gallery (1936–92)
The National Museum (1972–92)
The Museum of New Zealand Te Papa Tongarewa (1992–)

DIRECTORS OF THE NATIONAL MUSEUM

James Hector (1865–1903)
Augustus Hamilton (1903–13)
J. A. Thomson (1914–28)
W. B. Oliver (1928–47)
R. A. Falla (1947–66)
R.K. Dell (1966–80)
John Yaldwyn (1980–89)
Alan Baker (1990–93)
Cheryll Sotheran (1993–2001) and Cliff Whiting (1994–2000)

DIRECTORS OF THE NATIONAL ART GALLERY

E. D. Gore, secretary-manager (1936–48)
Stewart Maclennan (1948–69)
Melvin Day (1969–79)
Luit Bieringa (1980–90)
Jenny Harper (1990–3)

GLOSSARY

The following glossary is intended as an indicative guide only, and is compiled from major published sources, to which the reader is directed for further information. See: Williams (1971), Salmond (1975), Barlow (1991), Starzecka (1998), Neich (2001), Mead (2003).

amo – upright support posts at the end of gables on the front of the house
Aotearoa – modern Māori term for New Zealand
aroha – love, pity, show approval
atua – god, supernatural being

epa – small posts at the end wall of a house between *pou tahu* and *poupou*

haka – posture dance
hapū – subtribe or section of a large tribe
harakeke – flax
hei tiki – neck pendant in the form of a human figure
heke – rafter
heru – ornamental comb
hiki tapu – lift the tapu, ceremony for opening houses currently used for exhibitions (see also *tā i te kawa/kawanga whare*: Mead 2003: 361, 367)
hīnaki – eel pot
hoe – paddle
hui – meeting
Hori – colloquial term for Māori people, now considered impolite (also Hōri – George)
huia – extinct bird, tail feathers used as chiefly adornment

ihi – dread, fear, vitality
iwi – tribe, nation, people

kahu kiwi – kiwi feather cloak
kahu kurī – dogskin cloak
kai – food
kaiāwhina – guide (literally 'helper')

kāinga – home, village (unfortified)

kaiārahi – guide (literally one who leads)

kaitaka – cloak made of fine flax with ornamental border

kaitiaki – guardian, word designating Māori curators or other museum staff (literally one who cares)

kaiwhakairo – carver

kākaho – native reed used in *tukutuku* lattice work and the battens of a house

kākahu – garment, clothes

karakia – incantation, prayer

karanga – call of welcome to visitors in *pōwhiri* ceremony

kaumātua – elder, old man or woman

kaupapa – plan, proposal, policy, reason

kauri – native tree

kawa – cultural protocols (see *tikanga*)

kawakawa – green shrub

kete – flax basket

kiwi – native species of bird

kōauau – nose flute

koha – present, gift given at *pōwhiri*

kōiwi tangata – human bones

kōrere – drinking funnel

kōrero – say, speak, talk, conversation, story (Williams 1971: 141–2)

korowai – cloak ornamented with black tassles

kōruru – carved gable mask of a house

kōwhaiwhai – painted pattern on house rafters

kūaha/kūwaha – gateway, doorway of storehouse

kuia – old woman, grandmother

kupu – word, talk, saying, message (Williams 1971: 157)

maihi – carved gables on the front of a house

mana – power, authority, respect, prestige (Barlow and Williams 1991: 60–2)

manaakitanga – the hosting of visitors

manaia – carved figure in which the face and/or body is in profile (Neich 2001: 339)

mana motuhake – separate *mana*, independence

mana tangata – human authority, the power acquired by an individual based on skills in a particular field

mana taonga – the power and authority associated with the possession of *taonga*

mana whenua – the power associated with the possession of lands (Barlow 1991: 60–2)

manuhiri – visitors

mānuka – small native tree ('tea tree')

Māori – person of Māori descent, indigenous to Aotearoa New Zealand (Williams 1971: 179)

Māoritanga – explanation or meaning (Williams 1971: 179), in modern times denotes *Māoriness, Māori* culture (Salmond 1975: 1)

marae – space in front of meeting house, can also refer generally to all the community facilities around the house

marae ātea – space in front of meeting house where welcome ceremony takes place

māripi – knife

matapihi – window

mātauranga – knowledge

mauri – spark of life, life essence

mere – short flat club or cleaver often made of greenstone

mihi – greet, acknowledge

mirimiri – rub, stroke

moa – extinct species of native bird

mokamokai – dried human head often tattooed

mokemoke – solitary, lonely

mōkihi – raft made of reeds or rushes

moko – incised body adornment, tattoo

Moriori – the indigenous people of the Chatham Islands 800km East of New Zealand, descended from the same Polynesian settlers as the Māori

muka – processed flax prepared for weaving

ngutukākā – climbing plant, name of painted pattern in house decoration

oha – relic, keepsake

pā – fortified village (sometimes anglicized as 'pah'), former name for *marae* complex

paepae – threshold of house, line of *kaumātua* at welcome ceremony

Pākehā – person of European descent, as opposed to Māori

Papa – short for *Papatūānuku,* mother earth

papa – earth, ground, flat surface such as slab, board or rock

papahou – form of Māori treasure box from northern New Zealand

pare – lintel over a door or window

pātaka – storehouse

patu – short club

patu onewa – stone club

pāua – brightly coloured sea shell (abalone)

pepeha – proverb, saying (see also *whakataukī*)

piupiu – skirt made from flax

pou – post, pole

pounamu – greenstone, jade (New Zealand nephrite)

poupou – carved side wall post or slab of a house

poutahu – central post of front wall inside a house

poutokomanawa – central freestanding post inside a house supporting the ridgepole

poutuarongo – central post of rear wall inside a house

pōwhiri – welcome ceremony

pūkana – exaggerated facial gesture used in *haka* etc.

punga – anchor

pūtorino – bugle flute

rākau momori – dendriglyphs, or carvings in the bark of a living tree

rākau whakapapa – genealogy staff

rangatahi – youth, young people

rangatira – chief

rangatiratanga – chieftainship, chiefly authority, power or sovereignty

rauawa – strakes of a canoe

raupō – native bullrush used for thatching etc.

rawa – goods, property

rei niho – ear pendent made from the ivory of sea mammal

taiaha – two-handled fighting or ceremonial staff

taihoa – wait, by and by

tangata – adult person (sing.), people (pl.)

tangata whenua – people of the land, indigenous people (Māori)

tangi, tangihanga – funeral ceremony (Barlow 1991: 120–4)

tāniko – ornamental border of a cloak

taonga – property procured by the spear (Lee and Kendell 1820) property, treasure (Tregear 1891) property, anything highly prized (Williams 1971) highly prized object (Mead 2003)

taonga tuku iho – treasures handed down (literal), gift of the ancestors, precious heritage (Mead 2003)

tapu – sacred, set apart (Barlow 1991: 125–29)

tātua – belt, girdle

tauihu – carved stern post of a war canoe

tauira – example, copy, pattern, pupil

taurapa – carved prow of a war canoe

Te Papa Tongarewa – a receptacle of treasured possessions (Māori name for Museum of New Zealand)

tekoteko – freestanding carved figure, usually at the front apex of a house *tewhatewha* – long-handled club

tikanga – customary rules or habits, set of beliefs associated with Māori cultural practices and procedures (see *kawa* Mead 2003: 8, 11–12)

tiki – carved figure of human form

tikitiki – topknot of hair

tiriti – treaty

tohunga – skilled person, priest, expert

toki – adze blade

tongarewa, tongarerewa – variety of greenstone, ear ornament, something precious (adjective)

tōtara – native timber favoured for carving

tukutuku – stitched latticework panels between posts in a house interior

tūmeke – startle, modern slang approximating to the English phrase 'too much!'

tūpāpaku – corpse

tupuna/tipuna – ancestor

wahaika – short wooden club

waharoa – gateway

waiata – song

waiata-ā-ringa – action songs, also called *Kapa haka*

waiata tawhito – ancient songs

wairua – soul, spirit, spirituality

waka – canoe, vessel or container

waka huia – carved feather box, treasure box

waka taua – war canoe

waka tiwai – small canoe without attached sides, usually river canoe

waka tūpāpaku – burial chest for bones and human remains

wana – inspire fear, awe, sublimity

wehi – fearsomeness, awe, respect

whai – string games

whaikōrero – oration, formal speech

whakairo – to ornament with a pattern (Williams 1971), in modern usage refers to wood carving generally

whakamaumahara – remembrance, memorial

whakapapa – genealogy

whakataukī, whakatauākī – proverb, saying

whakawae – door jamb

whānau - family

whare – house

whare kai – dining room

wharenui – big house
wharepuni – small dwelling house
whare rūnanga – meeting house
whare wānanga – school of learning
whare whakairo – carved house
whāriki – mat
whenua – land, afterbirth
whiri – plaited hem of cloak

urupā – burial ground, cemetery

BIBLIOGRAPHY

PRIMARY SOURCES

CORRESPONDENCE, FILES AND OTHER ARCHIVAL MATERIAL

MUSEUM OF NEW ZEALAND TE PAPA TONGAREWA ARCHIVES, WELLINGTON

Major series consulted as follows (for details of file items see in text references):

MU 1 Dominion Museum: Registered files 1913–49.
MU 2 Dominion Museum: Registered files 1918–77.
MU 5 National Museum: Registered files 1976–89.
MU 6 National Art Gallery: Miscellaneous exhibitions.
MU 7 Dominion Museum: Cuttings re museums and art galleries 1926–8.
MU 13 Colonial Museum: Outwards correspondence letter books 1865–1904.
MU 14 Colonial/Dominion Museum: Subject files 1880–1969.
MU 15 National Museum, Betty McFadgen: Correspondence files, 1967–91.
MU 16 Dominion/National Museum: General subject files 1885–1991.
MU 28 National Museum, John Yaldwyn: Correspondence 1980–7.
MU 29 National Museum: General file Te Maori 1984–7.
MU 30 National Museum: Te Maori 1981–6.
MU 32 National Museum: McFadgen/Te Maori publicity 1984–7.
MU 33 National Museum: McFadgen/Te Maori newspaper clippings 1982–7.
MU 62 National Museum: Arapata Hakiwai 'Taonga Maori' general files 1988–90.
MU 63 National Museum: Hakiwai 'Taonga Maori' visitors' books 1989–90.
MU 75 National Museum: Yaldwyn 'Taonga Maori' exhibition files 1986–90.
MU 82 Colonial Museum: Hamilton Maori art publication 1877–98.
MU 83 Colonial Museum: Hamilton Maori related scrapbooks c.1890–9.
MU 94 Colonial Museum: Registered inwards correspondence c.1871–1912.
MU 95 Colonial Museum: Registered inwards correpondence 1884–1913.
MU 130 Colonial Museum: Visitors' books 1868–99.
MU 136 Colonial/Dominion Museum: Christchurch Exhibition 1906–7.
MU 144 Dominion Museum: Hamilton diaries 1905, 1909, 1913.
MU 147 Colonial Museum: Hector & Hamilton miscellaneous inwards correspondence.
MU 152 Dominion Museum: Miscellaneous Hamilton correspondence 1903–13.
MU 157 Dominion Museum: Maori related clippings c.1910–51.

MU 158 Colonial Museum: Subject files 1904–7.

MU 160 Dominion Museum: Index of Maori terms c.1910–13.

MU 188 Colonial Museum: Hector registered correspondence 1870s–1880s.

MU 203 Dominion Museum: Miscellaneous files on new building Buckle Street 1926–36.

MU 206 Colonial/Dominion Museum: Hamilton loose papers c.1903–13.

MU 207 Dominion Museum: Thomson miscellaneous files 1914–28.

MU 208 Dominion Museum: Oliver miscellaneous files 1928–47.

MU 215 Museum of New Zealand building project, Wylie videos c.1995–7.

MU 218 National Museum: Designs for Maori Hall 1970s–1980s.

MU 240–268 National Museum: Director's reports, National Museum Council 1983–8.

MU 286 New Zealand Institute: Published proceedings and transactions 1868–1904.

MU 289 Museum of New Zealand: videotapes of related events c.1992–6.

MU 361 Museum of New Zealand: Project office exhibition development documents

MU 465 Colonial Museum: CD ROMs vols 1–9 of tissue letter books 1865–1905.

MU 487 National Museum: Te Maori general file.

MU 496 National Museum: 'Nga taonga o te Motu' submissions 1986–7.

MU 504 National Museum: Temporary exhibitions 1980s.

ALEXANDER TURNBULL LIBRARY, WELLINGTON

Files consulted include:

A.C. Barker museum album, PAI-q-166-052.

Elsdon Best misc. notebooks c.1914, ATL Ms 188, 189, 190, 197, 199.

Samuel Carnell collection, PAColl-3979, G 19389-1/1.

James Cowan collection, C 1140.

Herbert Deverill albums, G4706 ½.

T.E. Donne's scrapbook, qms 0622.

T.W. Downes papers, Mss micro-0109.

Augustus Hamilton papers, qMS-0906.

L.B. Inch, 'History of the Dominion Museum 1936', Ms 1070.

Walter Mantell family papers, Ms 0305.

D.L. Mundy photograph albums, PA1-f-042.

W.J. Phillipps, Ms papers 4316.

Preston album, PA 1-0-423-05-1.

Larry Pruden papers, Ms 6664-15.

Sebley photographs albums, ATL PA4-1063 and PA4-1361.

James Stack, Ms papers 2778.

Henry Stowe papers, Mss 006-63.

K.A. Webster, Ms papers 3522.

Utiku collection, photo album F180916 ½

Williams early Maori imprint, 709a. and P box q 499M.

ARCHIVES NEW ZEALAND TE RUA MAHARA O TE KAWANATANGA, WELLINGTON

Series consulted include:

AALZ Dominion Museum
   Miscellaneous files.
MA Native Office/Maori Affairs
   Series 1, 1906/1413 Maori antiquities.
   Series 5, Correspondence.
IA Colonial Office/Internal Affairs
   Series 1, Correspondence Colonial Secretary's Office 1865–79.
   Series 4, Registered files Colonial Secretary's Office.
   Series 25, International exhibitions, newspaper clippings.
   Series 29, International exhibitions.
TO Department of Tourism and Health Resorts
   Series 1, Carving 1902–59.
   Series 1/20, Miscellaneous correspondence.
AJZ Maori Purposes Fund Board
   W4644/27 9/5/63 'Te Maori' exhibition 1983–4.
   W4644/6 2/2/15 'Te Maori' art exhibition 1987.
AAAC Department of Foreign Affairs/External Relations and Trade
   W5158/190 MPO 333 'Te Maori' exhibition 1984–5.
AAQT Communicate New Zealand/National Publicity Studios
ACC 3537 Tourist & Publicity photographic collection.

HOCKEN COLLECTIONS, UARE TAOKA O OTAKOU UNIVERSITY OF OTAGO, DUNEDIN

Scrapbook relating to the New Zealand and South Seas Exhibition 1889–90 Ms 0451/038.
Dr T.M. Hocken papers Journals, notebooks and letters Misc Ms 210
Jock McEwan, 'The future of Māori culture', Hocken lecture c. 1972 Misc Ms 0423
Hone Tuwhare, Convenor's report May 29, 1974 New Zealand Conference of Māori Artists and
   Writers: Papers Misc Ms 210
James Hector papers Ms 0445–4/16

AUCKLAND MUSEUM TAMAKI PAENGA HIRA, AUCKLAND

Augustus Hamilton papers Ms 131
Auckland Museum Annual Reports 1890–1914

OFFICIAL REFERENCE WORKS

AJHR – Appendices to the Journals of the House of Representatives, Wellington: Government Printer,
   1867–1902.
AGMANZ Journal – Art Gallery and Museums Association of New Zealand Journal, 1969–89,
   Wellington: Art Gallery and Museums Association of New Zealand.

AR – Annual Reports (of the Museum of New Zealand Te Papa Tongarewa and its predecessors) 1865–2001, Wellington.

NZPD – *New Zealand Parliamentary Debates*, 1900–40, Wellington: Government Printer.

TNZI – *Transactions and Proceedings of the New Zealand Institute*, 1868–1903, Wellington: New Zealand Institute.

SECONDARY SOURCES: BOOKS, ARTICLES, CATALOGUES, FILMS, INTERVIEWS, ETC.

A Concept for the Museum of New Zealand Te Papa Tongarewa (1991), Wellington: Project Development Board.

ADMISSIONS *Charges: The Issues* (1994), Wellington: The Museum of New Zealand Te Papa Tongarewa.

A Guidebook to the National Art Gallery (1969), Wellington: National Art Gallery.

ALLEN, N. (1998), 'Maori Vision and the Imperialist Gaze', in T. Barringer and T. Flynn (eds), *Colonialism and the Object: Empire, Material Culture and the Museum*, Birmingham: Routledge.

AMES, E. (2004), 'From the Exotic to the Everyday: The Ethnographic Exhibition in Germany', in V. R. Schwartz and J. Przyblyski (eds), *The Nineteenth Century Visual Culture Reader*, London and New York: Routledge.

ANDERSON, B. (1991), *Imagined Communities: Reflections on the Origin and Spread of Nationalism*, London and New York: Verso.

ANDERSON, N. (2000), Unpublished interview 28 July, Wellington: Te Papa Archives.

APPADURAI, A. (1986), *The Social Life of Things: Commodities in Cultural Perspective*, Cambridge: Cambridge University Press.

APPENDICES *to the Journals of the House of Representatives (AJHR)*, Wellington: Government Printer, 1867–1902

APPIAH, K. A. (2006), 'Whose Culture Is It?' *New York Review of Books*, 9 February, 53(2): 38–41.

ARAEEN, R., Cubitt, S. and Sardar, Z. (eds) (2002), *The Third Text Reader*, London and New York: Continuum.

ARMSTRONG, M. (1993), 'A Jumble of Foreigness: The Sublime Musayums of Nineteenth Century Fairs and Expositions', *Cultural Critique*, Winter: 199–250.

ATLICK, R. (1978), *The Shows of London*, Cambridge, MS and London: Harvard University Press.

AUDIENCE *Research with Aboriginal and Torres Strait Islander Communities* (2000), Canberra: National Museum of Australia.

BALLANTYNE, K. M. (1930), 'Notes on Maori Art', *Art in New Zealand*, 3(9): 39–47.

BALLANTYNE, T. (2001), *Orientalism and Race: Aryanism in the British Empire*, Basingstoke: Palgrave-Macmillan.

BALLARA, A. (1993), 'Mahupuku, Hamuera Tamahau 1837–1842? – 1904', *Dictionary of New Zealand Biography*, vol. 2. Retrieved 23 March 2006 from http://www.dnzb.govt.nz/.

—— (1996), 'Ratana, Tahupotiki Wiremu 1873–1939', *Dictionary of New Zealand Biography*, vol. 3. Retrieved 23 March 2006 from: http://www.dnzb.govt.nz/.

BANN, S. (1984), *The Clothing of Clio: A Study of the Representation of History in Nineteenth-century Britain and France*, Cambridge: Cambridge University Press.

—— (1998), 'Art History and Museums', in M. Cheetham, M. Holly and K. Moxley (eds), *The Subjects of Art History: Historical Objects in Contemporary Perspective*, Cambridge: Cambridge University Press.

—— (2003), 'The Return to Curiosity: Shifting Paradigms in Contemporary Museum Display', in A. McClellan (ed.) *Art and its Publics: Museum Studies at the Millennium*, Oxford: Blackwell.

BARBER, D. (1984), 'Te Maori', *Air New Zealand Pacific Way*, 4: 8–13, 18.

BARKER, E. (ed.) (1999), *Contemporary Cultures of Display*, New Haven, CT: Yale University Press in association with the Open University.

BARLOW, C. (1991), *Tikanga Whakaaro: Key Concepts in Maori Culture*, Auckland: Oxford University Press.

BARFIELD, T. (ed.) (1997), *The Dictionary of Anthropology*, Oxford: Blackwell.

BARROW, T. (1976), *A Guide to the Maori Meeting House: Te Hau ki Turanga*, Wellington: National Museum.

—— (1978), *Maori Art of New Zealand*, Wellington: Reed and UNESCO.

BEATSON, D. and Beatson, P. (1994), *The Arts in Aotearoa New Zealand*, Palmerston North: Sociology Department, Massey University.

BECKER, H. (1982), *Art Worlds*, Berkeley: University of California Press.

BELGRAVE, M. (2005), *Historical Frictions: Maori Claims and Reinvented Histories*, Auckland: Auckland University Press.

BELICH, J. (1996), *Making Peoples: A History of the New Zealanders from Polynesian Settlement to the End of the Nineteenth Century*, Auckland: Allen Lane, Penguin.

—— (2001), *Paradise Reforged: A History of the New Zealanders from the 1880s to the Year 2000*, Auckland: Allen Lane and Penguin.

BELL, L. (1992), *Colonial Constructs: European Images of Maori 1840–1914*, Auckland: Auckland University Press.

BELOVARI, S. (1997), 'Invisible in the White Field: The Chicago Field Museum's construction of Native Americans, 1893–1996', PhD thesis, Sociology, Urbana: University of Illinois.

BENEDICT, B. (1983), *The Anthropology of World's Fairs: San Francisco's Panama Pacific International Exposition of 1915*, London: Lowie Museum of Anthropology: Scolar Press.

BENEDICT, B. (1994), 'Rituals of Representation: Ethnic Stereotypes and Colonized People at World's Fairs', in R. Rydell and N. Gwinn (eds), *Fair Representations: World's Fairs and the Modern World*, Amsterdam: VU University Press.

BENNETT, T. (1995), *The Birth of the Museum: History, Theory, Politics*, London: Routledge.

—— (2004), *Pasts Beyond Memory: Evolution, Museums, Colonialism*, London and NY: Routledge.

—— EMMISON, M. and Frow, J. (1999), *Accounting for Tastes: Australian Everyday Cultures*, Melbourne: Cambridge University Press.

—— AND Carter, C. (eds) (2001), *Culture in Australia: Policies, Publics and Programs*, Cambridge: Cambridge University Press.

BEST, E. (1916), *Maori Storehouses and Kindred Structures: Dominion Museum Bulletin No.5*, Wellington: Government Printer.

—— (1924), *The Maori as He Was*, Wellington: Government Printer.

BINNEY, J. (1995), *Redemption Songs: A Life of Te Kooti Arikirangi Te Turuki*, Auckland: Auckland University Press, Bridget Williams Books.

—— BASSETT, J. and Olssen, E. (1990), *The People and the Land: Te Whenua me te Iwi: An Illustrated History of New Zealand 1820–1920*, Wellington: Allen & Unwin.

BISHOP, C. (1998), *Kei mura [sic] a mua – The Past Determines the Future: The Relationship between Museums and Maori People in New Zealand,* Museology and Globalisation, International Committee for Museology, Australia, Melbourne: International Council of Museums.

BLACK, B. (2000), *On Exhibit: Victorians and their Museums*, Charlottesville and London: University Press of Virginia.

BLACKLEY, R. (1987), 'The Exhibitions of Maori Art in Auckland 1884–85', *Antic*, 3: 116–22.

—— (1997), *Goldie*, Auckland: Auckland Art Gallery, David Bateman.

—— (2004), 'Centennial Exhibitions of Art', in W. Renwick (ed.), *Creating a National Spirit: Celebrating New Zealand's Centennial*, Wellington: Victoria University Press.

BLAKE, P. (1984), 'Sacred Treasures of the Maoris', *Time*, 24 September: 40–42, 64.

BLEDISLOE, C. B. (1934), *The Proper Function and Scope of a National Art Gallery and Museum: Address Given when Laying the Foundation-stone of the National Art Gallery and Dominion Museum at Wellington, 14 April 1934*, Auckland: Wilson & Horton.

BOUQUET, M. (2000), 'Figures of Relations: Reconnecting Kinship Studies and Museum Collections', in J. Carsten (ed.), *Cultures of Relatedness: New Approaches to the Study of Kinship*, Cambridge: Cambridge University Press.

BOURDIEU, P. (1984), *Distinction: A Social Critique of the Judgement of Taste*, London: Routledge & Kegan Paul.

—— (1995), *The Rules of Art: Genesis and Structure of the Literary Field*, Stanford, CA: Stanford University Press.

—— AND Darbel, A. (1991), *The Love of Art: European Art Museums and their Public*, Oxford and Cambridge: Polity Press, Blackwell.

BOSCH, A. (1974), 'Te Hau ki Turanga: A Rare Masterpiece', *Te Maori*, February, 6(2): 34–5.

BRASCH, C. (1954), 'Round the Galleries: Wellington', *Landfall*, 30 June: 127–9.

BROOKING, T. (1999), *Milestones: Turning Points in New Zealand History*, Palmerston North: Dunmore.

BROWN, D. (1995), 'Te Hau ki Turanga', *The Journal of the Polynesian Society*, March 105(1): 7–26.

BROWN, G. H. (1981), *New Zealand Painting 1940–1960: Conformity and Dissension,* Wellington: Queen Elizabeth II Arts Council of New Zealand.

—— AND Keith, H. (1969), *An Introduction to New Zealand Painting 1839–1967*, Auckland: Collins.

—— AND Keith, H. (1988), *An Introduction to New Zealand Painting 1839–1980*, 2nd edn. Auckland: David Bateman/Collins.

BROWN, M. (2000), 'The Public Art Gallery and the Construction of the Canon of Modernist New Zealand Art', *Predictions: The Role of Art at the End of the Millennium*, Victoria University of Wellington, Art Association of Australia and New Zealand.

BROWN, M. (2002), 'Representing the Body of the Nation: The Art Exhibitions of New Zealand's National Museum', *Third Text*, 16(3): 285–94.

BROWN, M. F. (2003), *Who Owns Native Culture?* Cambridge, MA: Harvard University Press.

BRUNT, P. (2004), 'Since "Choice!": Exhibiting the New Maori Art', in A. Smith and L. Wevers (eds), *On Display: New Essays in Cultural Studies*, Wellington: Victoria University Press.

BUCK, P. (1921), 'Maori Decorative Arts', *Transactions and Proceedings of the New Zealand Institute*, 53: 452–70.

—— (1924), 'The Evolution of Maori Clothing', *The Journal of the Polynesian Society*, 33(129): 25–47.

BURTON, A. (1996), 'Making a Spectacle of Empire: Indian Travellers in Fin-de-Siècle London', *History Workshop Journal*, 42: 127–46.

BUTLER, P. (1996), 'Te Maori Past and Present: Stories of Te Maori', MA thesis, Museum Studies, Palmerston North: Massey University.

BUTTS, D. (1984), 'Co-operative Redevelopment Planning: First Steps', *Art Gallery and Museums Association of New Zealand Journal*, December (15.4): 23–4.

—— (2003), 'Maori and Museums: The Politics of Indigenous Recognition', PhD thesis, Museum Studies, Palmerston North: Massey University.

BYRNES, G. (1990), 'Savages and Scholars: Some Pakeha Perceptions of the Maori 1890s–1920s', MA thesis, History, Hamilton: University of Waikato.

—— (2003), *The Waitangi Tribunal and New Zealand History*, Auckland: Oxford University Press.

CALHOUN, A. (2000), *The Arts and Crafts Movement in New Zealand, 1870–1940: Women Make their Mark*, Auckland: Auckland University Press.

CAMERON, F. (2000), 'Shaping Maori Identities and Histories: Collecting and Exhibiting Maori Material Culture at the Auckland and Canterbury Museums from the 1850s to the 1920s', PhD thesis, Social Anthropology, Palmerston North: Massey University.

CANNADINE, D. (2001), *Ornamentalism: How the British Saw Their Empire*, London: Allen Lane, Penguin.

CAPE, P. (1979), *New Zealand Painting since 1960: A Study in Themes and Developments*, Auckland: Collins.

CASSELLS, R. (1985), 'Maori "Taonga" and the art gallery/museum dichotomy', *Art Gallery and Museums Association of New Zealand Journal*, 16(1): 25–7.

CASEY, D. (2001), 'Indigenous Identities: Australian and International Perspectives', Museums Australia Conference, Perth, 25 April 2001, Museums Australia Conference paper archive. Retrieved 23 March 2006 from: www.museumsaustralia.org.au/.

CATALOGUE of the Colonial and Vienna Exhibition, held at Christchurch, Canterbury, New Zealand, 1872–3 (1873), Christchurch: Christchurch Times Office.

CATALOGUE of the Colonial Museum, Wellington New Zealand (1870), Wellington: Government Printer.

CHAKRABARTY, D. (2000), *Provincializing Europe: Postcolonial Thought and Historical Difference*, Princeton and Oxford: Princeton University Press.

CHAMBERLAIN, J. (2000), 'Museum Wars: Behind the Scenes at the Museums', *North and South*, April (169): 46–54.

CHAPMAN, W. R. (1985), 'Arranging Ethnology: AHLF Pitt Rivers and the Typological Tradition', in G. Stocking (ed.), *Objects and Others: Essays on Museums and Material Culture*, Madison: University of Wisconsin.

CLIFFORD, J. (1985), 'Histories of the Tribal and Modern', *Art in America*, April: 164–77.

—— (1988), *The Predicament of Culture: Twentieth-century Ethnography, Literature, and Art*, Cambridge, MA: Harvard University Press.

—— (1997), *Routes: Travel and Translation in the Late Twentieth Century*, Cambridge, MA: Harvard University Press.

—— (2001), 'Indigenous Articulations', *The Contemporary Pacific*, 13(2): 468–90.

COCKBURN, R. (1989), *The National Art Gallery and National Museum of New Zealand: An Evaluation of the Silver Miracle exhibition*, Wellington: Victoria University: Recreation and Leisure Studies Programme.

—— (1990), *The National Art Gallery and National Museum of New Zealand: An Evaluation of the Exhibition Treasures and Landmarks*, Wellington: Victoria University Recreation and Leisure Studies Programme.

COLLINGE, H.R. (1999), 'Changing Museology as Viewed Through the Life Biography of Kave, De Hine Aligi', MA thesis, Anthropology, Auckland: Auckland University.

COLONIAL and Indian Exhibition 1886: Official Catalogue (1886), London: William Clowes & Sons.

CONDLIFFE, J. B. (1971), *Te Rangi Hiroa; the Life of Sir Peter Buck*, Christchurch: Whitcombe and Tombs.

CONN, S. (1998), *Museums and American Intellectual Life, 1876–1926*, Chicago: University of Chicago Press.

CONTEMPORARY Maori Art (1976), Hamilton: Waikato Art Museum exhibition catalogue.

COOMBES, A. (1991), 'Ethnography and the Formation of National Cultural Identities', in S. Hiller (ed.), *The Myth of Primitivism: Perspectives on Art*, London: Routledge.

—— (1994), *Reinventing Africa: Museums, Material Culture and Popular Imagination in Late Victorian and Edwardian England*, London: Yale University Press.

CORBEY, R. (1995), 'Ethnic Showcases, 1870–1930', in J. Nederveen Pieterse and B. Parekh (eds), *The Decolonization of Imagination: Culture, Knowledge and Power*, London and New Jersey: Zed Books.

COSSONS, N. (2000), *Museums in the New Millennium*, Public lecture, 9 August, Wellington: Te Papa.

COWAN, J. (1910), *Official Record of the New Zealand International Exhibition of Arts and Industries Held at Christchurch, 1906–7: A Descriptive and Historical Account*, Wellington: Government Printer.

—— (1929), 'The Art Craftmanship of the Maori', *Art in New Zealand*, 2(6): 121–31.

—— (1939), *New Zealand's First Century: The Dominion's Scene and Story*, Wellington: New Zealand Government Department of Tourist and Publicity.

CRAIG, E. (1964), *Man of the Mist: A Biography of Elsdon Best*, Wellington: A.H. & A.W. Reed.

CRARY, J. (1990), *Techniques of the Observer: On Vision and Modernity in the Nineteenth Century*, Cambridge, MA: The MIT Press.

CRIMP, D. and Lawler, L. (1993), *On the Museum's Ruins*, Cambridge, MA: MIT Press.

CUNDALL, F. (ed.) (1886), *Reminiscences of the Colonial and Indian Exhibition*, London: William Clowes & Son.

CURNOW, A. (ed.) (1960), *The Penguin Book of New Zealand Verse*, Harmondsworth: Penguin.

—— AND Marsh, N. (1945), 'A Dialogue by Way of Introduction', *Yearbook of the Arts in New Zealand* (1): 2.

CURNOW, J. and Graham, E. R. (1998), 'Graham, George Samuel 1874–1952', *Dictionary of New Zealand Biography*, vol. 4. Retrieved 23 March, 2006 from: http://www.dnzb.govt.nz/.

CYCLOPEDIA of New Zealand Vol. 1. (1897), Wellington: Cyclopedia Co. Ltd.

DANSEY, H. (1971), 'Family Possessions: Part of Maoritanga', *Te Maori*, 2(3): 13–14.

DAVIDSON, J. (ed.) (1989), *Taonga Maori: Treasures of the New Zealand Maori People*, Sydney: Australian Museum.

—— (2000). Unpublished interview, 15 August, Wellington: Te Papa Archives.

DAVIS, F. (1976), 'Maori Art, no. 9: Māori Statements in a European Idiom', *Education*, (9): 28–30.

DAVISON, G. (2002), *Museums and National Identity*, Museums Australia annual conference Adelaide, 20 March 2002. Museums Australia Conference paper archive. Retrieved 23 March 2006 from: www.museumsaustralia.org.au/.

DAY, K. (2005), 'James Butterworth and the Old Curiosity Shop', New Plymouth, Taranaki', *Tuhinga* 16: 93–126.

DAY, M. (1972), *Contemporary New Zealand Painting: A Selection of Recent Acquisitions,* Wellington: National Art Gallery.

DELL, R. (1965A), *Dominion Museum, 1865–1965*, Wellington: Dominion Museum.

—— (1965B), *The First Hundred Years of the Dominion Museum,* Dominion Museum, Wellington, TPA Dell Ms papers 5156.

—— (1972), 'James Hector and the Geological Survey', *New Zealand's Heritage: The Making of a Nation,* 3(33): 887–901.

—— (1990), 'Hector, James 1834–1907', *Dictionary of New Zealand Biography*, vol. 1. Retrieved 23 March 2006 from: http://www.dnzb.govt.nz/.

'HAMILTON, Augustus 1853–1913', *Dictionary of New Zealand Biography*, vol. 2. Retrieved 23 March 2006 from: http://www.dnzb.govt.nz/.

DENNIS, J. (1996), 'McDonald, James Ingram 1865–1935', *Dictionary of New Zealand Biography*, vol. 3. Retrieved 23 March 2006 from: http://www.dnzb.govt.nz/.

—— GRACE, P. and Ramsden, I. (eds) (2001), *The Silent Migration: Ngati Poneke Young Maori Club 1937–48*, Wellington: Huia.

D'HARNONCOURT, R. Linton, R. and Wingert, P. (1946), *Arts of the South Seas*, New York: Museum of Modern Art and Simon & Schuster.

DIAS, N. (1994), 'Looking at Objects: Memory, Knowledge in Nineteenth-century Ethnographic Displays', in G. Robertson, M. Mash, L. Tickner, J. Bird, B. Curtis, M. Mash, T. Putnam, G. Robertson, L. Tickner (eds), *Travellers' Tales: Narratives of Home and Displacement*, London & New York: Routledge.

DIBLEY, B. (1997), 'Telling Times: Narrating Nation at the New Zealand International Exhibition, 1906–7', *Sites*, 34: 1–18.

—— (2005), 'The Museum's Redemption: Contact Zones, Government and the Limits of Reform', *International Journal of Cultural Studies*, 8(1): 5–27.

DIRLIK, A., Bahl, V. and Gran, P. (eds) (2000), *History after the Three Worlds: Post-Eurocentric Historiographies,* Lanham: Rowman & Littlefield.

DOMINION Museum (1940s), Movietone, 35 mm, New Zealand Film Archive, Wellington 5384.

DOMINION Museum Bulletin, No. 3 (1911), Wellington: Government Printer.

DUNCAN, C. (1995), *Civilizing Rituals: Inside Public Art Museums*, New York: Routledge.

DURIE, M. (1994), *Whaiora: Maori Health Development*, Auckland: Oxford University Press.

DURING, S. (1992), 'Post-colonialism', in K.K. Ruthven (ed.), *Beyond the Disciplines, The New Humanities: Papers from the Australian Academy of the Humanities Symposium, 1991*, Canberra: Australian Academy of the Humanities.

DYSON, L. (2005), 'Reinventing the Nation: British Heritage and the Bicultural Settlement in New Zealand', in J. Littler, R. Naidoo, J. Littler and R. Naidoo (eds), *The Politics of Heritage: The Legacies of Race*, London and New York: Routledge.

ECCLES, A. (1925), *The First New Zealand Exhibition and Dunedin in 1865*, Dunedin: Otago Witness.

EDEN, T. and Kay, R. (1983), *Portrait of a Century: The History of the New Zealand Academy of Fine Arts, 1882–1982*, Wellington: Millwood.

ELLIS, N. (1998), 'Sir Apirana Ngata and the School of Maori Arts', *Art New Zealand*, Summer 89: 58–61, 87.

ERIKSON, H., Neumann, K. and Thomas, N. (eds) (1999), *Quicksands: Foundational Histories in Australia and Aotearoa New Zealand*, Sydney: University of New South Wales Press.

EVANS, J. and. Hall, S. (1999), *Visual Culture: The Reader*, London: Sage and Open University Press.

EVANS, R. (1999), 'Tribal Involvement in Exhibition Planning and Conservation Treatment: A New Institutional Approach', *ICOM Ethnographic Conservation Newsletter*, 19: 13–16.

FABIAN, J. (1983), *Time and the Other: How Anthropology Makes its Object*, New York: Columbia University Press.

—— (1991), *Time and the Work of Anthropology: Critical Essays, 1971–1991*, Philadelphia: Harwood Academic Publishers.

FAGGETTER, R. (1998), 'Review: Te Papa Tongarewa Museum of New Zealand', *Australian Museum National Newsletter*, August: 30–1.

FALLA, R. (1950), 'Are Museums Quite Dead?' *Education*, March 3(1): 41–2.

FINDLEN, P. (1994), *Possessing Nature: Museums, Collecting and Scientific Culture in Early Modern Italy*, Berkeley: University of California Press.

FIRTH, R. (1925), 'The Maori Carver', *The Journal of the Polynesian Society*, 35(136): 277–91.

FISHER, P. (1991), *Making and Effacing Art: Modern American Art in a Culture of Museums*, Cambridge, MA: Harvard University Press.

—— (1996), 'Local Meanings and Portable Objects: National Collections, Literatures, Music and Architecture', in G. Wright (ed.), *The Formation of National Collections of Art and Archaeology*, Washington: National Gallery of Art.

FITZGERALD, C. and MacLennan, P. (1994), *Mana Whenua: Front-end Evaluation*. Wellington: The Museum of New Zealand Te Papa Tongarewa: Visitor and Market Research.

FITZGERALD, M. (2001), Unpublished interview, 28 August, Wellington: Te Papa Archives.

FLERAS, A. and Spoonley, P. (1999), *Recalling Aotearoa: Indigenous Politics and Ethnic Relations in New Zealand*, Auckland: Oxford University Press.

FOSTER, H. (ed.) (1987), *Discussions in Contemporary Culture: DIA Art Foundation*, Seattle: Bay Press.

—— (ED.) (1988), *Vision and Visuality: DIA Art Foundation discussions in contemporary culture, number 2*, Seattle: Bay Press.

FOUCAULT, M. (1970), *The Order of Things: An Archaeology of the Human Sciences*, London: Tavistock Publications.

—— (1972), *The Archaeology of Knowledge*, London,: Tavistock Publications.

—— (1984), 'Nietzsche, Genealogy, History', in P. Rabinow (ed.), *The Foucault Reader*, Harmondsworth: Penguin.

FOWLER, L. (1974), *Te Mana o Turanga: The Story of the Carved House Te Mana o Turanga on the Whakato Marae at Manutuke Gisborne*, Auckland: Historic Places Trust.

FYFE, G. (2000), *Art, Power, and Modernity: English Art Institutions, 1750–1950*, London and New York: Leicester University Press.

GALBREATH, R. (1989), 'Colonisation, Science and Conservation: The Development of Colonial Attitudes Towards the Native Life of New Zealand with Particular Reference to the Career of the Colonial Scientist Walter Lawry Buller (1838–1906)', PhD thesis, History, Hamilton: University of Waikato.

—— (1990), 'Buller, Walter Lawry 1838–1906', *Dictionary of New Zealand Biography*, vol. 1. Retrieved 23 March 2006 from: http://www.dnzb.govt.nz/.

GARLAND, M. (1951), 'New Zealand Painting in the National Art Gallery', *Arts Yearbook*, 7: 130–5.

GATHERCOLE, P. (1979), 'Henry Devenish Skinner: 1886–1978', *Asian Perspectives*, 22(1): 107–12.

—— (1999), 'Review: 'Maori' at the British Museum', *Journal of Museum Ethnography*, 11: 139–43.

GELL, A. (1992), 'The Technology of Enchantment and the Enchantment of Technology', in J. Coote and A. Shelton (eds), *Anthropology, Art, and Aesthetics*, Oxford: Clarendon Press.

—— (1998), *Art and Agency: An Anthropological Theory*, Oxford: Clarendon Press.

—— (1999), 'Vogel's Net: Traps as Artworks and Artworks as Traps', in E. Hirsch (ed.), *The Art of Anthropology: Essays and Diagrams.* London: London School of Economics Monographs on Social Anthropology/The Athlone Press.

GIBBONS, P. (1992), 'Going Native: A Case Study of Cultural Appropriation in a Settler Society, with Particular Reference to the Activities of Johannes Andersen in New Zealand during the First Half of the Twentieth Century', PhD thesis, History, Hamilton: University of Waikato.

GILLESPIE, R. (2001), 'Making an Exhibition: One Gallery, One Thousand Objects, One Million Critics', *Meanjin*, 60(4): 118–19.

GLENN PENNY, H. (2002), *Objects of Culture: Ethnology and Ethnographic Museums in Imperial Germany*, Chapel Hill and London: The University of North Carolina Press.

GOLDSMITH, M. (2001), 'Te Papa/Our Place and the Grammar of New Zealand Museumhood', Conference of Social Anthropologists of Aotearoa/New Zealand, Palmerston North, 22–25 November.

—— (2003), ' "Our place" in New Zealand Culture: How the Museum of New Zealand Constructs Biculturalism', *Ethnologies Comparées*, Spring. Retrieved 6 February 2004 from: http://alor.univ-montp.3.fr/cerce/.

GOODMAN, D. (1999), 'Fear of Circuses: The Founding of the National Museum of Victoria', in J. Evans and D. Boswell (eds), *Representing the Nation: Histories, Heritage, and Museums: A Reader*, London: Routledge.

GORBEY, K. (1984), 'A New National Art Gallery of New Zealand', *Art Gallery and Museums Association of New Zealand Journal*, 15(2): 7–10.

—— (1991), 'The Challenge of Creating a Bicultural Museum', *Museum Anthropology*, 15(4): 7–8.

—— (2000), Unpublished interview, March 16, Wellington: Te Papa Archives.

GORST, J. (1908), *New Zealand Revisited: Recollections of the Days of My Youth*, London: Isaac Pitman & Sons.

GRABURN, N. H. (1976), *Ethnic and Tourist Arts: Expressions from the Fourth World*, Berkeley, CA: University of California Press.

GRAHAM, B. (1995), 'Trafficking Authenticity: Aspects of Non-Maori use of Maori Cultural and Intellectual Property', *New Zealand Museums Journal*, 25(1): 31–4.

GRAHAM, J. (1965), *Maori Paintings: Pictures from the Partridge Collection of Paintings by Gottfried Lindauer*, Auckland: Reed.

GREENBERG, R., Ferguson, B. and Nairne, S. (1996), *Thinking About Exhibitions*, London and New York: Routledge.

GREENBLATT, S. (1991), *Marvellous Possessions: The Wonder of the New World*, Chicago: Chicago University Press.

GREENHALGH, P. (1988), *Ephemeral Vistas: The Expositions Universalles, Great Exhibitions and World Fairs, 1851–1939*, Manchester: Manchester University Press.

GRIFFITHS, T. (1996), *Hunters and Collectors: The Antiquarian Imagination in Australia*, Melbourne: Cambridge University Press.

GROSSBERG, L. (1986), 'Post Modernism and Articulation: An Interview with Stuart Hall', *Journal of Communication Enquiry*, 10(2): 45–60.

HAKIWAI, A. (1990), 'Once Again the Light of Day: Museums and Maori Culture in New Zealand', *Museum*, 42(1): 42–4.

—— (1999), 'Kaitiakitanga – Looking after Culture: Insights from 'Within' – Two Curatorial Perspectives', *ICOM Ethnographic Conservation Newsletter*, 19: 10–12.

—— (2000), Unpublished interview, 26 July, Wellington: Te Papa Archives.

—— (2005), 'The Search for Legitimacy: Museums in Aotearoa, New Zealand – a Maori Viewpoint', in G. Corsane (ed.), *Heritage, Museums and Galleries: An Introductory Reader*, London and New York: Routledge.

HALL, S. (1997), *Representation: Cultural Representations and Signifying Practices*, London: Sage/Open University.

HAMILTON, A. (1901A), *The Art Workmanship of the Maori Race in New Zealand*, Dunedin: New Zealand Institute.

—— (1901B), *National Collection of the Ethnology of the Maori People*, Dunedin: *Otago Daily Times*.

—— (1902A), *Notes for the Information of Members of both Houses of Parliament, in the Matter of the National Maori Museum Proposed to be Erected in Wellington to Carry Out the Provisions of the Maori Antiquities Act of 1901, and to be a Permanent Memorial to the Past History of the Maori People*, Dunedin: Fergusson & Mitchell.

—— AND Percy Smith, S. (1902B), 'Suggestions for the Establishment of a Maori Museum', *Appendices to the Journals of the House of Representatives* 1902 G-8: 1–3.

HAMILTON, G. H. (1978), *The Pelican History of Art: Painting and Sculpture in Europe 1880–1940*, Harmondsworth: Penguin.

HANHAM, S. (2000), 'The Te Maori exhibition: An Examination of its Organisation and Impacts as Seen by those Closely Involved with It', MA thesis, Museum and Heritage Studies, Wellington: Victoria University.

HARKER, R. (1986), 'Museum Object: Cultural Artefact', Museum Education Association of New Zealand Seminar '86: Interpretation and Evaluation, New Plymouth, August.

——, MAHAR, C. and Wilkes, C. (eds) (1990), *An Introduction to the Work of Pierre Bourdieu: The Practice of Theory*, London: Macmillan.

HARPER, J. (1990), 'Questions of Access', Extending Parameters: Research Forum, Queensland Art Gallery, Sydney: Australia Council for the Arts.

—— (1991), 'A Fresh Perspective on New Zealand Art', Australian Museums: Collecting and Presenting in Australia, Council of the Australian Museum Association, Canberra, 21–4 November 1990.

—— (1997), 'The Bicultural Buffer Zone: Art, Maori Art, Museums and their Markets', Art Association of Australia Conference, Canberra, 4–5 October.

HEALY, C. (1997), *From the Ruins of Colonialism: History as Social Memory*, Melbourne: Cambridge University Press.

HEDLEY, R. (2004), 'Prototype Theory and the Concept of Taonga: Implications for Treaty-related Issues such as the Display and Conservation of Taonga Maori', *He Puna Korero: Journal of Maori and Pacific Development*, 5(1): 49–68.

HELLER, S. (1997), 'The Museum of the Twenty-first Century: A Preview', *ART News*, November: 196–9.

HENARE, A. (2003), 'Artifacts in Theory: Anthropology and Material Culture', *Cambridge Anthropology*, 23(3): 54–66.

—— (2005), *Museums, Anthropology and Imperial Exchange*, Cambridge: Cambridge University Press.

HERLE, A., Stanley, N., Stevenson, K., Welsch, R. (eds) (2002), *Pacific Art: Persistence, Change, and Meaning*, Honolulu: University Press of Hawai'i.

HIDES, S. (1997), 'The Genealogy of Material Culture and Cultural Identity', in S. Pearce (ed.), *Experiencing Material Culture in the Western World*, London and Washington: Leicester University Press.

HILL, K. (2005), *Culture and Class in English Public Museums, 1850–1914*, Aldershot: Ashgate.

HILLIARD, C. (2000), 'Textual Museums: Collection and Writing in History and Ethnology, 1900–1950', in B. Dalley and B. Labrum (eds), *Fragments: New Zealand Social and Cultural History*, Auckland: Auckland University Press.

HIPANGO, H. W. (1969), 'Te Haerenga ki Rawahi: From the Writings of H. W. Hipango', *Te Wharekura*, 16: 17–31.

HOBBS, J. (1999). 'Te Papa Biographical Index,' Unpublished compendium in two volumes, Wellington: Te Papa Library.

HOBSBAWN, E. and Ranger, T. (eds) (1983), *The Invention of Tradition*, Cambridge: Cambridge University Press.

HODGSON, T. (1990), *Colonial Capital: Wellington 1865–1910*, Auckland: Random.

HOGAN, H. M. (1997), *Hikurangi ki Homburg: Henare Kohere and Terei Ngatai with the Maori Coronation Contingent 1902*, Christchurch: Clerestory Press.

—— (2003), *Bravo, Neu Zeeland: Two Maori in Vienna 1859–1860*, Christchurch: Clerestory Press.

HOOPER-GREENHILL, E. (1992), *Museums and the Shaping of Knowledge*, London and New York: Routledge.

—— (1998), 'Perspectives on Hinemihi: A Maori Meeting House', in T. Barringer and T. Fynn (eds), *Colonialism and the Object: Empire, Material Culture and the Museum*, London: Routledge.

HORNIBROOK, N. (1996), 'Thomson, James Allan 1881–1928', *Dictionary of New Zealand Biography*, vol. 3. Retrieved 23 March 2006 from: http://www.dnzb.govt.nz/.

HUDSON, K. (1987), *Museums of Influence*, Cambridge: Cambridge University Press.

IHIMAERA, W. and Ellis, N. (eds) (2002), *Te ATA: Maori Art from the East Coast, New Zealand*, Auckland: Reed.

IMPEY, O. and MacGregor, A. (eds) (1985), *The Origins of Museums: The Cabinet of Curiosities in Sixteenth- and Seventeenth-century Europe*, Oxford: Oxford University Press.

INTERCOLONIAL *Exhibition of Australia, Melbourne, 1866–67: Official Record* (1867), Melbourne: Blundell & Co.

IRVINE-SMITH, F.L. (1948), *The Streets of My City: Wellington, New Zealand*, Wellington: Reed.

JACKNIS, I. (1985), 'Franz Boas and Exhibits: On the Limitations of the Museum Method of Anthropology', in G. Stocking (ed.), *Objects and Others: Essays on Museums and Material Culture*, Madison: University of Wisconsin Press.

—— (2002), *The Storage Box of Tradition: Kwakiutl Art, Anthropologists, and Museums, 1881–1981*, Washington, DC: Smithsonian Institution Press.

JACKSON, M. (1988), 'The Treaty of Waitangi and the Museum of New Zealand/Te Marae Taonga o Aotearoa', National Museum unpublished policy report, Wellington: Te Papa Library.

JACKSON Rushing, W. (1992), 'Marketing the Affinity of the Primitive and the Modern: Rene d'Harnoncourt and "Indian Art of the United States"', in J. Berlo (ed.), *The Early Years of Native American Art History*, Seattle, WA: University of Washington Press.

JAHNKE, R. (1991), 'Kohia ko Taikaka anake', *New Zealand Craft*, June 36: 32–5.

—— (1999), 'Voices Beyond the Pae', in N. Thomas and D. Losche (eds), *Double Visions: Art Histories and Colonial Histories in the Pacific*, Melbourne: Cambridge University Press.

JENKINS, D. (1994), 'Object Lessons and Ethnographic Displays: Museum Exhibitions and the Making of American Anthropology', *Comparative Studies in Society and History*, 36(2): 242–70.

JOHNSTON, E. (1999), 'Representing the Pacific at International Exhibitions 1851–1940', PhD thesis, History, Auckland: Auckland University.

JONAITIS, A. (1981), 'Creations of Mystics and Philosophers: The White Man's Perceptions of Northwest Coast Indian Art from the 1930s to the Present', *American Indian Culture and Research Journal*, 5(1): 1–45.

KAA, Te O. and Kaa, W. (eds) (1996), *Mohi Turei: Ana tuhinga i roto i te reo Maori*, Wellington: Victoria University Press.

KAEPPLER, A. (1978), *'Artificial Curiosities': An Exposition of Native Manufactures Collected on the Three Pacific Voyages of Captain James Cook, R.N.*, Honolulu: Bishop Museum Press.

KAHN, M. (1995), 'Heterotopic Dissonance in the Museum Representation of Pacific Islands Cultures', *American Anthropologist*, June 97(2): 324–38.

'KALEIDOSCOPE Reviewed: Te Maori' (1984), Derek Fox, director, 32 minutes. Television New Zealand 44155, Wellington: New Zealand Film Archive.

KARP, I. and Lavine, S. (eds) (1991), *Exhibiting Cultures: The Poetics and Politics of Museum Display*, Washington: Smithsonian Institution Press.

KAWHARU, H. (1989), *Waitangi: Maori and Pakeha Perspectives of the Treaty of Waitangi*, Auckland: Oxford University Press.

KENDALL, R. and Lee, S. (1820). *Grammar and Vocabulary of the Language of New Zealand,* London: Church Missionary Society.

KERNOT, B. (1987), 'Te Maori Te Hokinga Mai: Some Reflections', *Art Gallery and Museums Association of New Zealand Journal,* 18(2): 3–7.

—— (1999), 'Imaging the Nation: The New Zealand International Exhibition 1906–7 and the Model Maori pa', in C. Anderson, B. Craig and B. Kernot (eds), *Art and Performance in Oceania,* Bathurst: Crawford House Publishing.

KING, C. R. (1998), *Colonial Discourses, Collective Memories, and the Exhibition of Native American Cultures and Histories in the Contemporary United States,* New York: Garland Publishing.

KING, M. (1992), 'Between Two Worlds', in G. Rice (ed.), *The Oxford History of New Zealand,* 2nd edn, Auckland: Oxford University Press.

—— (2000), *Wrestling with the Angel: A Life of Janet Frame,* Auckland: Viking.

—— (2003), *The Penguin History of New Zealand,* Auckland: Penguin Books.

KIRKBY, G. (1978), 'The Need for a Creative Arts Centre in New Zealand', Pacific Arts Association: The Second International Symposium on the Art of Oceania, Victoria University, Wellington, 1–8 February.

KIRSHENBLATT-GIMBLETT, B. (1994), 'Destination Museum: Issues of Heritage, Museums and Tourism', Seminar paper, Wellington City Gallery, Museum Directors Federation of Aotearoa/ New Zealand, Wellington.

—— (1995), 'American Jewish Life: Ethnographic Approaches to Collection, Presentation and Interpretation in Museums', in P. Hall and C. Seeman (eds), *Folklife and Museums: Selected Readings,* New York: Altamira Press.

—— (1998), *Destination Culture: Tourism, Museums, and Heritage,* Berkeley: University of California Press.

KOHIA ko Taikaka Anake: New Zealand's Largest Exhibition of Contemporary Maori Art (1993), Wellington: Museum of New Zealand catalogue.

KULIK, G. (1998), 'Designing the Past: History Museum Exhibitions from Peale to the Present', in W. Leon and R. Rosenzweig (eds), *History Museums in the United States,* Urbana and Chicago: University of Illinois Press.

LABRUM, B. (2002), '"Bringing Families Up to Scratch": The Distinctive Workings of Maori State Welfare, 1944–1970', *The New Zealand Journal of History,* 36(2): 161–84.

LATOUR, B. (2004), 'Why has Critique Run Out of Steam? From Matters of Fact to Matters of Concern', *Critical Inquiry,* 30: 225–48.

LEGGET, J. (1995), 'Biculturalism in Action', *Museums Journal,* 20: 22–5.

LEVINE, H. B. (1999), 'Reconstructing Ethnicity', *Journal of the Royal Anthropological Institute,* 5(2): 165–87.

LOWENTHAL, D. and Gathercole, P. (eds) (1994), *The Politics of the Past,* London and Boston: Routledge.

LUMLEY, R. (2005), 'The Debate on Heritage Reviewed', in G. Corsane (ed.), *Heritage, Museums and Galleries: An Introductory Reader,* London and New York: Routledge.

LYNCH, N. A. (2000), 'Culture Change and Development in New Zealand Archeology and Art History: An Interdisciplinary Approach', MA thesis, Anthropology, Auckland: Auckland University.

MacClancey, J. (ed.) (1997), *Contesting Art: Art, Politics and Identity in the Modern World*, Oxford and New York: Berg.

Macdonald, C. (1999), 'Race and Empire at Our Place: New Zealand's New National Museum', *Radical History Review*, 75: 80–91.

Macdonald, S. (ed.) (1998), *The Politics of Display: Museums, Science, Culture*, London and New York: Routledge.

—— and Fyfe, G. (eds) (1996), *Theorizing Museums: Representing Identity and Diversity in a Changing World*, Cambridge, MA: Blackwell.

Mackle, A. (1984), 'Protest and Provincialism', in (n.a.), *Aspects of New Zealand Art 1890–1940: From the Collections of the National Art Gallery*, Wellington: National Art Gallery.

Mackrell, B. (1985), *Hariru Wikitoria. An Illustrated History of the Maori Tour of England, 1863*, Auckland: Oxford University Press.

MacLeod, S. (2005), *Reshaping Museum Space: Architecture, Design, Exhibitions*, Oxford and New York: Routledge.

Mahuika, A. (1991), 'Maori Culture and the New Museum', *Museum Anthropology*, 15(4): 9–10.

Mané-Wheoki, J. (1996), 'Korurangi/Toihoukura: Brown Art in White Spaces', *Art New Zealand*, 78: 43–7.

Mainardi, P. (1993), *The End of the Salon: Art and the State in the Early Third Republic*, Cambridge: Cambridge University Press.

Mansfield, E. (ed.) (2002), *Art History and its Institutions: Foundations of a Discipline*, New York: Routledge.

Maori Art Treasures (1951), Wellington: New Zealand Film Archive.

Maori Arts and Culture No. 1: Carving and Decoration (1962), National Film Unit 5001, Wellington: New Zealand Film Archive.

Maori Portraits (1961), Wellington: National Art Gallery catalogue.

Marsh, J. (1999), 'Spectacle', in H.F. Tucker (ed.), *A Companion to Victorian Literature and Culture*, Malden and Oxford: Blackwell.

Martin, C. and Phillips, J. (1990), *The Sorrow and the Pride: New Zealand War Memorials*, Wellington: Historical Branch Internal Affairs, GP Books.

Mataira, K. (1961), 'Maori Arts are Our Heritage', *National Education: The Journal of the New Zealand Educational Institute*, August 43(468): 319.

Maxwell, A. (1999), *Colonial Photography and Exhibitions: Representations of the 'Native' and the Making of European Identities*, London and New York: Leicester University Press.

McCarthy, C. (2000), 'Mana Whenua Summative Evaluation Raw Data', Wellington: Te Papa Visitor & Market Research/Victoria University.

—— (2001), 'Mana whenua: Summative Evaluation Report', Wellington: Te Papa Visitor & Market Research/Victoria University.

—— (2002), *Forrester and Lemon of Oamaru, Architects*, Oamaru: North Otago Branch Committee of the New Zealand Historic Places Trust.

—— (2004), 'From Curio to Taonga: A Genealogy of Display at New Zealand's National Museum, 1865–2001', PhD thesis, Museum and Heritage Studies, Wellington: Victoria University.

—— (2005), 'Objects of Empire? Displaying Maori at International Exhibitions, 1873–1924', *Journal of New Zealand Literature*, 23(1): 52–70.

—— (2006), 'Hailing the Subject: Māori Visitors, Museum Display and the Sociology of Cultural Reception', *New Zealand Sociology* 21(1): 108–30.

—— AND Labrum, B. (2005), 'Museum Studies and Museums: Bringing Together Theory and Practice', *Te Ara Journal of Museums Aotearoa* 30(2): 4–11.

McCAULEY, L. (1996), *Te Huka a Tai: Maori Art and History Resource Centre. Formative Evaluation Study One*, Wellington: Te Papa Visitor and Market Research.

McCLELLAN, A. (ed.) (2003), *Art and its Publics: Museum Studies at the End of the Millennium*, Oxford and Malden, MA: Blackwell.

McCLURE, M. (2004), *The Wonder Country: Making New Zealand Tourism*, Auckland: Auckland University Press.

McCREDIE, A. (1999), 'Going Public: New Zealand Art Museums in the 1970s', MA thesis, Museum Studies, Palmerston North: Massey University.

McEVILLEY, T. (1992), *Art and Otherness: Crisis in Cultural Identity*, Kingston, NY: Documentext/ McPherson.

McINTYRE, D. and Wehner, K. (eds) (2001), *Negotiating Histories: National Museums: Conference Proceedings*, Canberra: National Museum of Australia.

McLAUGHLIN, A. (1975), 'Cliff Whiting: Art is Part and Parcel of his Life Style', *Te Maori*, 6(6): 24–5.

McLEAN, G. (2000), 'Where Sheep May Not Safely Graze: A Brief History of New Zealand's Heritage Movement, 1890–2000,' in A. Trapeznik (ed.), *Common Ground? Heritage and Public Places in New Zealand*, Dunedin: Otago University Press.

McLINTOCK, A.H. (ed.) (1966), *An Encyclopedia of New Zealand*, vol 1, Wellington: Government Printer.

McMANUS, G. (1988), 'Nga Whare Taonga me te Tangata Whenua o Aotearoa: Museums and the Maori People of New Zealand', MA thesis, Museum Studies, Leicester: Leicester University.

McQUEEN, H.C. (1942), *Education in New Zealand Museums: An Account of the Experiments Assisted by the Carnegie Corporation of New York*, Wellington: New Zealand Council for Educational Research.

MEAD, S.M. (Hirini) (1983), 'Indigenous Models of Museums in Oceania', *Museum*, 35(139): 98–101.

—— (ED.) (1984A), *Te Maori: Maori Art from New Zealand Collections*, New York: Abrams, American Federation of Arts.

—— (HIRINI) (1984B), 'Te Maori in New York', *Art New Zealand*, 33: 24–7.

—— (1985A), 'Te Maori Comes Home: The Walter Auburn Memorial Lecture', Auckland City Art Gallery, Auckland: Friends of the Gallery.

—— (1985B), 'Celebrating New Zealand's Cultural Diversity: A Maori Point of View', *Interpreting Cultural Diversity*, Museum Education Association of New Zealand Annual Conference, Wellington.

—— (1985C), 'Concepts and Models for Maori Museums and Culture Centres', *Art Gallery and Museums Association of New Zealand Journal*, 16(3): 3–5.

—— (1986A), *Magnificent Te Maori: Te Maori Whakahirahira*, Auckland: Heinemann.

—— (1986B), *Te Toi Whakairo: The Art of Maori Carving*, Wellington: Reed Methuen.

—— (1990), 'Tribal Art as Symbols of Identity', in A. Hanson and L. Hanson (eds), *Art and Identity in Oceania: Papers Presented to the Pacific Arts Association Symposium, New York, September 3–8, 1984*, Honolulu: University of Hawai'i.

—— (1993), 'The Maintenance of Heritage in a Fourth World Context: The Maori Case', in P. Dark, and Rose, R. (eds), *Artistic Heritage in a Changing Pacific*, Honolulu: University of Hawai'i Press.

—— (1997A), 'The Nature of Taonga', in *Landmarks, Bridges and Visions: Aspects of Maori Culture: Essays*, Wellington: Victoria University Press. Paper originally presented at the Taonga Maori Conference, National Museum, Wellington, 1990.

—— (1997B), *Maori Art on the World Scene: Essays on Maori Art*, Wellington: Ahua Design & Illustration Ltd; Matau Associates.

—— (2003), *Tikanga Maori: Living by Maori Values*, Wellington: Huia.

—— (2006), Unpublished interview, 4 April, Wellington: Te Papa Archives.

—— AND Grove, N. (2001), *Nga Pepeha a nga Tipuna: The Sayings of the Ancestors*, Wellington: Victoria University Press.

'MEMORANDUM Concerning the Colonial Museum' (1866), *Appendices to the Journals of the House of Representatives* D-9.

MERRIMAN, N. (1991), *Beyond the Glass Case: The Past, Heritage and the Public in Britain*, Leicester and London: Leicester University Press.

METGE, J. (1964), *A New Maori Migration: Rural and Urban Relations in Northern New Zealand*, Melbourne: Melbourne University Press.

MILLARD, R. (2001), *The Tastemakers: UK Art Now*, London: Thames & Hudson.

MITCHELL, T. (1991), *Colonising Egypt*, Los Angeles: University of California Press.

MITCHELL, W. J. T. (1994), *Picture Theory*, Chicago: University of Chicago Press.

—— (1996), 'What Do Pictures Really Want?' *October*, (77): 71–82.

MUCKLE, A. and Veracini, L. (2002), 'Reflections of Indigenous History inside National Museums of Australia and Aotearoa New Zealand and Outside of New Caledonia's Centre Cuturel Jean-Marie Tjibaou', *The Electronic Journal of Australian and New Zealand history*. Retrieved 17 February 2003 from: www.jcu.edu.au/aff/history/articles.

MULLER, C., Roberts, M. N. and Vogel, S. (1994), *Exhibitionism: Museums and African Art*, New York: Museum for African Art.

MUNZ, P. (2000), 'Te Papa and the Problem of Historical Truth', *History Now/Te Pae Tawhito o Te Wa*, 6(1): 13–16.

MURPHY, H. (1999), *Bicultural Developments in Museums of Aotearoa: A Way Forward/Te Kaupapa Tikanga-a-rua i roto i nga Whare Taonga o Aotearoa: Anei ko te Huarahi*, Wellington: Te Papa National Services.

MURPHY, R. (1983), 'The Politics of Maori Art', Insight documentary: Radio New Zealand, Wellington.

NATIONAL Art Gallery and Dominion Museum New Zealand: Souvenir Catalogue of Pictures and Works of Art for Opening Exhibition (1936), Wellington: National Art Gallery.

'NATIONAL Gallery and Museum' (1936), *Art in New Zealand*, 9(1): 19–26.

NEDERVEEN Pieterse, J. (1997), 'Multiculturalism and Museums: Discourse about Others in the Age of Globalisation', *Theory, Culture and Society*, 14(4): 123–46.

NEICH, R. (1978), 'Maori Art: An Introduction', in *Maori Art from the National Museum Collection*, Wellington: New Zealand Academy of Fine Arts.

—— (1980), 'A Survery of Visitor Attitudes to a Maori Art Exhibition', *Art Gallery and Museums Association of New Zealand Journal*, 11(2): 6–9.

—— (1984), 'Nga Taonga Hou o Aotearoa: New National Treasures', *Pacific Way*, 4: 50.

—— (1991), 'Jacob William Heberly of Wellington: A Maori Carver in a Changed world', *Records of the Auckland Institute and Museum*, 28: 69–148.

—— (1994), *Painted Histories: Early Maori Figurative Painting*, Auckland: Auckland University Press.

—— (2001), *Carved Histories: Rotorua Ngati Tarawhai Woodcarving*, Auckland: Auckland University Press.

—— (2002), Unpublished interview, 29 May, Wellington: Te Papa Archives.

NEILL, A. (2004), 'National Culture and the New Museology', in A. Smith and L. Wevers (eds), *On Display: New Essays in Cultural Studies*, Wellington: Victoria University Press.

NELSON, R. S. and Shiff, R. (eds) (1996), *Critical Terms for Art History*, Chicago: University of Chicago Press.

NEWHOUSE, V. (2005), *Art and the Power of Placement*, New York: Monacelli Press.

NEW Zealand and South Seas Exhibition, Dunedin, 1889–90: Official Catalogue (1889), Wellington: Government Printer.

NEW Zealand Centennial Exhibition: The Maori Court. Souvenir (1940), Wellington: Native Department.

NEW Zealand Court Catalogue: Centennial International Exhibition, Melbourne, 1888 (1888), Melbourne: Mason, Firth & McCutcheon.

NEW Zealand Exhibition, 1865: Reports and Awards of the Jurors and Appendix (1866), Dunedin: Mills, Dick & Co.

NGATA, A. (1929), 'Anthropology and the Government of Native Races in the Pacific', in J. Allen (ed.), *New Zealand Affairs*, Christchurch: Institute of Pacific Relations New Zealand Branch.

—— (1940), 'Maori Arts and Crafts', in I. Sutherland (ed.), *The Maori People Today: A General Survey*, Wellington: New Zealand Institute of International Affairs, New Zealand Council for Educational Research.

—— (1958A), 'The Origin of Maori Carving: Part One', *Te Ao Hou*, 6(2): 30–7.

—— (1958B), 'The Origins of Maori Carving: Part Two', *Te Ao Hou*, 6(3): 30–4.

NGA Taonga o te Motu: Treasures of the Nation (1985), Project Development Team for the National Museum of New Zealand: Department of Internal Affairs, Wellington.

OFFICIAL Guide to the Government Court: New Zealand Centennial Exhibition 1939–40 (1939), Wellington: Centennial Exhibition Company Ltd.

OFFICIAL Record of the Sydney International Exhibition, 1879 (1881), Sydney: Thomas Richards.

OLIVER, W. (2001), 'The Future Behind Us: The Waitangi Tribunal's Retrospective Utopia', in P. McHugh and A. Sharp (eds), *Histories, Power and Loss: Uses of the Past – A New Zealand Commentary*, Wellington: Bridget Williams Books.

—— (2002), *Looking for the Phoenix: A Memoir*, Wellington: Bridget Williams Books.

OLIVER, W. B. (1944), *New Zealand Museums: Present Establishment and Future Policy*, Wellington: Dominion Museum.

—— AND Markham, S. (1933), *A Report on the Museums and Art Galleries of Australia and New Zealand*, London: Museums Association.

ORANGE, C. (1987), *The Treaty of Waitangi*, Wellington: Port Nicholson Press.

ORBELL, M. (1978), 'Ethnic Identity', in P. Smith and R. Thorburn (eds), *Art in Schools: The New Zealand Experience*, Wellington: Department of Education, School Publications Branch.

—— (2002), *He Reta ki te Maunga/Letters to the Mountain: Maori Letters to the Editor, 1898–1905*, Auckland: Reed.

O'REGAN, H. (1999), 'If Its Good Enough for You Its Good Enough for Me: The Hypocrisy of Assimilation and Cultural Colonisation', in J. Brown and P. Sant (eds), *Indigeneity: Construction and Representation*, New York: Nova Science.

O'REGAN, S. (Tipene) (1984), 'Taonga Maori Mana Maori', *Art Gallery and Museums Association of New Zealand Journal*, 15(4): 15–18.

O'REGAN, T. (1986), 'Letter', *Art Gallery and Museums Association of New Zealand Journal*, 17(3): 28.

O'REGAN, G. (1997), 'Bicultural Developments in the Museums of Autearoa: What is the Current Status?' Wellington: Te Papa National Services, Museums Autearoa.

O'REILLY, R. (1968), 'Art and the Encyclopedia, No. 2: Maori Art', *Ascent*, 1(2): 51–62.

O'ROURKE, R. (ed.) (1994), *Te Hau ki Turanga: A Chronological Document Bank*, Wellington: Museum of New Zealand.

—— (ED.) (1996), *The Mummy and Coffin of the Lady Mehit-em-Wesekht: A Chronological Document Bank*. Wellington: Museum of New Zealand.

—— (2000), Unpublished interview, 8 July, Wellington: Te Papa Archives.

—— (ED.) (2001). *Two Diaries and a Field Notebook, July 1909 – August 1910 of the Late Augustus Hamilton and Associated Documentaton*, Wellington: Te Papa.

—— (ED.) (2003), *By the Seat of their Pants: Precorporate Museology at the National Museum 1930–1990*, Wellington: Te Papa.

ORSMAN, H. (ed.), (1997). *The Dictionary of New Zealand English: A Dictionary of New Zealandisms on Historical Principles*, Auckland: Oxford University Press.

OWENS, J. M. R. (2004), *The Mediator: A Life of Richard Taylor 1805–1873*, Wellington: Victoria University Press.

OXFORD English Dictionary (1989), 2nd edn, Oxford: Clarendon Press.

PAGE-ROWE, W. (1928), *Maori Artistry*, New Plymouth: Board of Maori Ethnological Research.

PALETHORPE, N. (1940), *Official History of the New Zealand Centennial Exhibition, Wellington, 1939–40*, Wellington: New Zealand Centennial Exhibition Company.

PANOHO, R. (1987–8), 'The Principle of Change in Maori Art', *Art New Zealand*, 45: 63–7.

PEARCE, S. (1992), *Museums, Objects and Collections: A Cultural Study*, London: Leicester University Press.

—— (ED.) (1997), *Experiencing Material Culture in the Western World*. London and Washington: Leicester University Press.

PEARSON, B. (1962), 'New Zealand Since the War: Maori People', *Landfall*, 16(1): 179–80.

PEVSNER, N. (1976), *A History of Building Types*, London: Thames & Hudson.

PHILADELPHIA International Exhibition, 1876: Official Catalogue of the British Section, Part One (1876), London: George Erye & William Spottiswoode.

Phillipps, W. J. (1938), 'Maori Carving: Native Schools Column', *The Education Gazette*, 1 April: 61.

—— (1940), 'Te hau-ki-turanga Maori House', *Art in New Zealand Quarterly*, 13(2): 82–5.

—— (1943), *Maori Designs*, Wellington: Harry Tombs.

—— (1946), *Maori Art*, Wellington: Harry Tombs.

Phillips, J. (1996), 'Our History, Our Selves: The Historian and National Identity', *The New Zealand Journal of History*, 30(2): 107–32.

Phillips, R. B. (2005), 'Making Sense Out/of the Visual: Aboriginal Presentations and Representations in Nineteenth-century Canada', in D. Cherry (ed.), *Art: History: Visual: Culture*, Malden/Oxford: Blackwell.

Pischief, E. (1998), 'Augustus Hamilton: Appropriation, Ownership, Authority', MA thesis, Museum Studies, Palmerston North: Massey University.

Pitt-Rivers, G. (1924), 'A Visit to a Maori Village: Being Some Observations on the Passing of the Maori Race and the Decay of Maori Culture', *The Journal of the Polynesian Society*, 33(129): 48–65.

Poata-Smith, E. (1996), 'He Pokeke Uenuku i Tu Ai: The Evolution of Contemporary Maori Protest', in P. Spoonley, D. Pearson and C. Macpherson (eds), *Nga Patai: Racism and Ethnic Relations in Aotearoa/New Zealand*, Palmerston North: Dunmore Press.

Pointon, M. (ed.) (1994), *Art Apart: Art Institutions and Ideology across England and North America*. Manchester and New York: Manchester University Press.

Pomian, K. (1990), *Collectors and Curiosities: Paris and Venice, 1500–1800*, London: Polity Press.

Pound, F. (1994), *The Space Between: Pakeha Use of Maori Motifs in Modernist New Zealand Art*, Auckland: Workshop Press.

Powell, A. (ed.) (1967), *The Centennial History of the Auckland Institute and Museum 1867–1967*, Auckland: Auckland Institute and Museum.

Preston, G. N. (1985), 'Review: Te Maori', *Pacific Arts Association Newsletter*, 20 January: 36–40.

Preziosi, D. (1997), 'Art, Art History, Museology', *Museum Anthropology*, 20(2): 5–6.

Prior, N. (2002), *Museums and Modernity: Art Galleries and the Making of Modern Culture*, Oxford: Berg.

Rabinow, P. (ed.) (1984), *The Foucault Reader*, Harmondsworth: Penguin.

—— (1986), 'Representations are Social Facts: Modernity and Post-modernity in Anthropology', in J. Clifford and G. Marcus (eds), *Writing Culture: The Poetics and Politics of Ethnography*, Berkeley: University of California Press.

Racevskis, K. (1989), 'Genealogical Critique: Michel Foucault and the Systems of Thought', in D. Aitkins and L. Morrow (eds), *Contemporary Literary Theory*, Amherst: The University of Massachusetts Press.

Rajchman, J. (1985), 'The Post Modern Museum', *Art in America*, 10: 110–17, 171.

—— (1988), 'Foucault's Art of Seeing', *October*, 44: 89–117.

Rasmussen, C. (ed.) (2001), *A Museum for the People: A History of Museum Victoria and its Predecessors, 1854–2000*, Carlton, Museum Victoria: Scribe Publications.

Rawiri, D. (1969), 'Visit to the Museum', *Te Ao Hou*, 66 (March–May): 15.

Reid, S. (2005), 'Francis Reid: The Democratic Politician Does Not Trouble Himself with Science,' Seminar presented at the Stout Research Centre, Victoria University of Wellington.

RENWICK, W. (1987), 'Emblems of Identity: Painting, Carving and Maori-Pakeha Understanding,' Audio-visual kit, Wellington: Department of Education.

—— (ED.) (2004), *Creating a National Spirit: Celebrating New Zealand's Centennial*, Wellington: Victoria University Press.

REPORTS *on the Vienna Universal Exhibition of 1873: Part One* (1874), London: George Eyre & William Spottisswoode.

REWI, B. (2001), Unpublished interview, 28 August, Wellington: Te Papa Archives.

RICE, R. (2002), 'Hauhau and Other Rebel Flags: Histories of Exchange, Acculturation and Appropriation in Nineteenth-century New Zealand', *The Journal of New Zealand Art History*, 23: 43–54.

—— (2003), 'Picturing Progress in Paradise: New Zealand on Display at International Exhibitions, 1873–1886', MA thesis, Art History, Wellington: Victoria University.

RICHARDSON, P. (1997), 'Building the Dominion: Government Architecture in New Zealand, 1840–1922', PhD thesis, Art History, Christchurch: Canterbury University.

ROGOFF, I. and Sherman, D. (ed.) (1994), *Museum Culture: Histories, Discourses, Spectacles*, Minneapolis: University of Minnesota Press.

ROYSTON, O. (1956), 'A visit to New Zealand', *The Museums Journal*, 57(10): 231.

RYDELL, R. (1984), *All the World's a Fair: Visions of Empire at American International Expositions*, Chicago: University of Chicago Press.

—— (1993), *World of Fairs: The Century-of-Progress Expositions*, Chicago: University of Chicago Press.

SAHLINS, M. (1993), 'Goodbye to *Triste Trope*: Ethnography in the Context of Modern World History', *The Journal of Modern History*, 65(1): 1–25.

—— (1995), *How 'Natives' Think: About Captain Cook, For Example*, Chicago and London: The University of Chicago Press.

SAID, E. (1989), 'Representing the Colonized: Anthropology's Interlocuters', *Critical Inquiry*, 15(2): 205–25.

—— (2001), *Reflections on Exile and Other Literary and Cultural Essays*, London: Granta.

SALMOND, A. (1975), *Hui: A Study of Maori Ceremonial Gatherings*, Auckland: Reed.

—— (1980), *Eruera: The Teachings of a Maori Elder*, Auckland: Oxford University Press.

—— (1991), *Two Worlds: First Meetings between Maori and Europeans 1642–1772*, Auckland: Viking.

SANDELL, R. (ed.) (2002), *Museums, Society, Inequality*, London and New York: Routledge.

—— AND Dodd, J. (eds) (2001), *Including Museums: Perspectives on Museums, Galleries and Social Inclusion*, Leicester: Research Centre for Museums and Galleries, Department of Museum Studies, University of Leicester.

SCHRENK, L. (2005). 'Catch a Star: The Presentation of Scientific Technology at Chicago's 1933–34 Century of Progress Exposition,' Paper presented at World's Fairs, Expositions and Current Museum Research, Smithsonian Institution, November.

SCHWIMMER, E. (1968), 'The Aspirations of the Contemporary Maori', in E. Schwimmer (ed.), *The Maori People in the 1960s: A Symposium*, Auckland: Longman Paul.

SCREVEN, C. (1976), 'Exhibit Evaluation: A Goal-referenced Approach', *Curator*, 19: 271–90.

SHELTON, A. (1994), 'Cabinets of Transgression: Renaissance Collections and the Incorporation of the New World', in J. Bird, B. Curtis, M. Mash, T. Putnam, G. Robertson, L. Tickner (eds), *Travellers' Tales: Narratives of Home and Displacement,* London and New York: Routledge.

SHINER, L. (2001), *The Invention of Art: A Cultural History,* Chicago and London: University of Chicago Press.

SIMPSON, E. (1964), 'The Visual Arts', in *The Arts in New Zealand: An Extract from the 1964 New Zealand Offical Yearbook,* Wellington: Government Printer.

SIMPSON, M. (ed.) (1994), *Te Mareikura,* Wellington: Huia Publishers.

SIMPSON, M. (1996), *Making Representations: Museums in the Post-colonial Era,* London and New York: Routledge.

SINCLAIR, K. (1959), *A History of New Zealand,* Harmondsworth: Penguin.

SISSONS, J. (1993), 'Best, Elsdon 1856–1931'. *Dictionary of New Zealand Biography,* vol. 2. Retrieved 23 March 2006 from: http://www.dnzb.govt.nz/.

—— (1998), 'The Traditionalisation of the Maori Meeting House', *Oceania,* 69(1): 36–47.

—— (2005), *First Peoples: Indigenous Cultures and their Futures,* London: Reaktion.

SKINNER, D. (2005), 'Another Modernism: Maoritanga and Maori Modernism in the Twentieth Century', PhD thesis, Art History, Wellington: Victoria University.

SLACK, J. (1996), 'The Theory and Method of Articulation in Cultural Studies', in K.-H. Chen and D. Morely (eds), *Stuart Hall: Critical Dialogues in Cultural Studies,* London and New York: Routledge.

SMART, B. (2002), *Michel Foucault,* London: Routledge.

SMART, J. (1986), 'Te Maori: A Pakeha view', *Art New Zealand,* 43: 83–4.

SMITH, B. (1989), *European Vision and the South Pacific,* 2nd edn, Melbourne: Oxford University Press.

SORRENSON, M.P.K. (1982), 'Polynesian Corpuscles and Pacific Anthropology: The Home Made Anthropology of Sir Apriana Ngata and Sir Peter Buck', *The Journal of the Polynesian Society,* 91(1): 7–27.

—— (ED.) (1987), *Na to Hoa Aroha: From Your Dear Friend. The Correspondence Between Sir Apirana Ngata and Sir Peter Buck 1925–1950,* vol. 2. Auckland: Auckland University Press, Maori Purposes Fund Board.

—— (1990), 'Mantell, Walter Baldock Durrant 1820–1895'. *Dictionary of New Zealand Biography,* vol. 1. Retrieved 23 March 2006 from http://www.dnzb.govt.nz/.

SOUVENIR: *New Zealand International Exhibition Christchurch 1906–7* (1907), Christchurch: Christchurch Press.

STACK, J. (1875), 'An Account of the Maori House Attached to the Christchurch Museum', *Transactions and Proceedings of the New Zealand Institute,* (8): 172–6.

STAFFORD, A. (1991), *Visitor Perception Survey Findings,* Wellington: A. J. Stafford & Associates.

STAINFORTH, L.S. (1990), 'Did the Spirit Sing? An Historical Perspective on Canadian Exhibitions of the Other', MA thesis, Canadian Studies, Ottawa: Carleton University.

STANISZEWSKI, M. A. (1995), *Seeing is Believing: Creating the Culture of Art,* New York: Penguin.

—— (1998), *The Power of Display: A History of Exhibition Installations at the Museum of Modern Art,* Cambridge, MA: MIT Press.

STARZECKA, D. C. (ed.) (1998), *Maori Art and Culture*, 2nd edn, London: British Museum, David Bateman.

STEAD, O. (ed.) (2001), *150 Treasures*, Auckland: Auckland War Memorial Museum/David Bateman.

STENHOUSE, J. (1996), 'A Disappearing Race Before We Came Here: Dr Alfred Kingcome Newman, the Dying Maori, and Victorian Scientific Racism', *The New Zealand Journal of History*, 30(2): 124–40.

STEPHENS, M. (2002), Unpublished interview, 21 March, Wellington: Te Papa Archives.

TAIKAKA (1991), Maia Matchitt, director, Simon Nixon Productions, 25 mins, Wellington: New Zealand Film Archive.

TAMARAPA, A. (1996A), 'Museum Kaitiaki: Maori Perspectives on the Presentation and Management of Maori Treasures and Relationships with Museums', in M. Ames and M. McKenzie (eds), *Curatorship: Indigenous Perspectives in Postcolonial Societies: Proceedings of Conference, May 1994*, Ottawa: Canadian Museum of Civilisation.

—— (1996B), 'Redefining the Keeping Place: Symposium Presentation and Roundtable Discussion', in M. Ames and M. McKenzie (eds), *Curatorship: Indigenous Perspectives in Post-colonial Societies, Proceedings of Conference, May 1994*, Canadian Museum of Civilization, Ottawa.

—— (2000), Unpublished interview 14 July, Wellington: Te Papa Archives.

TAMATI-QUENNELL, M. (1998), 'Lisa Reihana: Native Portraits n.19897', *Photofile*, November: 46–9.

'TAONGA Maori' (1989), *Muse: Magazine of the Australian Museum*, October–November: 4, 9.

TAONGA Maori Conference (1991), *Proceedings of the Conference November 18–27, 1990, National Museum*, Wellington: Cultural Conservation Advisory Council, Department of Internal Affairs.

TAPSELL, P. (1997), 'The Flight of Pareraututu: An Investigation of Taonga from a Tribal Perspective', *The Journal of the Polynesian Society*, 106(4): 323–74.

—— (2000), *Pukaki: A Comet Returns*, Auckland: Reed.

—— (ED.) (2006), *Ko Tawa: Maori Treasures of New Zealand*, Auckland: David Bateman and Auckland Museum.

'TARAWERA: A Memorial Exhibition' (1986), National Museum misc. series No. 14, Wellington: National Museum.

TAYLOR, B. (1999), *Art for the Nation: Exhibitions and the London Public 1747–2001*, Manchester: Manchester University Press.

TEAIWA, T. (2005), 'Native Thoughts: A Pacific Studies Take on Cultural Studies and Diaspora', in G. Harvey and C. D. Thompson Jnr (eds), *Indigenous Diasporas and Dislocations*, Aldershot: Ashgate.

TE Maori: He Tukunga Korero na te Komiti Whakahaere o Te Maori/A report by the Te Maori Management Committee (1988), Wellington: Te Maori Management Committee.

TE Papa Our Place: A Souvenir (1998), Wellington: Te Papa Press.

TE Punga Somerville, A. (2005), *Kanohi ki te Kanohi: Indigenous People Encounter One Another for a Change*, Unpublished paper, Pacific Studies seminar series, Wellington: Victoria University.

THOMAS, C. (1995), 'Professional Amateurs and Colonial Academics: Steps Towards Academic Anthropology in New Zealand 1860–1920', MA thesis, Auckland: Auckland University.

THOMAS, N. (1991), *Entangled Objects: Exchange, Material Culture, and Colonialism in the Pacific*, Cambridge, MA: Harvard University Press.

—— (1994), *Colonialism's Culture: Anthropology, Travel, and Government*, Carlton, Victoria: Melbourne University Press.

—— (1995A), *Oceanic Art*, London: Thames & Hudson.

—— (1995B), 'A Second Reflection: Presence and Opposition in Contemporary Maori Art', *Journal of the Royal Anthropological Institute*, 1: 23–46.

—— (1996), 'The Dream of Joseph: Practices of Identity in Pacific Art', *The Contemporary Pacific*, 8(2): 291–317.

—— (1999), *Possessions: Indigenous Art/Colonial Culture*, London: Thames & Hudson.

—— (2001), 'Indigenous Presences and National Narratives in Australasian Museums', in T. Bennett and D. Carter (eds), *Culture in Australia: Policies, Publics and Programs*, Cambridge: Cambridge University Press.

—— AND Losche, D. (eds) (1999), *Double Vision: Art Histories and Colonial Histories in the Pacific*, Cambridge: Cambridge University.

—— AND Pinney, C. (eds) (2001), *Beyond Aesthetics: Art and the Technologies of Enchantment*, Oxford: Berg.

THOMSON, G. (1927), *Official Record of the New Zealand and South Seas International Exhibition, Dunedin 1925–26*, Dunedin: New Zealand & South Seas Exhibition Company and Coulls, Somerville, Wilkie Ltd.

THOMSON, J. (1915), 'Special Reports: Some Principles of Museum Administration Affecting the Future Development of the Dominion Museum', *Appendices to the Journals of the House of Representatives* H-33: 9–19.

THOMSON, K. (1981), *Art Galleries and Museums of New Zealand*, Wellington: Reed.

TOWARDS Tomorrow (1956), John O'Shea, director, Wiremu Parker, narrator, Department of Education, Pacific Films, Wellington: New Zealand Film Archive.

TREGEAR, E. (1885), *The Aryan Maori*, Wellington: Government Printer.

—— (1891), *The Maori-Polynesian Comparative Dictionary*, Wellington: Lyon & Blair.

TUHIWAI Smith, L. (1999), *Decolonising Methodologies: Research and Indigenous Peoples*, Dunedin: University of Otago Press.

UNIVERSAL International Exhibition at Paris, 1889: New Zealand Courts Catalogue (1889), London: New Zealand Commission, Clowes and Sons, 1889.

VAN Meijl, T. (1996), 'Historicising Maoritanga: Colonial Ethnography and the Reification of Maori Traditions', *The Journal of the Polynesian Society*, 105(3): 311–46.

VERGO, P. (ed.) (1989), *The New Museology*, London: Reaktion Books.

VON Haast, H.F. (1948), *The Life and Times of Sir Julius von Haast: Explorer, Geologist, Museum Builder*, Wellington: Avery Press.

WALKER, P. (1991), 'The "Maori House" at the Canterbury Museum', *Interstices*, 4: 1–11.

WALKER, R. (1992), 'Maori People since 1950', in G. Rice (ed.), *The Oxford History of New Zealand*, 2nd edn, Auckland: Oxford University Press.

—— (2001), *He Tipua: The Life and Times of Sir Apirana Ngata*, Auckland: Viking.

WARD, A. (1993), 'Carroll, James 1857–1926' *Dictionary of New Zealand Biography* vol. 2. Retrieved 23 March 2006 from http://www.dnzb.govt.nz/.

WARD, M. (1996), 'What's Important about the History of Modern Art Exhibitions?' in R. Greenberg, B. Ferguson and S. Nairne (eds), *Thinking About Exhibitions*, London and New York: Routledge.

WATSON, C. (1997), 'Post-occupancy Evaluation for the Visitor Communications Group', Wellington: Te Papa Visitor Market Research/Watson Consultancy.

WEDDE, I. (2004), *Making Ends Meet: Essays and Talks, 1992–2004*, Wellington: Victoria University Press.

WEINER, A. (1992), *Inalienable Possessions: The Paradox of Keeping-While-Giving*, Berkeley: University of California Press.

WENDT, A. (1991), 'The Heartwood: Kohia ko Taikaka Anake Exhibition', *Australian Art Monthly*, 40: 16–18.

WERRY, M. L. (2001), 'Tourism, Ethnicity, and the Performance of New Zealand Nationalism, 1889–1914', PhD thesis, Performance Studies, Evanston, IL: Northwestern University.

WHITEHEAD, C. (2005), *The Public Art Museum in Nineteenth-century Britain: The Development of the National Gallery*, Aldershot: Ashgate.

WHITING, C. (2000), Unpublished interview, 19 January, Wellington: Te Papa Archive.

WILKENS, D. (2002), *When Famous People Come to Town*, Wellington: Four Winds Press.

WILLIAMS, H. (1971), *A Dictionary of the Maori Language*, 7th edn, Wellington: Government Printer.

WILLIAMS, P. (2003), 'Te Papa: New Zealand's Identity Complex,' *The Journal of New Zealand Art History*, 24: 11–24.

—— (2005), 'A Breach on the Beach: Te Papa and the Fraying of Biculturalism', *Museum and Society* 3(2): 81–97. Leicester University Museum Studies online journal. Retrieved 28 September 2005 from http://www.le.ac.uk/museumstudies/m&s/.

WILLIAMS, R. (2004), *Art Theory: An Historical Introduction*, Oxford: Blackwell.

WILLIAMS, W. L. (1871), *A Dictionary of the Maori Language*, 3rd edn, London: Williams & Norgate.

WILSON, R. (1976), 'Ralph Hotere's Song Cycle Banners', *Art New Zealand*, 2: 9–10.

WINGERT, P. (1953), *Art of the South Pacific Islands*, London: Thames & Hudson.

WITCOMB, A. (2003), *Re-imagining the Museum: Beyond the Mausoleum*, London and New York: Routledge.

WIZEVICH, K. (1993), 'Creation and Reception of Exhibitions: Comparison of Provider Intentions and Visitor Response', PhD thesis, Architecture, Auckland: Auckland University.

WOLFE, R. (1993), 'Primitive Perceptions: Changing Attitudes towards Pacific Art', *Art New Zealand*, 69: 76–81.

WOLLEN, P. and Cooke, L. (eds) (1995), *Visual Display: Culture Beyond Appearances*, DIA discussions in contemporary culture, No. 10, Seattle: Bay Press.

INDEX

Italic numbers indicate illustrations.